Albert Harkness

**A Latin Reader**

Intended as a Companion to the Author's Latin Grammar

Albert Harkness

**A Latin Reader**
*Intended as a Companion to the Author's Latin Grammar*

ISBN/EAN: 9783337176136

Printed in Europe, USA, Canada, Australia, Japan

Cover: Foto ©Thomas Meinert / pixelio.de

More available books at **www.hansebooks.com**

A

# LATIN READER,

INTENDED AS A

## COMPANION

TO THE

## AUTHOR'S LATIN GRAMMAR.

WITH

REFERENCES, SUGGESTIONS, NOTES AND VOCABULARY.

BY

ALBERT HARKNESS,

PROFESSOR IN BROWN UNIVERSITY.

*REVISED EDITION.*

NEW YORK:
D. APPLETON AND COMPANY,
549 & 551 BROADWAY.
1876.

# PREFACE

THE object of the present revision is to adapt the Reader to the Revised Edition of the author's Grammar. Accordingly, all references are made to that edition.

But, in connection with this special object, it has been thought best to give the whole work a somewhat careful revision. Various slight changes have, therefore, been introduced in different portions of the volume. In Part First a few sentences and constructions, deemed too difficult, have given place to others, which will be found, it is hoped, better adapted to the wants of the learner.

The method of instruction adopted in the series of Latin text-books to which this volume belongs requires that the Reading Lessons should be accompanied by regular Exercises in translating English into Latin. Ample provision is made for such exercises in the author's Introduction to Latin Composition, which is intended to be put into the hands of the pupil when he begins the Reader, and to be used in weekly lessons throughout his entire preparatory course. That, in general, such exercises should form a regular progressive series, and be published in a separate volume, scarcely admits of a doubt; but, for the accommodation of certain schools, in which a large propor-

tion of the pupils pursue the study of the Latin only a very
limited time, it has been deemed advisable to insert Part
First of the Latin Composition in a special edition of the
Reader. This arrangement will furnish such schools the
full benefit of an elementary drill in Latin Composition,
without involving the necessity of procuring a separate
work upon that subject. The special edition will be en-
titled the "Reader with Exercises." The title of the regular edition will remain unchanged.

PROVIDENCE, *December* 15, 1874.

# PREFACE.

THE Latin Reader now offered to the public is intended as a companion to the author's Latin Grammar. It comprises Reading Lessons, Suggestions to the Learner, Notes, and a Vocabulary.

The Reading Lessons are abundantly supplied with references to the Grammar, and are arranged in two parts.

Part First presents a progressive series of exercises illustrative of grammatical forms, inflections, and rules. These exercises are intended to accompany the learner from the very outset in his progress through the Grammar, and thus to furnish him the constant luxury of using the knowledge which he is acquiring. They have been carefully selected from classical authors.

Part Second illustrates connected discourse, and comprises Fables, Anecdotes, and History. The Anecdotes have been selected from various classical sources; the other portions have been derived chiefly from the Lateinisches Elementarbuch of Professors Jacobs and Döring, though, in the Grecian History, Arnold's Historiae Antiquae Epitome, founded upon the work of Jacob and Döring, has furnished a few extracts. The Historical selections were, with a few exceptions, derived originally from the Latin historians Eutropius, Justin, and Cornelius Nepos.

The Suggestions to the Learner are intended to direct the unskilful efforts of the beginner, and thus to enable him to do for himself much which would otherwise require the aid of his teacher, and to do easily and pleasantly much which would otherwise be difficult and repulsive. They aim to point out to him the *process* by which he may most readily and surely reach the meaning and the structure of a Latin sentence, and then to teach him to embody that meaning in clear idiomatic English. Experience has abundantly shown the need of some such directions. The beginner's first efforts to solve the problem presented by a Latin sentence are too often little better than a series of unsuccessful conjectures, while his first translations are purely mechanical renderings, with little regard either to the thought of his author or to the proprieties of his mother tongue.

The Notes aim to furnish such collateral information as will enable the learner to appreciate the subject matter of his reading lessons, and such special aid as will enable him to surmount real and untried difficulties. Grammatical references can be employed only to solve grammatical difficulties; and, though for this purpose they are absolutely invaluable, it is yet a mistake to suppose that they can ever supply the place of commentary.

In the Vocabulary, the aim has been to give to each word the particular meanings which occur in the reading lessons, without omitting, however, its essential and leading signification.

At the solicitation of many eminent classical Professors and Teachers, the author has it in contemplation to publish an Introduction to Latin Composition, consisting of two parts, the first intended for the beginner, and the second for the more advanced student. Accordingly, the present work has been made simply a Reader, and all Exercises in writing Latin have been reserved for a future volume.

With this statement of the design and plan of the work, the author commits it to classical instructors, in the hope that, in their hands, it may render some useful service in the important work of classical instruction.

PROVIDENCE, *Aug. 21st,* 1865.

# CONTENTS.

## PART FIRST.

### GRAMMATICAL EXERCISES.

# PART SECOND.

## LATIN SELECTIONS.

# EXPLANATIONS OF REFERENCES AND ABBREVIATIONS.

THE reference numerals in the Latin text, and in the Suggestions, refer to the author's Latin Grammar, the Revised Edition.

In the Notes and Vocabulary, the Arabic numerals refer, when enclosed in parentheses, to articles in this work; and, when not thus enclosed, to articles in the Grammar.

Roman numerals refer to the Suggestions.

The following abbreviations occur:

| | | | |
|---|---|---|---|
| adj........ | adjective. | lit ......... | literally. |
| adv........ | adverb. | m .......... | masculine. |
| comp...... | comparative. | n .......... | neuter. |
| conj....... | conjunction. | part........ | participle. |
| defect..... | defective. | pass........ | passive. |
| dep........ | deponent. | plur. *or* pl.... | plural. |
| f ......... | feminine. | prep ....... | preposition. |
| impers.... | impersonal. | pron ....... | pronoun. |
| indec ..... | indeclinable. | subs ....... | substantive. |
| interj..... | interjection. | superl....... | superlative. |
| irreg...... | irregular. | | |

*PART FIRST.*

# GRAMMATICAL EXERCISES.

## NOUNS.

DEFINITION, GENDER, ETC.—39–42; 44–47.

FIRST DECLENSION.—48.

NOTE.—Before reading the Latin Exercises, the pupil is expected, in every instance, to learn carefully those portions of the Grammar which are embraced in the large type of the sections designated.

**1.** 1. Ală, alā, alae,[1] alam, alārum, alis, alas. 2. Victŏriă, victoriā, victoriae, victoriam, victoriārum, victoriis, victorias. 3. Causae, fortūnae, portae. 4. Causā, fortūnā, portā. 5. Causam, fortūnam, portam. 6. Causārum, fortuuārum, portārum. 7. Causis, fortūnis, portis. 8. Causas, fortūnas, portas.

SECOND DECLENSION.—51.

RULE II.—*Appositives.*—363; 352, 2.

**2.** 1. Domĭnus, domĭni, domĭno, domĭnum, domĭne, dominōrum, domĭnis. 2. Gener, genĕri, genĕro, genĕrum, generōrum, genĕris, genĕros. 3. Servi, anni. 4. Puĕri, socĕri. 5. Agri, magistri. 6. Templi, belli. 7. Servis, annis. 8. Puĕro, socĕro. 9. Agrōrum, magistrōrum. 10. Templa, bella.

---

[1] When the same Latin form may be found in two or more cases, the pupil is expected to give the meaning for each case.

11. Lucus, stellă. 12. Luci, stellae. 13. Lucum, stellam. 14. Luco, stellā. 15. Lucōrum, stellārum. 16. Lucis, stellis. 17. Lucos, stellas.

18. Dionysius tyrannus.[1] 19. Dionysio tyranno. 20. Dionysium tyrannum. 21. Tulliă regīnă. 22. Tulliae regīnae. 23. Tulliam regīnam. 24. Puer Ascanius.

### THIRD DECLENSION.—CLASS I.—57-61.

### RULE XVI.—*Genitive.*—395.

**3.** 1. Princĭpis, princĭpum. 2. Dux, duces. 3. Regem, reges. 4. Regis, milĭtis. 5. Regi, milĭti. 6. Rege, milĭte. 7. Reges, milĭtes. 8. Regum, milĭtum. 9. Regĭbus, militĭbus.

10. Virtus regis.[2] 11. Virtūtes regum.[2] 12. Vindex libertātis. 13. Vindĭces libertātis. 14. Nepotĭbus regis. 15. Virtūte regis. 16. Virtūte milĭtum.

17. Belli causă. 18. Belli causas.) 19. Victoriă regis. 20. Victoriae regis. 21. Gener judĭcis. 22. Sapientiă judĭcis. 23. Regis filiă. 24. Tulliă, regis filiă.

### THIRD DECLENSION.—CLASS II.—62-64.

### RULE XXXII.—*Cases with Prepositions.*—432-435.

**4.** 1. Nubi, nube, nubium. 2. Hostem, hostes, hostĭbus. 3. Carmĭna, carminĭbus. 4. Consŭlis, passĕris. 5. Consŭlum, passĕrum. 6. Consulĭbus, passerĭbus. 7. Leōni, virgĭni. 8. Leōnes, virgĭnes. 9. Patrem, pastōrem. 10. Patres, pastōres. 11. Opus, corpus. 12. Alăm avis. 13. Custōdes urbis.

14. Cicĕro consul.[1] 15. Cicerōnis consŭlis. 16. Cicerōnem consŭlem. 17. Nepos consŭlis.[2] 18. Nepōtes

---

[1] See Grammar, 363.    [2] 395.

consŭlis. 19. Nepōtes consŭlum. 20. Pater judĭcis. 21. Patres judĭcum. 22. Patrĭbus judĭcum.

23. Post Romŭli mortem.[1] 24. Apud Herodŏtum, patrem historiae. 25. Ad virtūtem. 26. Ante lucem. 27. Contra natūram. 28. Sermo de amicitiā.[2] 29. Pro patriā. 30. Sine labōre. 31. In amnem.[3] 32. In bello.

### FOURTH DECLENSION.—116.

**5.** 1. Fructŭs, cornūs. 2. Fructĭbus, cornĭbus. 3. Cantum, currum. 4. In currum. 5. In curru. 6. Solis ortus. 7. Ab ortu ad occāsum. 8. Ante solis occāsum.

### FIFTH DECLENSION.—120.

**6.** 1. Acies, aciem, aciēi. 2. Diēi, faciēi. 3. Rei. spei. 4. Diem, faciem. 5. Rem, spem. 6. Die, facie. 7. Re, spe.

8. In aciem. 9. In acie. 10. Facies urbis. 11. Spes fortūnae. 12. Contra spem. 13. Sine spe.

---

# ADJECTIVES.

### FIRST AND SECOND DECLENSIONS.—148–150.

RULE XXXIII.—*Agreement of Adjectives.*—438.

**7.** 1. Servus bonus. 2. Servi boni. 3. Servo bono. 4. Servum bonum. 5. Serve bone. 6. Servōrum bonōrum. 7. Servis bonis. 8. Servos bonos. 9. Regīnă bonă. 10. Regīnae bonae. 11. Regīnam bonam. 12. Regīnā bonā. 13. Regīnārum bonārum. 14. Regīnis bonis. 15. Regīnas bonas. 16. Exemplum bonum. 17. Exempli boni. 18. Exempla bona.

---

[1] 432, 433.   [2] 432, 434.   [3] 435, 1.

19. Puer pulcher.    20. Puellă pulchră.)    21. Tectum pulchrum.    22. Puĕri pulchri.    23. Puellae pulchrae. 24. Tecta pulchra.

25. Veră amicitiă.   26. Gladius longus.    27. Magnă gloriă.    28. Spes falsă.) 29. Sine magno labōre.    30. Modius aureōrum annulōrum.

### THIRD DECLENSION.—152–158.

**8.** 1. Dolor acer.    2. Sine dolōre acri.    3. Dolōres acres.    4. Hostis crudēlis.    5. Hostem crudēlem.    6. Hostium crudelium.    7. Hiems glaciālis.    8. Hiĕmcm glaciālem.   9. Carmen dulce.    10. Carmĭna dulcia. 11. Innumerabĭles fabŭlae.

### COMPARISON OF ADJECTIVES.—160–162.

**9.** 1. Triumphus clarus.    2. Triumphus clarior. 3. Triumphus clarissĭmus.    4. Triumphi clari.) 5. Triumphi clariōres.    6. Triumphi clarissĭmi.    7. Vir fortis. 8. Vir fortior.    9. Vir fortissĭmus.    10. Sapiens vir. 11. Sapientior vir.    12. Sapientissĭmus vir.

13. Fortissĭmi vĭri.    14. Fortissimōrum virōrum multitūdo.    15. Perītus dux.    16. Peritissĭmi duces. 17. Bella funestissĭma.

---

# PRONOUNS.

CLASSIFICATION AND DECLENSION OF PRONOUNS.—182–191.

RULE XXXIV.—*Agreement of Pronouns.*—445; 445, 1.

**10.** 1. Mei.    2. Tibi.    3. Inter se.²    4. Ad te. 5. Pro nobis.    6. Post me.    7. Ante nos.    8. Patriă meă.² 9. Nostră patriă.    10. Magister tuus.    11. Tuă mens.    12. Nostri milĭtes.    13. Nostrae amicitiae.

---

¹ 432.      ² 438, 1.

14. Ad salūtem vestram.  15. Ad vitam suam.  16. Hic'
vir.  17. Haec urbs.  18. Hoc regnum.  19. Hujus
viri.  20. In hac urbe.  21. Haec regna.  22. Illi viri.
23. Pro illis viris.  24. Ante 'hunc diem.  25. Sub hoc
rege.  26. Pastor illīus regiōnis.  27. Idem locus.  28.
In eundem locum.  29. Circa eandem horam.  30. Id
tempus.  31. Ab ipsā natūrā.  32. Ii ad quos.'  33. Quae
civitas?  34. Ab alĭquo.  35. Faustŭlus quidam,

---

## VERBS.

INTRODUCTION.—192-197;  199-203.
VERB SUM.—204.
RULE III.—*Subject Nominative.*—367.
RULE XXXV.—*Agreement of Verb with Subject.*—460.
RULE L.—*Predicate Nouns.*—362.

**11.** 1. Aristīdes' justus' fuit.'  2. Justus* est.'  3.
Justus erat.  4. Justi sumus.'  5. Justi fuerāmus.  6.
Justi erĭmus.  7. Justi simus.  8. Justi fuissēmus.
9. Cato sapiens erat.  10. Sapiens fŭĕrat.  11. Sapientes erĭtis.  12. Sapientes fuistis.  13. Sapiens es.  14.
Sapientes este.  15. Lex brevis est.  16. Lex brevis
esto.  17. Leges breves sunt.  18. Leges breves sunto.
19. Ego consul' fui.  20. Cicĕro consul fuit.  21. Cicĕro
consul fŭĕrat.

FIRST CONJUGATION.—205, 206.
RULE V.—*Direct Object.*—371.

**12.** 1. Amat, amant.  2. Amābat, amābant.  3.

---

* *Justus* agrees with the pronoun *is*, he, the omitted subject of *est.*
1 438, 1.       4 438.        6 460; 460, 2.
2 445.          5 460.        7 362.
3 367.

Amavĕrat, amavĕrant.    4. Amavĕrit, amavĕrint.    5. Amet, ament.

6. Laudat, laudātur.    7. Laudant, laudantur.    8. Laudābat, laudabātur.    9. Laudābant, laudabantur.    10. Laudet, laudētur.    11. Laudent, laudentur.

12. Oratiōnem¹ laudo.    13. Oratiōnem laudāmus. 14. Oratiōnes laudabĭmus.⟩   15. Oratio laudātur.    16. Oratiōnes laudantur.    17. Virtūtem amātis.    18. Virtūtem amabĭtis.    19. Virtus amātur.    20. Virtus amāta² est.    21. Ego patriam liberāvi.    22. Patriam liberavērunt.    23. Patria liberāta est.    24. Ancus urbem ampliāvit.    25. Marius fugātus³ est.    26. Fugāti erant.    27. Socrătes accusātus est.

\

SECOND CONJUGATION.—207, 208.

**13.** 1. Moneo, moneor.    2. Monēbam, monēbar. 3. Monēbo, monēbor.    4. Moneam, monear.    5. Monērem, monērer.    6. Monui, monuĭmus.    7. Monuĕrat, monuĕrant.    8. Monuĕris, monuerĭtis.    9. Monuĕrim, monĭtus sim.    10. Monuissēmus, monĭti essēmus. 11. Monēte, monentor.

12. Terrēbat, terrebātur.⟩   13. Terrēbant, terrebantur.    14. Terrēret, terrerētur.    15. Terrērent, terrerentur.    16. Terrĭtus sum, terrĭti sumus.    17. Terrĭtus es, terrĭti estis.    18. Terrĭtus est, terrĭti sunt.

19. Gloriam¹ veram² habes.    20. Gloriam habēbis. 21. Equĭtes gladios habēbant.    22. Gladios habuērunt. 23. Gladium habuisti.    24. Homo habet memoriam. 25. Cum Romānis⁴ pacem habuĭmus. ⸗26. Pacem habuerāmus.    27. Pacem habebĭmus.    28. Cyrus omnium in exercĭtu⁵ suo milĭtum nomĭna tenēbat.

---

¹ 371.         ³ 438.         ⁵ 435, 1.
² 460, 1.        ⁴ 432, 434.

THIRD CONJUGATION.—209, 210.

RULE LI.—*Use of Adverbs.*—582.

**14.** 1. Rego, regor. 2. Regĭmus, regĭmur. 3. Regit, regĭtur. 4. Regunt, reguntur. 5. Rege, regĭto. 6. Regendi, regendo. 7. Rectus eram, recti erāmus.

8. Spero, pareo, duco. 9. Speras, pares, ducis. 10. Sperāmus, parēmus, ducĭmus.ꞵ 11. Sperābam, parēbam, ducēbam. 12. Sperābant, parēbant, ducēbant. 13. Sperāvi, parui, duxi. 14. Speravĭmus, paruĭmus, duxĭmus. 15. Speravērunt, paruērunt, duxērunt.

16. Deus omnem hunc mundum regit. 17. Deus mundum semper¹ rexit. 18. Deus mundum regēbat. 19. Deus mundum reget. 20. Cicĕro ad Attĭcum² scribit.ꞵ 21. Ad te saepe scribam. 22. Cicĕro multos libros scripsit. 23. Ad amīcum de amicitiā³ scripsi. 24. Librum de senectūte scripsĕrat. 25. Quid dixisti? 26. Nihil dixi. 27. Quid dixistis? 28. Multa de amicitiā dixĭmus. 29. Haec recte dixistis. 30. Hic liber ad te scriptus est.

FOURTH CONJUGATION.—211, 212.

**15.** 1. Audiēbat, audiēbant. 2. Audiebātur, audiebantur. 3. Audiam, audiēmus. 4. Audiar, audiēmur. 5. Audīvit, audivērunt. 6. Audītus est, audīti sunt. 7. Audivĕram, audiverāmus. 8. Audītus eram, audīti erāmus.

9. Sperat, paret, ducit, scit. 10. Sperant, parent, ducunt, sciunt. 11. Sperābat, parēbat, ducēbat, sciēbat. 12. Sperabāmus, parebāmus, ducebāmus, sciebāmus. 13. Sperābo, parēbo, ducet, sciet.

14. Tullus bellum finīvit. 15. Bellum finivĕrat. 16.

---

¹ 582. ² 433. ³ 484.

Bellum finītum est. 17. Hic dies Graeciae libertātem finiet. 18. Cives templum custodiunt. 19. Templa custodiēmus. 20. Templum custodīte. 21. Brutus Macedoniam custodiēbat. 22. Hanc provinciam custodīmus. 23. Hoc audivīmus. 24. A vobis audīmur.

✝

VERBS IN IO, THIRD CONJUGATION.—221–223.

16. 1. Romāni urbem capiunt. 2. Urbes capiēbant. 3. Urbem capiēmus. 4. Haec urbs capiētur. 5. Urbes capientur. 6. Regŭlus captus est. 7. Milītes arma capiunt. 8. Scipio Carthagīnem cepit. 9. Praefecti regii Eretriam cepērunt. 10. Regis pater fugit. 11. Fugiēbat. 12. Lacedaemonii fugiunt. 13. Fugērunt. 14. Xerxes in Asiam fugĕrat.

DEPONENT VERBS.—225–230.

17. 1. Coriolānus populātur agrum¹ Romānum. 2. Pyrrhus Campaniam depopulātus est. 3. Milītes agros depopulabantur. 4. Hoc facīnus rex mirātur. 5. Hoc mirāmur. 6. Puer laudem merētur. 7. Laudem merēris. 8. Laudem merentur. 9. Gloria virtūtem sequĭtur. 10. Ascanium secūtus est Silvius. 11. Justitiam sequĭmur. 12. Justitiam sequēmur. 13. Cum Scipiōne honōrem partīmur. 14. Id opus inter se partiuntur.

PERIPHRASTIC CONJUGATION.—231, 232.

18. 1. Virtūtem laudatūri sumus. 2. Virtus laudanda est. 3. Quid laudatūrus es? 4. Bonitātem laudatūrus sum. 5. Omnia² sunt laudanda, quae³ conjuncta cum virtūte sunt. 6. Quid vituperandum est? 7. Omnia sunt vituperanda, quae cum vitiis conjuncta

¹ 371.     ² 441.     ³ 445.

sunt. 8. Gloriam veram habitūrus es. 9. Gloriam veram habitūri sumus. 10. Cicěro ad Attĭcum scriptū-rus erat. 11. Epistŏla scribenda est. 12. Orātor audi-endus est. 13. Seuatōres Cicerōnem auditūri erant.

---

# SYNTAX OF NOUNS.

### AGREEMENT OF NOUNS.

RULE I.—*Predicate Nouns.*—362.

**19.** 1. Mercurius *nuntius* erat. 2. Furius *consul* erät. 3. *Homo* sum.¹ 4. Bacchus erat vini' *deus.*' 5. Somnus est *imāgo* mortis. 6. Historia *testis* tempŏrum habētur. 7. Historia *magistra*' vitae habētur. 8. So-crätes *parens* philosophiae dicĭtur. ·9. Brutus *homo* mag-nus evasĕrat. ·10. Nos *causa*' belli sumus. 11. Nautius et Furius *consŭles*' erant.'

RULE II.—*Appositives.*—363.

**20.** 1. Dionysius *tyrannus* expulsus est. 2. Dema-rātus, regis *pater*, fugit. 3. Apud Herodŏtum, *patrem* historiae, sunt innumerabĭles fabŭlae.| 4. Hannĭbal Sa-guntum, foederātam *urbem*, expugnāvit. 5. *Themistŏcles*' veni ad te. ·6. Cato littĕras Graecas *senex*' didĭcit. 7. Junius aedem Salūtis, quam *consul* vovĕrat, *dictātor* dedicāvit. ·8. Socrätem, sapientissĭmum' *virum*, Athe-nienses interfecērunt.

---

| | | |
|---|---|---|
| ¹ 460, 2. | ⁴ 362, 1, 1). | ⁷ 363, 2. |
| ² 395. | ⁵ 362, 1, 2). | ⁸ 363, 3. |
| ³ 51, 5. | ⁶ 463, II. | ⁹ 162. |

## NOMINATIVE.

### RULE III.—*Subject Nominative.*—367. ⁑

**21.** 1. Cuncta *Graecia* liberāta est.   2. *Patria* mea est mundus. ⁚3. *Paulus* consul¹ regem ad Pydnam superāvit.⸱ 4. *Philosophia* inventrix legum fuit. ⸸5. Omnium malōrum *stultitia* est mater.   6. Non⁵ omnis *error* stultitia est.   7. Quot *homĭnes,*⁷ tot *sententiae.*

## VOCATIVE.

### RULE IV.—*Case of Address.*—369.

**22.** 1. Disce, *puer,* virtūtem.   2. Tu, mi⁴ *Cicĕro,* haec accipies. ⸸3. Te, *Minerva,* custos urbis, precor⸱ac quaeso. ⸱4. Audīte, *judĭces.* ⸱5. Disce, *puer,* virtūtes. ⸱6. *Amīci,* diem perdĭdi. ⸱7. Conservāte, *judĭces,* hunc homĭnem.

## ACCUSATIVE.

### RULE V.—*Direct   Object.*—371. ⸱

**23.** 1. Accēpi tuas *epistŏlas.*   2. Labor *omnia* vincit. 3. Anĭmus regit *corpus.*   4. Nostra *nos* patria delectat. 5. Miltiădes totam⁵ *Graeciam* liberāvit.  ⸱6. Sophŏcles *tragoedias* fecit.  ⸱7. Studia *adolescentiam* alunt, *senectūtem* oblectant.   8. Romŭlus *Romam* condĭdit.   9. Avaritia *probitātem* subvertit.   10. Virtus conciliat *amicitias.* 11. Virtus *amicitiam* gignit.

12. Vestri patres eam *vitam*⁵ vixērunt.   13. Mirum *somnium*⁵ somniāvi.   14. *Pacem*⁷ desperāvi.   15. Se-

---

¹ 363.          ⁴ 185.          ⁵ 371, 1, 3).
² 582.          ᵇ 151.          ⁷ 371, 3.
³ 460, 3.

quăni Ariovisti *crudelitātem*[1] horrēbant. 16. *Brutum* Romānae matrōnae luxērunt. 17. Milĭtes invădunt *urbem.*[2] 18. *Aciem*[3] circumvenērunt. 19. Caesar *agrum* Picēnum percurrit. 20. Periculosissĭmum[3] *locum* sum praetervectus. 21. Germāni *flumen* transiērunt.

RULE VI.—*Two Accusatives—Same Person.*—373. ·

**24.** 1. *Cicerōnem* universus popŭlus *consŭlem* declarāvit. 2. Romŭlus *urbem Romam* vocāvit. · 3. Fecit *herēdem filiam.* 4. Socrătes totīus[4] mundi *se civem* arbitrabātur. 5. Cato *cellam* penariam rei publĭcae nostrae, *nutrīcem* plebis Romānae *Siciliam* nomināvit. [5] 6. Praesta *te virum.* · 7. Senātus *Catilīnam hostem* judicāvit. · 8. Senātus *Paulum consŭlem* creāvit. 9. *Socrătem* Apollo *sapientissĭmum*[6] judicāvit. 10. *Mesopotamiam fertĭlem* effĭcit Euphrātes. 11. *Tiresiam sapientem* fingunt poētae. 12. *Polycrătem felīcem* appellābant.

RULE VII.—*Two Accusatives—Person and Thing.*—374.

**25.** 1. *Te* tua *fata* docēbo. · 2. *Hoc me* docuit usus, magister[8] egregius. · 3. Fortūna belli *artem victos*[7] docct. 4. Augustus *nepōtes* suos *littĕras* docuit. 5. Antigŏnus *iter omnes*[8] celat. 6. *Pacem te* poscĭmus. 7. Boeotii *auxilia regem* orābant. 8. Cato interrogātus est *sententiam.* ·9. Marcius omnes *artes* edoctus fuĕrat.

· 10. *Auxilium a Caesăre*[8] petiērunt.· 11. *Te illud*[10] admoneo. 12. *Te id* consŭlo. 13. Hannĭbal nonaginta

---

| | | |
|---|---|---|
| [1] 371, 3. | [5] 373, 8. | [8] 441, 1. |
| [2] 371, 4. | [6] 363. | [9] 374, 3, 8). |
| [8] 162. | [7] 575. | [10] 374. 5. |
| [4] 151. | | |

B

*millia*[1] pedĭtum *Ibērum*[1] traduxit.    14. Belgae *Rhenum*[1] transducti sunt.

## RULE VIII.—*Accusative of Time and Space.*—378.

**26.** 1. Servius Tullius regnāvit *annos* quattuor[2] et[3] quadraginta.   2. Appius Claudius caecus *annos* multos fuit.   3. Quaedam bestiŏlae unum *diem* vivunt.   4. Dionysius quinque et viginti natus *annos* dominātum occupāvit.   5. Caesar duas fossas quindĕcim *pedes* latas perduxit.   6. Mĭlĭtes aggĕrem altum *pedes* octoginta exstruxērunt.   7. Arăbes gladios habēbant longos quaterna *cubĭta.*   8. Urbs quinque diērum *iter* abest.

## RULE IX.—*Accusative of Limit.*—379.

**27.** 1. Cicĕro *Athēnas* venit.   2. Regŭlus *Carthagĭnem* rediit.   3. Hannĭbal *Capuam* concessit.   4. Cicĕro maxĭmum numĕrum frumenti[4] *Romam* misit.   5. Dionysius navigābat *Syracūsas.*   6. Curius elephantos quattuor *Romam* duxit.

‾7. Aurum *domum*[4] comportant. ⋆8. Ego *rus* ibo.[5] 9. Veni consŭlis *domum.*   10. Verres *Delum* venit. 11. Pausaniam *Cyprum* misērunt.   12. Hannĭbal *in hiberna*[7] *Capuam* concessit.   13. Legiōnes *ad urbem* addūcit.   14. Darīus *in Asiam* rediit.

15. Consŭles *Romam* redībant.   16. Cicĕro *domum* rediĕrat.   17. Consŭles *in Graeciam* venĕrant.   18. Publius Scipio *in Hispaniam* missus est.   19. Cives *rus* fugient.   20. *In Etruriam* missus erat.   21. Tullia *in forum* properāvit et regem salutāvit.

---

[1] 374, 6.      [4] 395.      [6] 295.
[2] 174.      [5] 379, 3 ; 119, 1.      [7] 379, 4.
[3] 308, 310, 1.

RULE X.—*Accusative of Specification.*—380.

**28.** 1. Equus tremit *artus*. 2. Aenēas' caedit nigrantes *terga* juvencos. 3. Hannĭbal *femur* ictus cecĭdit. 4. Hannĭbal *anĭmum* incensus est.

5. Haec vis valet *multum*.² 6. Haec vis *idem* potest. 7. Nervii *nihil* possunt. 8. Thebāni *nihil* moti sunt. 9. *Quid* hostis potest? 10. *Quid* venisti? 11. *Quid* plura³ dispŭto?

RULE XI.—*Accusative in Exclamations.*—381.

**29.** 1. O praeclāram *vitam*! 2. O *spectacŭlum* misĕrum! 3. O *tempŏra*, o *mores*! Senātus conjuratiōnem intellĭgit, consul videt. 4. O *vim* maxĭmam⁴ errōris! 5. O *clementiam* admirabĭlem!

\

DATIVE.

RULE XII.—*Dative with Verbs.*—384.

**30.** 1. Non *scholae*, sed *vitae* discĭmus. 2. Omnes homĭnes *libertāti* student. 3. Germāni *labōri* ac *duritiae* student. 4. Ego *philosophiae* semper vaco. 5. *Pietāti* summa⁵ trĭbuenda⁶ laus est. 6. Non solum *nobis* divĭtes sumus, sed *libĕris*, *amīcis*, maximēque *rei publĭcae*.

7. *Philosophiae* nos tradĭmus. 8. Graeci homĭnes honōres tribuunt iis *viris*, qui tyrannos necavērunt. 9. Non placĭdam *membris* dat cura quiētem. 10. Omnes, quum valēmus, recta consilia *aegrōtis*⁷ damus.

---

¹ 50.             ⁴ 165.          ⁶ 232.
² 380, 2.         ⁵ 163, 3.       ⁷ 441.
³ 165, 1.

2

**31. Dative of Advantage and Disadvantage.—385.**
—1. Probus' invĭdet nemĭni. 2. Homĭnes hominĭbus prosunt. 3. Nocet altĕri. •4. Consulātus meus placuit Catōni. • 5. Diōni crudelĭtas tyranni displicēbat. •6. Themistŏcles persuāsit popŭlo. `7. Parti` civium consŭlunt. ` 8. Milĭtes non mulierĭbus, non infantĭbus pepercērunt. 9. Nemo liber est, qui corpŏri servit.

**32. Dative with Compounds.—386.—1.** Pelopĭdas omnĭbus affuit pericŭlis. 2. Natūra sensĭbus• ratiōnem adjunxit. 3. Leges omnium• salūtem singulōrum• salūti antepōnunt. 4. Parva magnis saepe• conferuntur.• 5. Hannĭbal terrōrem injēcit exercitui Romanōrum. 6. Aristīdes interfuit pugnae navāli apud Salamīnem. 7. Consiliis interdum obstat fortūna. 8. Homĭnes hominĭbus plurĭmum' et prosunt et obsunt.. 9. Consŭles libertāti suas opes• postferēbant.• 10. Bona existimatio divitiis praestat. 11. Tu virtūtem praefer• divitiis. 12. Quidam succumbunt dolorĭbus. 13. Neque deĕro• neque superĕro• rei publĭcae.

**33. Dative of Possessor.—387.—1.** Fuēre Lydis multi reges. 2. Non semper idem florĭbus ¹⁰ est color, 3. Est honos eloquentiae.

**34. Dative of Apparent Agent.—388.—1.** Caesări omnia erant agenda. 2. Diligentia colenda est nobis. 3. Multa videnda sunt oratōri. 4. Cui non sunt haec audīta ?

**35. Miscellaneous Examples.—1.** Haec sententia

---

| | | |
|---|---|---|
| ¹ 441. | ⁵ 582. | ⁸ 133, 1. |
| ² 385, 3. | ⁶ 292, 2. | ⁹ 288. |
| ³ 386, 1. | ⁷ 380; 2. | ¹⁰ 83. |
| ⁴ 441, 1. | | |

consŭli placuit. 2. Romŭlus civitāti profuit. 3. Cives legĭbus parēbant. 4. Vobis summam¹ laudem tribuĭmus. 5. Darīus, rex Persārum, Graecis² bellum intŭlit. 6. Leonĭdas se³ perĭcŭlis obtŭlit.

**RULE XIII.—*Two Datives—To Which and For Which.*—390.**

**36.** 1. Virtūtes *hominĭbus decŏri* sunt. 2. Virtūtes *hominĭbus gloriae* sunt. 3. Probĭtas est *omnĭbus⁴ amōri*. 4. Crudelĭtas est *omnĭbus odio*. 5. Virtus neque datur *dono* neque accipĭtur. 6. Pausanias, rex⁵ Lacedaemoni-ōrum, venit *Atticis auxilio*..

7. Hoc *vitio mihi* dant. dabis, quod tu ipse fecisti? *castris praesidio* relinquit. locum delegērunt.

8. Idne⁶ *altĕri⁷ crimĭni* 9. Caesar legiōnes duas⁵ 10. Hunc *sibi domicilio*

**RULE XIV.—*Dative with Adjectives.*—391.**

**37.** 1. Verĭtas *mihi* grata est. 2. Gratissĭmae⁸ *mihi* tuae littĕrae¹⁰ fuērunt. 3. Patria *Cicerōni* erat caris-sĭma. 4. Id *Deo* est proxĭmum,¹¹ quod est optĭmum.¹² 5. Minĭme¹³ *sibi* quisque notus est. 6. *Morti* nihil est tam simĭle, quam somnus.¹⁴ 7. Homĭnum *genĕri* cultūra agrōrum est salutāris. 8. Belgae proxĭmi sunt *Germānis*. 9. *Iis*, qui vendunt, justitia necessaria est. 10. Pax *nobis* omnĭbus fuit optabĭlis.

**RULE XV.—*Dative with Derivatives.*—392.**

**38.** 1. Esto obtemperatio *institūtis* populōrum.

---

| | | |
|---|---|---|
| ¹ 163, 3. | ⁶ 346, II. 1. | ¹¹ 166. |
| ² 384, II. | ⁷ 441, 2. | ¹² 165. |
| ³ 448. | ⁸ 175. | ¹³ 305, 2; 165. |
| ⁴ 441. | ⁹ 162. | ¹⁴ 417, 1. |
| ⁵ 363. | ¹⁰ 132. | |

2. Insidiae *consŭli* non procedēbant. 3. Convenienter *natūrae* vivĭmus. 4. Philosŏphus *sĭbi* constanter convenienterquc dicit.

## GENITIVE.

( RULE XVI.—*Genitive with Nouns.*—395, 396.)

39.﹒1. Piĕtas fundamentum ¹ est omnium *virtūtum*. 2. Ira est initium *insaniae*. ﹒3. Sapientia est *rerum* divinārum et humanārum scientia.﹐ 4. Nona *diēi* hora erat.

I. SUBJECTIVE GENITIVE.—1. Vultus sermo ¹ quidam ⁾ tacĭtus ⁾ *mentis* est. 2. Nostri milĭtes impĕtum *hostium* sustinuērunt. 3. Themistŏcles non effūgit *civium* suōrum invidiam. 4. *Ventōrum* pater regit navem. 5. *Singulōrum* facultātes divitiae ¹ sunt *civitātis*.

II. OBJECTIVE GENITIVE.—1. Crescit amor *nummi*. 2. Anĭmi morbi sunt cupiditātes *divitiārum, gloriae, voluptātum*.

III. PARTITIVE GENITIVE.—1. Justitia nihil expĕtit *praemii*, nihil *pretii*. 2. Conon *pecuniae* quinquaginta talenta civĭbus suis donāvit. 3. Permagnum pondŭs *argenti* fuit. 4. Socrătes *omnium* ⁾ sapientissĭmus ⁴ judicātus est. 5. *Gallōrum* omnium fortissĭmi sunt Belgae. 6. Ubĭnam *gentium* ⁾ sumus ? 7. Satis *eloquentiae* ⁾ fuit, *sapientiae* parum.

IV. GENITIVE OF CHARACTERISTIC.—1. Tarquinius fratrem habuit Aruntem,⁷ mitis *ingenii* juvĕnem.

---

¹ 362.　　　　⁾ 396, III. 3) (2).　　　⁾ 396, III. 4) (2).
² 438; 438, 1.　⁴ 162.　　　　　　⁾ 396, III. 4) (1).
　　　　　　　　　　　　　　　　　⁷ 363.

2. Athenienses belli ducem' elĭgunt Perĭclem,' spectātae *virtūtis* virum.'    3. Classem' septuaginta' *navium* Athenienses Miltiädi' dedērunt.

. V. GENITIVE OF SPECIFICATION.—1. *Cyri* nomen' accēpit.   2. Quid sonat vox *voluptātis ?*   3. Virtūtes *continentiae, gravitātis, justitiae, fidci,* omni honōre' dignae sunt.   4. *Germaniae* vocabŭlum recens est.   5. *Domĭni* appellatiōnem semper' exhorruit Augustus.

RULE XVII.—*Genitive with Adjectives.*—399.

**40.** 1. Avĭda est *pericŭli* virtus.    2. Haec aetas *virtūtum* ferax est.   3. Conscia mens *recti* famae' mendacia' ridet.   4. Romāni appetentes '" *gloriae* atque '' avĭdi *laudis* fuērunt.   5. Multi *contentiōnis* sunt cupidiōres '" quam *veritātis.*   6. Epaminondas fuit perītus *belli, veritātis* dilĭgens.   7. Conon prudens *rei* militāris erat. 8. Socrătes se omnium *rērum* nescium " fingit.   9. Themistŏcles peritissĭmos '" *belli* navālis fecit Athenienses. 10. Homo *ratiōnis* '" est partĭceps.   11. Plena *errōrum* sunt omnia.   12. Omnes *virtūtis* compŏtes " beāti sunt. 13. *Viri* '" propria est fortitūdo.

RULE XVIII.—*Predicate Genitive.*—401–403.

**41.** 1. Damnatio est *judĭcum ;* poena, *legis.*   2. Imbecilli *anĭmi* est superstitio.   3. Xerxis' classis mille et ducentārum *navium* fuit.   4. Claudius erat *somni* brevissĭmi.   5. Permagni *momenti* est ratio.   6. Temerĭtas

---

¹ 373.     ⁷ 582.     ¹² 162.
² 363.     ⁸ 395.     ¹³ 373; 373, 3.
³ 384, II.     ⁹ 371, 3, 1).     ¹⁴ 399, 2, (3).
⁴ 176.     ¹⁰ 575 ; 353.     ¹⁵ 157, 2.
⁵ 371.     ¹¹ 587, I.     ¹⁶ 399, 3, 3).
⁶ 419, IV.

est florentis [1] *aetātis;* prudentia, senescentis.　7. Praeda parvi *pretii* fuit.　8. Thebae [2] *popŭli* Romāni factae [3] sunt.　9. Voluptātem virtus *minĭmi* [4] facit.　10. Divitiae a me [5] *minĭmi* [6] putantur.　11. Nulla possessio *pluris* [7] quam virtus aestimanda est.　12. Vendo meum frumentum non *pluris,* quam cetĕri.　13. Mentīri [8] non est *meum.* [9]　14. *Tuum* est mihi· [10] ignoscĕre.

Rule XIX.—*Genitive with Certain Verbs.*—406–408.

**42.** 1. *Eōrum* miserēre, [10] qui [11] in miseriis [12] sunt. 2. Anĭmus memĭnit [13] *praeteritōrum,* [14] praesentia cernit, futūra praevĭdet.　3. Reminiscĕre pristĭnae *virtūtis* Helvetiōrum.　4. Deōrum [15] immortalium *beneficia* [16] recordor.　5. Oblīti sunt *injuriārum.*　6. Habētis ducem memŏrem *vestri,* oblītum *sui.*　7. Aliōrum vitia cernit, obliviscĭtur *suōrum.*　8. *Flagitiōrum* suōrum recordabĭtur.　9. Planci *merĭti* recordor.

10. Magni [17] *rei* publĭcae intĕrest.　11. Illud *Cicerōnis* maxĭme interfuit.　12. Hoc regis nihil [17] intĕrest. 13. *Scipiōnis* meminĕrat.　14. *Sui* oblītus ĕrat.　15. Miserentur *sociōrum.*　16. *Atheniensium* maxĭme interĕrat.

Rule XX.—*Accusative and Genitive.*—410.

**43.** 1. *Te* vetĕris *amicitiae* commonefacio.　2. Tiberius *judĭces* [18] *legum* admonēbat.

---

| | | |
|---|---|---|
| [1] 575. | [7] 549. | [13] 297, I. |
| [2] 131, 1, 2). | [8] 404, 1. | [14] 575; 295, 2. |
| [3] 279; 294. | [9] 385. | [15] 45, 6. |
| [4] 403; 165. | [10] 271, 2. | [16] 407, 1. |
| [5] 414, 5. | [11] 445. | [17] 408, 3. |
| [6] 165, 1. | [12] 435, 1. | [18] 93. |

3. *Te* convinco non *inhumanitātis* solum, sed etiam [1] *amentiae.* 4. Fannius *Verrem* insimŭlat *avaritiae* et *audaciae.* 5. Cicĕro *Verrem avaritīae* coarguit. 6. Orestes accusātur *matricidii.* 7. Nicomēdes *furti* damnātus est.

8. Nonne [2] *te* misĕret *mei ?* 9. Num [2] hujus *te gloriae* paenitēbat? 10. *Me* non solum piget *stultitiae* meae, sed etiam pudet. 11. *Me* civitātis *morum* [2] piget taedetque. [3]

### ABLATIVE.

RULE XXI.—*Ablative of Cause, Manner, Means.*—*414.*

**44.** I. CAUSE.—1. Caesar *beneficiis* ac *munificentiā* magnus habebātur, *integritāte* vitae, Cato. [3] 2. Quidam *vitiis* suis gloriąntur. 3. Gubernatōris ars *utilitāte,* non *arte* laudātur. 4. *Avaritiā* et *luxuriā* Romāna civĭtas laborābat. 5. Nimio *gaudio* paene [5] desipiēbam. 6. Adolescentes senum [7] *praeceptis* gaudent. 7. Laetus *sorte* tuā vives sapienter. [5] 8. Campāni fuērunt superbi *bonitāte* agrōrum.

II. MANNER.—1. Miltiădes summā [8] *aequitāte* res Chersonēsi constituit. 2. Athenienses *vi* summā proelium commisērunt. 3. Sidĕra [9] cursus suos conficiunt maxĭmā [10] *celeritāte.* 4. Athenienses *cum silentio* [11] audīti sunt. 5. *Cum virtūte* vivĭmus. 6. Pausanias epulabātur *more* Persārum.

III. MEANS, INSTRUMENT.—1. Servius Tullius *virtūte*

---

[1] 587, I. 5.     [5] 367, 3.     [8] 84.
[2] 346, II. 1.     [6] 582.     [10] 165.
[3] 83.     [7] 66.     [11] 414, 3.
[4] 587, I. 3.     [9] 163, 3.

regnum tenuit. 2. Nemo fit ' *casu* bonus. 3. Avārus
animus nullo satiātur *lucro.* 4. Trahĭmur omnes *studio*
laudis.' 5. Magnos homĭnes *virtūte* metīmur, non *fortūnā.* 6. Dido ' vitam suam *gladio* finīvit. 7. *Voluptāte*
capiuntur homĭnes, ut *homo* pisces.' 8. Minuuntur atrae
*carmĭne* curae. 9. Boni nullo *emolumento* impelluntur
iu fraudem.'

IV. Agent.—1. Alcibiădes erudītus est *a Socrăte.*
2. *A Deo* omnia ' facta sunt.' 3. Sacra *ab Numā* insti-
tūta sunt. 4. *A multis* ' ipsa ' virtus contemnĭtur.

Rule XXII.—*Ablative of Price.*—416.

**45.** 1. Ego " spem *pretio* non emo. 2. Vas Corin.
thium magno *pretio* mercātus sum. 3. Viginti *talentis*
unam " orationem Isocrătes vendĭdit. 4. Si prata *magno*
aestĭmant, quanti " est aestimanda " virtus? 5. Fanum
*pecuniā* grandi vendĭtum est. 6. Otium non *gemmis* "
venāle est.

Rule XXIII.—*Ablative with Comparatives.*—417.

**46.** 1. Vilius argentum est *auro, virtutĭbus* aurum.
2. Lux *sonĭtu* est velocior. 3. Amōris simulatio pejor "
est *odio.* 4. Nihil est veritātis *luce* dulcius. 5. Nihil est
*ratiōne* melius." 6. *Lacrĭmā* nihil citius arescit.
7. Tullus Hostilius ferocior quam *Romŭlus* " fuit.
8. Sol major " est quam *terra.* 9. Natūra nihil habet

---

| | | |
|---|---|---|
| ' 294. | ' 441, 1. | " 402, III. 1. |
| ' 396, II. | ' 294 ; 294, 2. | " 232. |
| ' 68. | ' 452. | " 416, 1, 4). |
| ' 367, 3. | " 446. | " 165. |
| ' 435, 1. | " 175. | " 417, 1. |
| ' 414, 5. | | |

praestantius quam *honestātem.*[1]  10. Timoleon sapientius[2] tulit[3] secundam fortūnam quam *adversam.*  11. Major famae sitis est quam *virtūtis.*[1]

#### RULE XXIV.—*Ablative of Difference.*—418.

⚹ **47.** 1. Patṛia mihi[4] vitā meā *multo* est carior.  2. Pompeius *biennio* major fuit quam Cicĕro.[1]  3. Hic locus aequo *spatio* ab castris[5] Ariovisti et Caesăris abĕrat.  4. Numa Pompilius *annis* permultis ante fuit quam[6] Pythagŏras.  5. Homēri[7] etsi incerta sunt tempŏra, tamen *annis* multis fuit ante Romŭlum.[8]

#### RULE XXV.—*Ablative in Special Constructions.*—419.

**48.** I. UTOR, FRUOR, ETC.—1. Multi *beneficio* Dei perverse utuntur.  2. *Recordatiōne* nostrae amicitiae[9] fruor.  3. Commŏda, *quibus* utĭmur, a Deo[10] nobis[11] dantur.  4. Lux, *quā* fruĭmur, a Deo nobis datur.  5. Virtūtis munĕre functus sum.  6. Solus potītus est *imperio* Romŭlus.  7. Numĭdae plerumque *lacte*[12] et *carne*[13] vescebantur.

II. FIDO, CONFIDO, ETC.—1. *Prudentiā consiliō*que[14] fidĭmus.  2. Quis aut corpŏris *firmitāte* aut fortūnae *stabilitāte* confīdet?  3. Juvĕnis nitĭtur *hastā.*

III. PLENTY AND WANT.—1. Abundārunt[15] semper *auro* regna Asiae.  2. Capua fortissimōrum virōrum *multitudĭne* redundat.  3. Antiochīa eruditissĭmis *homi-*

---

| | | |
|---|---|---|
| [1] 417, 1. | [6] 523, 2, 2). | [11] 384, I. |
| [2] 582, 305. | [7] 395. | [12] 74. |
| [3] 292. | [8] 432, 433. | [13] 72, 3. |
| [4] 391. | [9] 396, II. | [14] 587, I. 3. |
| [5] 434. | [10] 414, 5. | [15] 234. |

*nĭbus* affluēbat.    4. Nihil honestum est quod ¹ *justitiā* vacat.    5. Nulla ² vitae pars vacat *officio*.    6. Nunquam eminentia *invidiā* caret.    7. Magna negotia magnis *adjutorĭbus* egent.    8. Deus *bonis* ³ omnĭbus explēvit mundum.    9. Hectŏra ⁴ *vitā* spoliāvit Achilles.    10. Caesări tradĭta urbs est, nuda ⁵ *praesidio*, referta *copiis*.   11. *Virtūte* multi ⁶ praedĭti sunt.

IV. Dignus, Indignus, etc.—1. Virtus *imitatiōne*, non *invidiā* digna est.    2. Quam multi indigni *luce* sunt, et tamen dies orĭtur.⁷    3. Sapientia *eo* contenta est, quod adest.    4. *Intelligentiā* vestrā frētus sum.

V. Opus and Usus.—1. *Magistratĭbus* opus est.    2. Multis ⁸ *duce* opus est.    3. Nihil ⁹ opus est *simulatiōne*. 4. *Navĭbus* consŭli usus est.    5. Quantum ⁹ argenti ¹⁰ est tibi opus ?    6. Nobis exempla permulta opus sunt.

Rule XXVI.—*Ablative of Place.*—421.

**49.** 1. *In Italiā* bellum fuit.    2. Haec ab Romānis *in Graeciā* gesta sunt.    3. Iphicrătes *in Thraciā* vixit. 4. Caesar *ab urbe* proficiscĭtur.    5. Darīus *ex Asiā* in Eurōpam ¹¹ exercĭtum trajēcit.    6. Talis *Romae* Fabricius, qualis Aristīdes *Athēnis* fuit.

7. Tarquinius Superbus mortuus est *Cumis*. · 8. Numa Pompilius *Curĭbus* habitābat.    9. *Syracūsis* est fons aquae dulcis, cui ¹² nomen Arethūsa est.    10. Demarātus, Tarquinii regis pater, fugit Tarquinios ¹³ *Corintho*.   11. Haec *terrā marī*que ¹⁴ gesta sunt.    12. Conon plurĭmum ¹⁵ vixit *Cypri*, Timotheus *Lesbi*.

---

| | | |
|---|---|---|
| ¹ 445. | ⁶ 258, 2. | ¹¹ 435, 1. |
| ² 151. | ⁷ 419, 3. | ¹² 387. |
| ³ 441, 1. | ⁸ 380, 2. | ¹³ 379. |
| ⁴ 68. | ⁹ 419, 3, 2). | ¹⁴ 422, I, 1). |
| ⁵ 438. | ¹⁰ 396, III. | ¹⁵ 380, 2; 165. |
| | | ¹⁶ 424, 1. |

RULE XXVII.—*Ablative of Source and Separation.*—425.

**50.** 1. Praeclārum *a majorĭbus* accepĭmus morem.[1]
2. Hoc *a senĭbus*[2] audivĭmus. 3. Disce, puer, virtūtem
*ex me*, fortūnam *ex aliis.* 4. Collatīnus *ex urbe* migrāvit.
5. *Jove*[3] nate, Hercŭles, salve.
6. Abstĭnent *pugnā.* 7. Lacedaemonii de diutĭnā
*contentiōne* destitērunt. 8. Zama quinque diērum iter[4]
*ab Carthagĭne* abest. 9. Ariovistus millĭbus[5] passuum
sex *a* Caesăris *castris*[6] consēdit. 10. Tu, Jupĭter, Catilīnam *a tectis* urbis, *a moenĭbus*, *a vitā fortunis*que civium omnium arcēbis. 11. Dionysius tyrannus *Syracūsis*
expulsus est. 12. Aristīdes nonne[7] expulsus est *patriā?*
13. Themistŏcles imperātor bello Persĭco *servitūte* Graeciam liberāvit. 14. Robustus anĭmus omni est liber
*curā* et *angōre.*

RULE XXVIII.—*Ablative of Time.*—426, 427.

**51.** 1. Augustus obiit[8] sexto et septuagesĭmo aetātis
*anno.* 2. Socrătes suprēmo[9] vitae *die* de immortalitāte
animōrum multa disseruit. 3. Timoleon proelia maxĭ-
ma[10] natāli *die* suo fecit omnia. 4. Quā *nocte* natus est
Alexander, *eādem* Diānae Ephesiae templum deflagrāvit.
5. Solis *occāsu* suas copias Ariovistus in castra reduxit.
6. Nemo mortalium omnĭbus *horis* sapit. 7. Laelius
sermōnem de amicitiā habuit paucis *diēbus*[11] post mortem Africāni. 8. Roscius litem[12] decīdit abhinc *annis*
quattuor. 9. Carthāgo septingentesĭmo *anno* postquam
condĭta erat, delēta est.

---

| | | |
|---|---|---|
| [1] 83. | [4] 378, 2. | [9] 163, 3. |
| [2] 66. | [5] 132. | [10] 165. |
| [3] 66, 3 ; 425, 3. | [6] 346, II. 1. | [11] 427. |
| [4] 378. | [8] 295, 3. | [12] 82, 6. |

RULE XXIX.—*Ablative of Characteristic.*—428.

**52.** 1. Caesar Procillum, *summā* ¹ *virtūte* adolescentem, ad Ariovistum misit. 2. Aristotĕles, vir⁸ *summo ingenio, scientiā, copiā*, prudentiam cum eloquentiā conjunxit. 3. Cato *singulāri* fuit *prudentiā*⁸ et *industriā*. 4. Appius homo fuit *summā prudentiā, multā* etiam *doctrīnā*. 5. Hannibălis nomen erat *magnā* apud omnes *gloriā*. 6. Agesilāus *statūrā* fuit *humĭli* et *corpŏre exiguo*. 7. Caesar fuit *excelsā statūrā, colōre candĭdo, nigris ocŭlis*.

RULE XXX.—*Ablative of Specification.*—429.

**53.** 1. Sunt quidam homĭnes⁴ non *re*, sed *nomĭne*. 2. *Doctrīnā* Graecia Romānos et omni litterārum *genĕre* superābat. 3. Mardonius, *natiōne* Medus, a Pausaniā⁸ fugātus est. 4. Helvetii relĭquos Gallos *virtūte* praecēdunt. 5. Ancus regnāvit annos⁸ quattuor et viginti, cuilĭbet⁷ superiōrum⁸ regum belli pacisque et *artĭbus* et *gloriā* par.

RULE XXXI.—*Ablative Absolute.*—430 & 431.

**54.** 1. Cognĭto Caesăris *adventu*, Ariovistus legātos ad eum mittit. 2. Ite,⁸ *deis* ¹⁰ bene *juvantĭbus*. 3. Pythagŏras, *Tarquinio Superbo regnante*, in Italiam venit. 4. *Virtūte exceptā*, nihil amicitiā ¹¹ praestabilius est. 5. Germāni pellĭbus ¹² utuntur, magnā corpŏris *parte nudā*. 6. Natus est Augustus, *Cicerōne* et *Antonio consulĭbus*.

---

| | | |
|---|---|---|
| ¹ 163, 3. | ⁵ 414, 5. | ⁹ 295. |
| ² 363. | ⁶ 378. | ¹⁰ 51, 6. |
| ³ 428, 1, 2). | ⁷ 191, II.; 391. | ¹¹ 417. |
| ⁴ 362. | ⁸ 163, 3. | ¹² 419. |

7. Romāni, *Scipiōne duce, ponte facto,* superavērunt
Ticinum flumen.
                .

RULE XXXII.—*Cases with Prepositions.*—432–435.

**55. I. Accusative.**—1. Sophŏcles ad summam *senec-*
*tūtem* tragoedias fecit.   2. Adolescentes senum praeceptis
ad virtūtum[1] *studia* ducuntur.   3. Piětas est justitia adversus *deos.*   4. Ante *lucem* galli canunt.   5. Epaminondas Lacedaemonios vicit apud *Mantinēam.*   6. Legiōnes
Etruscōrum cis *Padum* fusae sunt.   7. Utilitātis derelictio contra *natūram* est.   8. Justitia erga *deos* religio[3]
dicitur, erga *parentes,* piětas.   9. Ratio conciliat inter
*se*[3] homĭnes.   10. Amicitia est propter *se* expetenda.[4]
11. Anĭmus per *somnum* curis[5] vacuus est.   12. Post
*me* erat Aegīna.   13. Secundum *flumen* paucae statiōnes
videbantur.   14. Germāni trans *Rhenum* incŏlunt.

**II. Ablative.**—1. A primā[6] *aetāte* me philosophia
delectāvit.   2. Cantābit vacuus coram *latrōne* viātor.
3. Sex menses[7] cum *Antiŏcho* philosŏpho fui.   4. Scipio
ob egregiam victoriam de *Hannĭbăle* appellātus est Africānus.   5. Virtus ex *viro* appellāta est.   6. Cato prae
*cetĕris* floruit.   7. Caesar legiōnes pro *castris* constituit.
8. Vita nihil sine magno *labōre* dedit mortalĭbus.[8]   9.
Aqua erat *pectorĭbus* tenus.[9]

**III. Accusative or Ablative.**—1. In *amnem* ruunt.
2. Gallia est divīsa in *partes* tres.   3. Homo doctus in *se*
semper divitias habet.   4. Sub ipsa *moenia* progressi
sunt.   5. Saepe est etiam sub *pallio* sordĭdo sapientia.
6. Virtus omnia subter *se* habet.

---

[1] 396, II.       [4] 232.       [7] 378.
[2] 362.       [5] 419, III.       [8] 384, II.
[3] 448, 1.       [6] 441, 6; 160.       [9] 434, 4.

# SYNTAX OF ADJECTIVES.

RULE XXXIII.—*Agreement of Adjectives.*—438, 439.

**56.** 1. *Vera* amicitia *sempiterna* est.  2. *Verae* amicitiae *sempiternae* sunt.  3. Venit hiems *glaciālis.*  4. Fugit *irreparabĭle* tempus.  5. Nihil est ab *omni* parte *beātum.*  6. *Atra* nubes condĭdit lunam.  7. Hora *quota* est ?  8. *Qualis* est *tua* mens ?  9. Nemo nascĭtur *dives.*
10. Stultitia et temerĭtas *fugienda*[1] sunt.  11. Labor voluptasque, *dissimillĭmă*[2] natūrā,[3] inter se sunt *juncta.*
12. Non terret *sapientem*[4] mors.  13. *Fortes*[4] fortūna adjŭvat.  14. *Primā*[5] luce *summus* mons a Labiēno tenebătur.[5]  15. Feriunt *summos* fulgŭra montes.  16. Roscius *assiduus*[7] ruri[8] vixit.  17. Philosophiae[9] nos *totos* tradĭmus.  18. Themistŏcles *absens* proditiōnis[10] est *accusātus.*  19. Triumphus *clarior* quam *gratior*[11] fuit.

---

# SYNTAX OF PRONOUNS.

RULE XXXIV.—*Agreement of Pronouns.*—445.

**57.** 1. Omne anĭmal *se ipsum*[12] dilĭgit.  2. Ad *quas* res aptissĭmi erĭmus, in *iis* elaborabĭmus.  3. Nihil expĕdit, *quod* non decet.  4. Non est vir[13] fortis, *qui*[14] labōrem fugit.

**58.** PERSONAL AND POSSESSIVE.—446–449.—1. Omnia

---

[1] 460; 439, 3.
[2] 163, 2; 439, 3.
[3] 414.
[4] 441.
[5] 441, 6.
[6] 468.
[7] 443.
[8] 424, 2; 421, II.
[9] 384, II.
[10] 410, II.
[11] 444, 2.
[12] 452.
[13] 362.
[14] 445, 6.

animalia *se* dilĭgunt. 2. *Te'* *tua*,' *me* delectant *mea*.
3. Ad amīcum de amicitiā scripsi. 4. *Ego* beātus sum.
5. In philosophiae studio aetātem consumpsi. 6. Aristīdes non effūgit civium *suōrum* invidiam.

**59.** DEMONSTRATIVE.—450–452.—1. *Haec* est tyrannōrum vita. 2. *Nos ipsi'* consolāmur. 3. *Ille* est vir.
4. Ab *ipso* Graccho *eădem haec* audīmus. 5. Homo habet memoriam et *eam'* infinītam.

**60.** RELATIVE.—453.—1. In mundo Deus est, *qui*
regit, *qui* gubernat, *qui* cursus astrōrum, mutatiōnes
tempŏrum, rērum vicissitudĭnes conservat. 2. Riden-
tur,' mala *qui* compōnunt carmĭna. 3. *Eădem* est utilitātis, *quae'* honestātis, regŭla. 4. Servi morĭbus' iisdem
erant, *quĭbus'* domĭnus. 5. Anĭmal hoc provĭdum,
sagax, acūtum, memor, plenum ratiōnis,' *quem'* vocā-
mus homĭnem, generātum est a Deo. 6. Perutĭles
Xenophontis libri sunt; *quos* '⁰ legĭte studiōse.

**61.** INTERROGATIVE.—454.—1. O dii'' immortāles,''
*quam* rem publĭcam habēmus, in *quā* urbe vivĭmus? 2.
*Quae* in me est facultas?

**62.** INDEFINITE.—455–459.—1. Exspectābam '³ *alĭ-
quem* meōrum.'⁴ 2. Veni Athēnas,'⁵ neque me *quisquam*
ibi agnōvit. 3. Aut *nemo*, aut, si *quisquam*, Cato sapiens fuit. 4. *Quidam* consŭlem laudant. 5. Optĭmum '⁶
*quidque*'' rarissĭmum est. 6. Consŭlum *alter* '⁸ exercĭtum
perdĭdit, *alter* vendĭdit.

| | | |
|---|---|---|
| ¹ 371. | ⁷ 428. | ¹³ 468. |
| ² 441, 1. | ⁸ 399, 2, 2). | ¹⁴ 441, 1. |
| ³ 452, 1. | ⁹ 445, 4. | ¹⁵ 379. |
| ⁴ 451, 2. | ¹⁰ 453. | ¹⁶ 165; 441, 2. |
| ⁵ 453, 2. | ¹¹ 51, 5. | ¹⁷ 458, 1. |
| ⁶ 451, 5. | ¹² 360. | ¹⁸ 151. |

# SYNTAX OF VERBS.

## AGREEMENT.

RULE XXXV.—*Verb with Subject.*—460–463.

**63.** 1. Homĭnes, dum *docent,*[1] *discunt.* 2. Tantum *scimus,*[2] quantum memoriā *tenēmus.* 3. Ego libertātem *pepĕri ;* ego patriam *liberāvi.*[3] 4. *Crescit* amor nummi, quantum[3] ipsa pecunia *crescit.* 5. Pars perexigua Romam inermes[4] *delāti sunt.* 6. Uterque[5] eōrum exercĭtum ex castris *edūcunt.*[6] 7. Corinthus, totīus Graeciae lumen, *exstinctum*[7] *est.* 8. Ratio et oratio *conciliat*[8] inter se homĭnes. 9. Castor et Pollux ex equis *pugnavērunt.*[9]

## INDICATIVE—TENSES AND USE.

RULE XXXVI.—*Use of Indicative.*—474.

**64.** PRESENT.—466, 467.—1. Virtus ab omnĭbus *laudātur.* 2. Nulla *habēmus* arma contra mortem. 3. In proelio cita mors *venit,* aut victoria laeta.

**65.** IMPERFECT.—468, 469.—1. Laelius oratiōnem suam *exornābat.* 2. *Exspectābam* adventum Menandri. 3. Lycurgi leges *vigēbant.* 4. Ut Romae[10] consŭles, sic Carthagĭne quotannis bini reges *creabantur.*

**66.** FUTURE AND FUTURE PERFECT.—470, 473.—1. Ro-

---

[1] 460, 2.  [5] 151, 4.  [8] 463, I.
[2] 460, 2, 1).  [6] 461, 3.  [9] 463, II.
[3] 380, 2.  [7] 462.  [10] 421, II.
[4] 438, 6.

mam¹ quum *venĕro*, quae' *perspexĕro*, *scribam* ad tc.
2. Ut sementem *fecĕris*, ita *metes*. 3. Si te' *rogavĕro*
alĭquid,' non *respondēbis ?*

**67.** PERFECT AND PLUPERFECT.—471, 472.—1. Hostes, ubi primum nostros equĭtes *conspexērunt*,' celerĭter
nostros *perturbavērunt*. 2. Ipse semper cum Graecis
Latīna *conjunxi*. 3. Civĭtas haec semper a me *defensa
est*. 4. Lacedaemoniōrum gens fortis *fuit*, dum Lycurgi
leges vigēbant. 5. Summā curā' exspectābam adventum
Menandri, quem' ad te *misĕram*. 6. Hannĭbal tres modios aureōrum annulōrum Carthagĭnem *misit*, quos
manĭbus' equĭtum Romanōrum' *detraxĕrat*.

SUBJUNCTIVE.—TENSES AND USE.

RULE **XXXVII.**—*Sequence of Tenses.*—480, 481.

**68.** 1. Ego vos hortor, ut amicitiam omnĭbus rebus'
humānis *anteponātis*.'⁰ 2. Philosophia nos docuit, ut
nosmet'' ipsos *noscerēmus*.'² 3. Dubĭtant nonnulli de
mundo, casūne '' ipse *sit effectus*,'⁴ an mente divīnā. 4.
Epaminondas quaesīvit, salvusne '⁵ *esset* clipeus. 5. Epaminondas rogāvit, *essentne fusi* hostes. 6. Ego in causis
publĭcis ĭta sum versātus, ut *defendĕrim* multos.

RULE **XXXVIII.**—*Potential Subjunctive.*—485, 486.

**69.** 1. *Quaerat* quispiam, cujusnam '⁶ causā '⁷ mun
dus factus sit.'⁶ 2. *Videas* rebus '' injustis justos '

---

¹ 379.
² 445, 6.
³ 374.
⁴ 460, 2.
⁵ 414, 3.
⁶ 445.

⁷ 434, 1.
⁸ 438.
⁹ 386.
¹⁰ 489, 490.
¹¹ 184, 6.
¹² 492, 2; 374, 4.

¹³ 526, II. 1.
¹⁴ 525.
¹⁵ 526, I.
¹⁶ 188, 3.
¹⁷ 414.
¹⁸ 441, 545.

maxĭme¹ dŏlēre.² 3. Equĭdem *vellem*,³ ut redīres. 4. Forsĭtan *quaeras* qui iste terror sit. 5. Hoc sine ullā⁴ dubitatiōne *confirmavĕrim.* 6. Quid *faciātis ?*⁵ 7. Quis haec *faciat ?* 8. Quid *videātur* Deo⁶ magnum in rebus humānis?

RULE XXXIX.—*Subjunctive of Desire.*—487; 488.

**70.** 1. *Imitēmur* majōres nostros. 2. *Valeant* cives mei; *sint* incolŭmes, *sint* beāti; *stet* haec urbs praeclāra. 3. Religio et fides *anteponātur*⁷ amicitiae.⁸ 4. Orātor *imitētur* Demosthĕnem. 5. Is qui impĕrat aliis⁹ *serviat* ipse nulli¹⁰ cupiditāti. 6. In rebus prospĕris superbiam arrogantiamque *fugiāmus.* 7. Ne quis, tanquam parva, *fastidiat* grammaticae elementa.

RULE XL.—*Subjunctive of Purpose or Result.*—489.

**71.** UT AND NE.—490–493.—1. Romāni ab arātro abduxērunt Cincinnātum, ut dictātor *esset.*¹¹ 2. Phaëthon optāvit, ut in currum¹² patris¹³ *tollerētur.*¹⁴ 3. Caesar ad Lamiam scripsit, ut ad ludos omnia *parāret.*¹⁴ 4. Timoleon orāvit omnes, ne id *facĕrent.*¹⁵ 5. Decrēvit senātus, ut consul *vidēret,*¹⁴ ne quid res publĭca detrimenti¹⁶ *capĕret.*¹⁴ 6. Discipŭlos id unum¹⁷ moneo, ut praeceptōres¹⁸ non minus, quam ipsa studia *ament.*¹⁴

**72.** UT AND UT NON.—494–496.—1. Tanta vis probĭtātis est, ut eam in hoste etiam *diligāmus.* 2. Dives est, cui¹⁹ tanta possessio est, ut nihil *optet* amplius. 3. Epaminondas adeo fuit veritātis²⁰ dilĭgens, ut ne joco²¹ qui-

---

| | | |
|---|---|---|
| ¹ 305, 2 ; 165. | ⁸ 386. | ¹⁵ 374, 4. |
| ² 550. | ⁹ 385. | ¹⁶ 396, III. |
| ³ 293. | ¹⁰ 151. | ¹⁷ 374, 5 |
| ⁴ 151. | ¹¹ 480. | ¹⁸ 371. |
| ⁵ 486, II. | ¹² 435. | ¹⁹ 387. |
| ⁶ 384. | ¹³ 77, II. 1. | ²⁰ 399. |
| ⁷ 463, 1. | ¹⁴ 492. | ²¹ 414, 3. |

dem[1] *mentirētur.* 4. Quis est tam miser, ut non Dei munificentiam *sensĕrit?* 5. Alcibiădes erat eā sagacităte,[2] ut decĭpi[3] non *posset.*[1]

**73.** Quo, Quin, Quominus.—497–499.—1. Lex brevis est, quo facilius ab imperītis *teneătur.* 2. Nunquam accēdo ad te, quin abs te *abeam*[4] doctior. 3. Quis dubĭtet,[5] quin in virtute divitiae *sint?* 4. Quid obstat, quomĭnus Deus *sit* beătus?

**74.** Relative.—500, 501.—1. Caesar equitātum, qui *sustinēret* hostium impĕtum, misit. 2. Non tu is es, quem nihil *delectet.* 3. Ego is sum, qui nihil unquam meā, potius quam meōrum civium causā,[6] *fecĕrim.*[7] 4. Nihil est quod Deus efficĕre[8] non *possit.* 5. Nullum est anĭmal praeter homĭnem, quod *habeat* notitiam alĭquam Dei. 6. Inventi sunt multi,[10] qui non modo pecuniam,[11] sed vitam etiam profundĕre[12] pro patriā parāti[13] *essent.*

Rule XLI.—*Subjunctive of Condition.*—503–513.

**75.** Dum, Modo, Dummodo.—505.—1. Odĕrint,[14] dum *metuant.* 2. Multi omnia recta[15] neglĭgunt, dummŏdo potentiam *consequantur.* 3. Omnia postposui, dummŏdo praeceptis[15] patris *parērem.*

**76.** Ac si, Ut si, Quasi, etc.—506.—1. Regem laudavērunt ac si hostes *vicisset.* 2. Patres metus cepit,[16] velut si jam ad portas hostis *esset.* 3. Quid[17] testĭbus[18] utor, quasi res dubia *sit.*

---

| | | |
|---|---|---|
| [1] 602, III. 2. | [7] 414. | [13] 438. |
| [2] 428. | [8] 481; I. 2; 460. | [14] 487, 297. |
| [3] 552, 1. | [9] 552, 1. | [15] 385. |
| [4] 290. | [10] 411. | [16] 222. |
| [5] 295, 3. | [11] 371. | [17] 380, 2. |
| [6] 486, II. | [12] 552, 3. | [18] 419. |

**77.** Si, Nisi, etc. : Qui=Si is, etc.—507–513.—1.
Anĭmum rege, qui, nisi *paret, impĕrat.*' 2. Si beātam
vitam *volŭmus*' adipisci,' virtūti opĕra *danda est.* 3.
Thucydĭdis oratiōnes ego laudo ; imitāri neque *possim,*'
si *velim,*' nec *velim* fortasse, si *possim.* 4. Non *possem*'
vivĕre, nisi in litteris *vivĕrem.*' 5. Consilium, ratio, sententia nisi *essent*' in senĭbus,' non summum' consilium'
majōres nostri *appellassent* '⁰ senātum.

RULE XLII.—*Subjunctive of Concession.*—515, 516.

**78.** Licet, Quamvis, etc.—1. Licet ipsa vitium '' *sit*
ambitio, frequenter tamen causa virtūtum est.'' 2. Non
est magnus pumilio, licet in monte *constitĕrit.* 3. Quam-
vis se '' ipso contentus *sit* sapiens,'' amīcis '' illi opus est.
4. Ego, qui sero Graecas littĕras *attigissem,* tamen complūres Athēnis '' dies '' sum commorātus.

**79.** Etsi, Tametsi, Etiamsi.—1. Eloquentiae '' stu-
dendum est, etsi eā '' quidam perverse *abutuntur.* 2.
Hoc, etiamsi nobilitātum non *sit,*²⁰ tamen honestum est ;
etiamsi a nullo '' *laudētur,* est laudabĭle.

RULE XLIII.—*Subjunctive of Cause.*—517–520.

**80.** Quum, Qui.—518, 519.—1. Quum vita sine amīcis metus '' plena *sit,* ratio ipsa monet amicitias compa-
rāre. 2. Quum *sint* in nobis consilium, ratio, prudentia,

---

| | | |
|---|---|---|
| ' 508. | ⁹ 373. | ¹⁶ 421. |
| ² 293. | ¹⁰ 510, 1 ; 234. | ¹⁷ 378. |
| ³ 552. | ¹¹ 362. | ¹⁸ 384. |
| ⁴ 509, 289. | ¹² 460, 2. | ¹⁹ 419. |
| ⁵ 510. | ¹³ 419, IV. | ²⁰ 460, 2. |
| ⁶ 510; 463, II. | ¹⁴ 441. | ²¹ 151. |
| ⁷ 66. | ¹⁵ 419, 3. | ²² 399, 2, 2). |
| ⁸ 163. 3. | | |

necesse est, Deum ¹ haec ipsa habēre ² majōra.   3. Quum
*venissem* ³ Athēnas,⁴ sex menses ⁵ cum Antiŏcho, nobilis-
simo ⁶ philosŏpho,⁷ fui.   4. Caninius fuit mirificā vigilan-
tiā,⁸ qui suo toto consulātu ⁹ somnum non *vidĕrit.*¹⁰

**81.** Quod, Quia, etc.—520.—1. Plato escam ¹¹ malōrum appellat voluptātem, quod eā ¹² homĭnes *capiantur,*
velut hamo pisces.   2. Nemo unquam est oratōrem, quod
Latīne *loqueretur,* admirātus.   3. Mater irata est, quia
non *rediĕrim.*

RULE XLIV.—*Subjunctive of Time with Cause.*—521–523.

**82.** 1. Dum relĭquae naves *convenīrent,* ad horam
nonam exspectāvit.   2. Quievēre ¹³ milĭtes, dum praefectus arma ¹⁴ *inspicĕret.*   3. Tragoedi quotidie, antĕquam
*pronuntient,* vocem sensim excĭtant.   4. Ante ¹⁵ vidēmus
fulguratiōnem, quam sonum *audiāmus.*   5. Caesar ad
Pompeii castra ¹⁶ pervēnit, priusquam Pompeius *sentīret.*¹⁷

RULE XLV.—*Subjunctive in Indirect Questions.*—525.

**83.** 1. Nescis, quantas vires virtus *habeat.*¹⁸   2. Nomen tantum virtūtis usurpas; quid ¹⁹ ipsa *valeat,* ignōras.
3. Lepĭdus declarāvit quantum *habēret* odium servitūtis.²⁰
4. Caesar equitātum omnem praemittit, qui ²¹ videant,²²
quas in partes iter *faciant.*   5. Non intellĭgunt homĭnes,
quam magnum vectīgal ²³ *sit* parsimonia.²⁴   6. In orato-

| | | |
|---|---|---|
| 545; 45, 6. | ⁹ 426. | ¹⁷ 523, 2. |
| ² 549. | ¹⁰ 519. | ¹⁸ 525, 2; 480. |
| ³ 518, II. 1. | ¹¹ 373. | ¹⁹ 380, 2. |
| ⁴ 379. | ¹² 414. | ²⁰ 396, II. |
| ⁵ 378. | ¹³ 235. | ²¹ 445, 5. |
| ⁶ 162. | ¹⁴ 131, 1, 4). | ²² 500. |
| ⁷ 363. | ¹⁵ 523, 3, 2). | ²³ 362. |
| ⁸ 428. | ¹⁶ 132; 379, 4. | ²⁴ 367. |

rĭbus Graecis, admirabĭle est, quantum inter omnes unus
*excellat.* 7. Mihi non minŏri ¹ curae ² est, qualis res publĭca post mortem meam *futūra sit,* quam qualis hodie *sit.*

RULE XLVI.—*Subjunctive by Attraction.*—527.

**84.** 1. Me admŏnes, ut me intĕgrum, quoad *possim,*
servem.³ 2. Quid est, cur non orātor de rebus iis elo-
quentissĭme dicat,⁴ quas *cognōrit.* 3. Jussit ut, quae
*venissent,* naves Euboeam petĕrent.⁵ 4. In Hortensio
memoria fuit tanta, ut, quae secum *commentātus esset,*
ea verbis ⁶ iisdem ⁶ reddĕret,⁷ quibus *cogitavisset.* 5. Recordatiōne ⁶ nostrae amicitiae sic fruor, ut beāte vixisse ⁶
videar,⁷ quia cum Scipiōne *vixĕrim.*¹⁰

RULE XLVII.—*Subjunctive in Indirect Discourse.*—529.

**85.** 1. Socrātes dicēbat,¹¹ omnes ¹² in eo, quod *scīrent,*
satis ¹³ esse ¹⁴ eloquentes. 2. Apud Hypănim ¹⁵ fluvium,
Aristotĕles ait,¹⁶ bestiŏlas quasdem nasci, quae unum
diem *vivant.* 3. Ariovistus Caesāri ¹⁷ respondit: quid
sibi *vellet ?* ¹⁸ cur in suas possessiōnes *venīret ?* jus esse
belli, ut, qui *vicissent,* iis,¹⁹ quos *vicissent,* quemadmŏ-
dum *vellent, imperārent.* 4. Legatiōni Ariovistus respondit: si quid ipsi²⁰ a Caesāre opus *esset,*²¹ sese ad eum
ventūrum fuisse;²² si quid ille a se *velit,* illum ad se
venīre²³ oportēre. 5. Divĭco ita cum Caesāre egit: si
pacem popŭlus Romānus cum Helvetiis *facĕret,*²³ in eam

---

<table>
<tr><td>¹ 165.</td><td>⁹ 549, 4, 1).</td><td>¹⁷ 384.</td></tr>
<tr><td>² 390.</td><td>¹⁰ 481, I. 2.</td><td>¹⁸ 293.</td></tr>
<tr><td>³ 489.</td><td>¹¹ 469, II.</td><td>¹⁹ 385.</td></tr>
<tr><td>⁴ 525.</td><td>¹² 545.</td><td>²⁰ 452, 5.</td></tr>
<tr><td>⁵ 414.</td><td>¹³ 582.</td><td>²¹ 532, 2.</td></tr>
<tr><td>⁶ 186.</td><td>¹⁴ 530, I.</td><td>²² 549, 2.</td></tr>
<tr><td>⁷ 489, 494.</td><td>¹⁵ 85, III. 1.</td><td>²³ 533, 3.</td></tr>
<tr><td>⁸ 419</td><td>¹⁶ 297, II. 1.</td><td></td></tr>
</table>

partem itūros ' Helvetios,' ubi eos Caesar esse *voluisset ; '*
sin bello persĕqui ' *perseverāret, reminiscerētur* pristinae
vırtūtis ' Helvetiōrum.

IMPERATIVE—TENSES AND USE.

RULE XLVIII.—*Imperative.*—535.

**86.** 1. *Sperne* voluptātes. 2. *Consulĭte* vobis,' Patres ' conscripti, *prospicĭte* patriae, *conservāte* vos,' conjŭges, libĕros, fortunasque vestras ; popŭli Romāni nomen
salutemque *defendĭte.* 3. *Vive* memor leti ; ' fugit hora.
4. Valetudĭnem tuam *cura* diligenter. 5. Virtūtes *excĭta,*
si forte dormiunt. 6. Poëmăta dulcia *sunto.*' 7. Impius '' ne '* *audēto* '* placāre donis iram deōrum. 8. Consŭles militiae summum jus *habento,* nemĭni *parento.* 9.
*Noli* '* te oblivisci '* Cicerōnem esse. 10. *Cura* ut quam
primum '* venias.'*.

INFINITIVE—TENSES AND USE.

*Tenses of Infinitive.*—540–544.

RULE XLIX.—*Subject of Infinitive.*—545.

*Predicate after Infinitive.*—546, 547.

*Infinitive as Subject.*—549.

**87.** 1. *Virum bonum esse,* semper est utĭle.'' 2. Omnĭbus bonis '* expĕdit, *salvam esse rem publĭcam.* 3. A
Deo *mundum* necesse '' est *regi.* 4. Concedendum est '*

---

| | | |
|---|---|---|
| ' 530, I.; 545, 3; 295. | ' 448. | '' 538, 2. |
| ' 545. | ' 399, 2, 2). | '' 305, 6. |
| ' 532, 4 | '' 537, II. | '' 535, 1, 1). |
| ' 552. | '' 441. | '' 438, 3. |
| ' 406, II. | '' 538, 1. | '' 441, 384. |
| ' 384. | '' 271, 3. | '' 301, 2. |
| ' 369. | | |

C

in virtūte solā *posĭtam esse beātam vitam*. 5. *Laelium doctum fuisse* tradĭtum est. 6. *Lectĭtavisse*[1] Platōnem studiōsc Demosthĕnes dicĭtur.[1] 7. Non *esse*[2] *cupĭdum* pecunia[3] est. 8. Non *esse emācem* vectīgal est. 9. *Contentum* suis rebus[4] *esse* maxĭmae[5] sunt divitiae. 10. *Dĭligĕre* parentes[6] *prima*[7] naturae lex[3] est. 11. Lycurgi temporĭbus[8] Homĕrus *fuisse* dicĭtur. 12. *Imperāre* sibi maxĭmum est imperium. 13. Parentes suos non *amāre*[7] impĭĕtas est. 14. Constat ad salūtem civium *inventas esse leges.* 15. Pecuniam *praeferre*[9] amicitiae[10] sordĭdum est. 16. Nihil est tam angusti anĭmi,[11] quam *amāre* divitias. 17. Ex malis *eligĕre* minĭma oportet.

*Infinitive as Object.*—550, 551.

**88.** 1. *Ferre* labōrem consuetūdo docet. 2. *Vincĕre* scis, Hannĭbal,[12] victoriā[13] *uti* nescis. 3. Magister tuus te magnā mercēde[14] nihil[15] *sapĕre*[16] docuit. 4. Num sum vel Graece *loqui*, vel Latīne docendus? 5. Non omnes sciunt *referre*[17] beneficium. 6. A Graecis[18] Galli urbes moenĭbus[19] *cingĕre* didicērunt. 7. Non *utĭlem* arbĭtror *esse* futurārum rerum *scientiam.* 8. Concēde *nihil esse bonum*, nisi quod honestum sit.[20] 9. Nonne poëtae post mortem *nobilitāri* volunt? 10. *Syracūsas maxĭmam esse Graecārum urbium*[21] *omnium* audivistis. 11. Socrătes parens[22] philosophiae jure[23] *dici* potest.[24] 12. Nunquam putāvi *fore*,[25] ut supplex ad te venīrem.[25] 13. Cato *esse* quam *vidēri* bonus[22] malēbat.[26]

---

| | | |
|---|---|---|
| [1] 549, 4, 1). | [10] 386, 1. | [19] 414. |
| [2] 545, 2, 2). | [11] 401. | [20] 531. |
| [3] 362. | [12] 369. | [21] 396, 2, 3). |
| [4] 419, IV. | [13] 419. | [22] 547, L |
| [5] 165. | [14] 416 | [23] 414. |
| [6] 371. | [15] 371, 3. | [24] 290. |
| [7] 166. | [16] 374, 4. | [25] 544. |
| [8] 426. | [17] 202, 2. | [26] 293. |
| [9] 292, 2. | [18] 425. | |

*Infinitive in Special Constructions.—553.*

**89.** 1. Consilium erat *continuāre*[1] bellum. 2. Bene et beäte vivĕre est honeste et recte *vivĕre*. 3. Postumio negotium dabātur *vidēre*,[2] ne quid[3] res publĭca detrimenti[4] capĕret.[2] 4. Fuit fama Themistŏclem venēnum suā sponte[5] *sumpsisse*. 5. Consilium fuit in Graeciam *redīre*. 6. Fama est Romŭlum Romam *condidisse*. 7. Fama est Homērum caecum *fuisse*.

SUBJECT AND OBJECT CLAUSES.—554–558.

**90.** SUBJECT CLAUSES.—555, 556.—1. Quaerĭtur, quid faciendum sit.[7] 2. Verum[8] est amicitiam inter bonos esse. 3. Relĭquum est, ut certēmus[9] officiis[10] inter nos. 4. Accēdit quod[11] patrem[12] amo.

**91.** OBJECT CLAUSES.—557, 558.—1. Non dubĭto, tu quid responsūrus sis.[7] 2. Rogāvi pervenissentne[11] Agrigentum. 3. Sentīmus nivem esse albam; dulce, mel. 4. Democrĭtus dicit innumerabĭles esse mundos. 5. Memĭni gloriātum esse Hortensium,[13] quod nunquam bello[15] civīli interfuisset.[16]

GERUNDS AND GERUNDIVES.—559–566.

**92.** GENITIVE.—563.—1. Sapientia ars[17] *vivendi* putanda est. 2. Caesar *loquendi* finem facit. 3. Mihi[18] *discendi*, tibi *docendi* facultātem otium praebet. 4. *Legendi* semper occasio est, *audiendi*, non semper. 5. Epa-

---

| | | |
|---|---|---|
| [1] 553, I. | [7] 525. | [13] 526, I. |
| [2] 553, II. | [8] 438, 3. | [14] 545. |
| [3] 190, 1. | [9] 495, 2. | [15] 386. |
| [4] 396, 2, 3). | [10] 414. | [16] 529. |
| [5] 492. | [11] 554, IV. | [17] 362. |
| [6] 414, 2. | [12] 447. | [18] 384, II. |

minondas studiōsus erat *audiendi.*'    6. Maxĭme' sum cupĭdus te' *audiendi.*    7. Demosthĕnes *Platōnis* studiōsus *audiendi* fuit.    8. Multi propter gloriae cupiditātem cupĭdi sunt *bellōrum gerendōrum.*    9. *Exercendae memoriae* gratiā,' quid quoque die' audiĕrim,' commemŏro vespĕre.

**93. DATIVE.—564.—1.** Crassus *disserendo*' par non erat.   2. *Solvendo*' civitātes non erant.   3. Numa *sacerdotĭbus*' *creandis* anĭmum adjēcit.   4. Mons *pecŏri* bonus *alendo* erat.   5. Consul *placandis diis* dat opĕram.   6. Sunt nonnulli *acuendis* puerōrum *ingeniis* non inutĭles lusus.

**94. ACCUSATIVE.—565.—1.** Homo ad *intelligendum*[10] et ad *agendum* est natus.   2. Breve tempus aetātis satis longum est ad bene[11] *vivendum.*   3. Bene sentīre rectēque facĕre[12] satis est ad bene beatēque *vivendum.*   4. Pythagŏras Lacedaemŏna[13] ad *cognoscendas* Lycurgī *leges* contendit.   5. Ubii navium magnam copiam ad *transportandum exercĭtum* pollicebantur.   6. Catilīna, nobilissĭmi genĕris[14] vir, sed ingenii pravissĭmi, ad *delendam patriam* conjurāvit cum audacissĭmis viris.

**95. ABLATIVE.—566.—1.** Nihil[15] *agendo*[16] homĭnes male agĕre[17] discunt.   2. Lycurgi leges laborĭbus erudiunt juventūtem, *venando, currendo, algendo, aestuando.*   3. Omnis loquendi èlegantia augētur *legendis oratorĭbus*[18] et *poëtis.*   4. Virtūtes cernuntur in *agendo.*   5. Multa[19] de bene beatēque *vivendo* a Platōne disputāta sunt.

---

' 399, 2, 2).      ' 391, 1.      13 379 ; 68.

' 305, 2 ; 165.      ' 384.      14 396, IV.

' 371.      ' 384, II.      15 371.

' 414, 2.      10 433.      16 414.

' 426.      11 559.      17 550.

' 525 ; 234.      12 549.      18 441, 1.

SUPINE.—567–570.

RULE L.—*Supine in* UM.—569.

*Supine in* U.—570.

**96.** 1. Lacedaemonii Agesilāum *bellātum* miscrunt in Asiam. 2. Themistŏcles Argos¹ *habitātum* concessit. 3. Hannĭbal patriam⁸ *defensum* revocātus est. 4. Veientes pacem *petītum* oratōres Romam mittunt. 5. Quod optĭmum⁸ *factu*⁴ videbĭtur, facies. 6. Quid est tam jucundum *cognĭtu* atque *audītu*, quam sapientĭbus sententiis⁵ ornāta oratio? 7. Plerāque *dictu*, quam re⁶ sunt faciliōra.⁷

PARTICIPLES.—571–581.

**97.** 1. Alexander *moriens*⁸ annŭlum dedit Perdiccae. 2. Hippias in Marathonia pugnā cecĭdit, arma contra patriam *ferens.*⁹ 3. Apelles pinxit Alexandrum Magnum fulmen *tenentem* in templo Ephesiae Diānae. 4. Sol *occĭdens*¹⁰ noctem confĭcit. 5. Terra *mutāta*¹¹ non mutat mores. 6. Dionysius tyrannus, Syracūsis¹⁸ *expulsus*, Corinthi¹⁹ puĕros docēbat. 7. Hannĭbal imperātor¹⁴ *factus* omnes gentes Hispaniae bello subēgit. 8. Sacerdos *vincta* in custodiam datur. 9. Regĭbus *exactis*, consŭles creāti sunt. 10. *Perdĭtis*¹⁵ rebus omnĭbus, tamen ipsa¹⁶ virtus se sustentāre¹⁷ potest. 11. Athenienses, non *exspectāto*¹⁸ auxilio, in proelium egrediuntur.¹⁹ 12. Sperne

| | | |
|---|---|---|
| ¹ 379. | ⁸ 578, I. | ¹⁴ 362, 3. |
| ² 371. | ⁹ 292. | ¹⁵ 578, IV. |
| ³ 165. | ¹⁰ 578, II. | ¹⁶ 452. |
| ⁴ 570, 429. | ¹¹ 580. | ¹⁷ 552, 1. |
| ⁵ 414. | ¹⁸ 425. | ¹⁸ 581. |
| ⁶ 429. | ¹³ 421, II. | ¹⁹ 225. |
| ⁷ 163, 2. | | |

voluptātes ; nocet *empta* dolōre [1] voluptas.   13. Dilapsi sunt in oppĭda, moenĭbus [2] se *defensūri*.[3]   14. Puĕris sententias *ediscendas* [3] damus.   15. Lentŭlus attribuit urbem *inflammandam* Cassio,[4] totam Italiam *vastandam* Catilīnae.

---

## SYNTAX OF PARTICLES.

### RULE LI.—*Use of Adverbs.*—582–585.

### CONJUNCTIONS, 587, 588.

**98. ADVERBS.**—1. Sapientis [5] anĭmus *semper* vacat vitio,[6] *nunquam* turgescit ; *nunquam* sapiens irascĭtur. 2. *Semper* in proelio iis [7] maxĭmum [8] est pericŭlum qui [9] *maxĭme* timent.   3. *Ut* secunda [10] *moderāte* tulĭmus,[11] *sic* adversam fortŭnam *fortĭter* ferre debēmus.

**99. CONJUNCTIONS.**—1. Horae cedunt *et* dies *et* menses *et* anni.   2. *Neque* pecuniae *neque* tecta magnifĭca [12] *neque* opes [13] *neque* imperia *neque* voluptātes in bonis rebus numerandae sunt.   3. Attĭcus *neque* mendacium dicēbat *neque* pati potĕrat.   4. Virtus *nec* erĭpi *nec* surrĭpi potest unquam ; *neque* naufragio [14] *neque* incendio amittĭtur. 5. *Aut* labōres *aut* sumptus suscipĕre nolunt.[15]   6. Est philosŏphi [16] habēre [17] non vagam, *sed* certam sententiam. 7. Jus suā sponte [18] est expetendum ; *etĕnim* omnes viri boni jus ipsum amant.

---

| | | |
|---|---|---|
| [1] 416. | [7] 387. | [13] 133, 1. |
| [2] 414. | [8] 165. | [14] 414, 4. |
| [3] 578, V. | [9] 445. | [15] 293. |
| [4] 384, II. | [10] 441, 1. | [16] 401. |
| [5] 441. | [11] 292. | [17] 549. |
| [6] 419, III. | [12] 164. | [18] 414, 2. |

# PART SECOND

# LATIN SELECTIONS.

## FABLES.

**NOTE.**—It is recommended that, in reading the Fables and Anecdotes, special attention should be given to *Gender* and to the *Declension of Nouns, Adjectives and Pronouns.*

### The Kid and the Wolf.

**100.** Hoedus, stans[1] in tecto domus,[2] lupo[3] praetereunti maledixit. Cui lupus, "*Non tu,*" inquit,[4] "*sed tectum mihi maledicit.*"

Saepe locus[5] et tempus homines[6] timidos audaces[7] reddit.[8]

### The Oxen.

**101.** In eōdem prato pascebantur[9] tres[10] boves[11] in maxĭmā concordiā, et sic ab omni ferūrum incursiōne[12] tuti erant. Sed dissidio[13] inter illos orto, singŭli a feris[14] petīti et laniāti sunt.

Fabŭla docet, quantum boni sit[15] in concordiā.

---

| | | |
|---|---|---|
| [1] 438, 1. | [6] 72, 2. | [11] 66. |
| [2] 119, 1. | [7] 373, 3. | [12] 100, 3. |
| [3] 384. | [8] 463, I. | [13] 431. |
| [4] 297, II. 2. | [9] 468. | [14] 414, 5. |
| [5] 141. | [10] 175. | [15] 525. |

### The Woman and the Hen.

**102.** Mulier quaedam habēbat gallīnam, quae ei[1]
quotidie ovum pariĕbat aureum.  Hinc suspicāri[2] coepit,[3]
illam auri massam intus celāre, et gallīnam occīdit.  Sed
nihil in eā repĕrit, nisi quod[4] in aliis gallīnis reperīri
solet.[5]  Ităque dum majorĭbus[6] divitiis[7] inhiābat, etiam
minōres perdĭdit.

### The Peasant and the Mouse.

**103.** Mus[8] a rustĭco deprehensus tam acri morsu
ejus digĭtos vulnerāvit, ut ille eum dimittĕret,[9] dicens:
"*Nihil, mehercŭle, tam pusillum est, quod de salūte*[10] *des-
perāre debeat,*" *modo se defendĕre velit.*[12]

### The Fox and the Grapes.

**104.** Vulpes[13] uvam in vite conspicāta ad illam subsiliit omnium virium[14] suārum contentiōne,[15] si eam forte
attingĕre posset.  Tandem defatigāta ināni labōre discē-
dens dixit: "*At nunc etiam acerbae sunt, nec eas in viā
repertas*[16] *tollĕrem.*"[17]

Haec fabŭla docet, multos ea contemnĕre, quae se
assĕqui posse despērent.[18]

### The Wolf and the Crane.

**105.** In faucĭbus lupi os inhaesĕrat.  Mercēde[19] igĭtur
condūcit gruem,[20] qui illud extrăhat.[21]  Hoc grus longi-
tudĭne[22] colli facĭle effēcit.  Quum autem mercēdem

---

[1] 384, II.
[2] 552.
[3] 297; 460, 2.
[4] 445, 3.
[5] 271, 3.
[6] 165.
[7] 386.
[8] 115, 1.
[9] 489; 494.
[10] 73, E. 2; 115, 2.
[11] 500.
[12] 505.
[13] 43, 3.
[14] 66.
[15] 414; 100, 3.
[16] 578, III.
[17] 503; 503, 2.
[18] 501, I.
[19] 416; 104, 1.
[20] 66, 2.
[21] 100, 1.

postulăret,[1] subrīdens lupus et dentĭbus[2] infrendens, "*Num tibi*," inquit, "*parva merces[3] vidētur, quod caput incolŭme ex lupi faucĭbus extraxisti ?*".

### The Trumpeter.

**106.** Tubĭcen[4] ab hostĭbus captus, "*Ne[5] me*," inquit, "*interficĭte ; nam inermis sum, neque[6] quidquam habeo praeter hanc tubam.*" At hostes, "*Propter hoc ipsum*," inquiunt, "*te interimēmus, quod, quum ipse pugnandi[7] sis[8] imperītus, alios ad pugnam incitāre soles.*"

Fabŭla docet, non solum maleficos[9] essę puniendos, sed etiam eos, qui alios ad male faciendum [10] irrītent.[11]

### The Husbandman and his Sons.

**107.** Agricŏla senex, quum mortem [12] sibi [13] appropinquāre sentīret,[14] filios convocāvit, quos,[15] ut fiĕri [16] solet, interdum discordāre novĕrat,[17] et fascem virgulārum afferri [18] jubet. Quibus allātis, filios hortātur, ut hunc fascem frangĕrent. Quod [19] quum facĕre non possent, distribuit singŭlas virgas, iisque celerĭter fractis, docuit illos, quam firma res [20] esset[21] concordia, quamque imbecillis discordia.

### The Mice.

**108.** Mures aliquando habuērunt consilium, quomŏdo sibi [22] a fele cavērent. Multis aliis[23] propositis,

| | | |
|---|---|---|
| [1] 518, II. | [9] 441; 545. | [17] 278, 3. |
| [2] 110, 1. | [10] 559, 565. | [18] 292, 2; 551. |
| [3] 362. | [11] 501, I. | [19] 453. |
| [4] 76, 1. | [12] 110; 105. | [20] 362. |
| [5] 538, 1. | [13] 380. | [21] 525. |
| [6] 587, I. 2. | [14] 518, II. | [22] 385, 3. |
| [7] 563; 399. | [15] 545. | [23] 431. |
| [8] 518, I. | [16] 294. | |

omnĭbus placuit, ut ei,[1] tintinnabŭlum annecterētur;[2] sic enim ipsos[3] sonĭtu admonĭtos eam fugĕre posse. Sed quum jam inter mures quaererētur,[4] qui feli tintinnabŭlum annectĕret,[5] nemo repertus est.

Fabŭla docet, in suadendo[6] plurĭmos[7] esse audāces, sed in ipso pericŭlo timĭdos.[7]

### The Enemies.

**109.** In eādem navi[8] vehebantur duo,[9] qui inter se capitalia odia exercēbant. Unus[8] eōrum in prorā, alter[10] in puppi[11] residēbat. Ortā tempestāte ingenti, quum omnes de vitā desperārent, interrŏgat is, qui in puppi sedēbat, gubernatōrem, *utram* [10] *partem navis prius submersum iri existimāret.* Cui gubernātor, "*Proram*," respondit. Tum ille, "*Jam mors mihi non molesta est, quum inimīci mei mortem adspectūrus sim.*"[12]

### The Tortoise and the Eagle.

**110.** Testūdo aquĭlam magnopĕre orābat, ut sese volāre docēret.[13] Aquĭla ei ostendēbat quidem, eam [14] rem [15] petĕre natūrae [16] suae contrariam; sed illa nihĭlo [17] minus instābat, et obsecrābat aquĭlam, ut se volŭcrem facĕre vellet.[18] Ităque ungŭlis arreptam aquĭla sustŭlit in sublīme, et demīsit illam, ut per aërem ferrētur.[19] Tum in saxa incĭdens comminūta interiit.[19]

Haec fabŭla docet, multos cupiditatĭbus suis occaecātos consilia prudentiōrum respuĕre, et in exitium ruĕre stultitiā [20] suā.

---

| | | |
|---|---|---|
| [1] 386. | [8] 62, III. | [15] 371. |
| [2] 495, 2. | [9] 441; 175. | [16] 391. |
| [3] 545. | [10] 151. | [17] 418. |
| [4] 518, II. | [11] 62, III. | [18] 293. |
| [5] 525. | [12] 517. | [19] 295, 3. |
| [6] 566, II. | [13] 489. | [20] 414, 2. |
| [7] 165; 441. | [14] 545. | |

### The Lion.

**111.** Societātem junxĕrant[1] leo, juvenca, capra, ovis. Praedā autem, quam cepĕrant, in quattuor partes aequāles divīsā,[2] leo, " *Prima*," ait,[3] " *mea est ; debētur enim haec praestantiae meae. Tollam et secundam, quam merētur*[4] *robur*[5] *meum. Tertiam vindĭcat sibi*[6] *egregius labor meus. Quartam qui sibi arrogāre voluĕrit,*[7] *is*[8] *sciat,*[9] *se habitūrum me inimīcum sibi."*[10] Quid facĕrent[11] imbecilles bestiae, aut quae sibi leōnem infestum habēre vellet ?[12]

---

## ANECDOTES.

### Anaxagoras.

**112.** Anaxagŏram ferunt,[13] nuntiātā[3] morte filii, dixisse : "*Sciēbam me genuisse mortālem.*"[15]

### Thales.

**113.** Thales interrogātus, quid esset " Deus, " *Quod*," inquit, " *initio*[16] *et fine caret.*"

**114.** Thales interrogātus, quid esset difficĭle,[16] " *Se ipsum*," inquit, "*nosse.*"[17] Interrogātus, quid esset facĭle : "*Altĕrum*," inquit, "*admonēre.*"

**115.** Thales rogātus, quid maxĭme commūne esset hominĭbus,[18] " *Spes*," respondit, " *hanc enim et illi habent, qui aliud nihil.*"

**116.** Quum Thales interrogarētur,[19] quid esset omnium vetustissĭmum, respondit : " *Deus, quod nunquam esse coepit.*"[20]

---

| | | |
|---|---|---|
| [1] 463, II. | [8] 451. | [15] 419, III. |
| [2] 431, 2, (1). | [9] 487. | [16] 163, 2. |
| [3] 297, II. | [10] 391. | [17] 234, 2. |
| [4] 225. | [11] 485 ; 486, II. | [18] 391. |
| [5] 77, IV. | [12] 292. | [19] 518, II. |
| [6] 384, II. ; 449, I. | [13] 357, L | [20] 297. |
| [7] 485. | [14] 525. | |

### Socrates.

**117.** Socrătes, in pompā quum magna vīs auri argentīque ferrētur,[1] "*Quam multa non desidĕro,*" inquit.

**118.** Sapientissĭmus Socrătes dicēbat,[2] *scire se*[3] *nihil, praeter hoc ipsum, quod nihil sciret:*[4] *relĭquos hoc etiam nescīre.*

### Scipio Africanus.

**119.** Scipio Africānus nunquam ad negotia publĭca accedēbat, antĕquam in templo Jovis[5] precātus esset.[6]

**120.** Scipio Africānus Ennii poētae imagĭnem[7] in sepulcro gentis Corneliae collocāri jussit,[8] quod Scipiōnum res gestas carminĭbus suis illustravĕrat.[9]

### Antigonus and the Cynic.

**121.** Ab Antigŏno Cynĭcus quidam petiit[10] talentum. Respondit,[11] *plus*[12] *esse, quam quod*[13] *Cynĭcus petĕre debēret.*[4] Repulsus petiit denarium. Respondit rex, *mi-nus*[13] *esse quam quod*[13] *regem decēret dare.*[14]

### Cicero.

**122.** Cicĕro Dolabellae[15] dicenti, se[16] triginta annos habēre,[17] "*Verum est,*" inquit, "*nam hoc jam ante viginti annos audīvi.*"

### The Lacedaemonians.

**123.** Lacedaemonii, Philippo minitante[18] per littĕras, se omnia quae conarentur[19] prohibitūrum,[20] quaesivĕrunt, *num se esset*[21] *etiam mori prohibitūrus.*

---

| | | |
|---|---|---|
| [1] 518, II. | [8] 471, II. | [15] 384. |
| [2] 469, II. | [9] 472. | [16] 545. |
| [3] 545. | [10] 234. | [17] 551, I. |
| [4] 531. | [11] 460, 2. | [18] 431, 2, (1). |
| [5] 66, 3. | [12] 165. | [19] 531. |
| [6] 523, II. 2. | [13] 371 ; 445, 6. | [20] 545, 3. |
| [7] 72, 3. | [14] 549. | [21] 525. |

**124.** Leonĭdas, Lacedaemoniōrum rex, quum Xerxes scripsisset,[1] "*Mitte arma;*" respondit, "*Veni et cape.*"

**125.** Quum ad Leonĭdam quidam milĭtum[2] dixisset,[1] "*Hostes sunt prope nos;*" "*Et nos,*"[3] inquit, "*prope illos.*"

**126.** E Lacedaemoniis[4] unus, quum Perses hostis in colloquio dixisset[1] glorians, "Solem[5] prae jaculōrum multitudĭne[6] et sagittārum non videbĭtis," "*In umbrā igĭtur,*" inquit, "*pugnabĭmus.*"

**127.** Lacedaemonius quidam quum riderētur,[1] quod claudus in pugnam iret,[7] "*At mihi,*" inquit, "*pugnāre, non fugĕre est propositum.*"

### Solon.

**128.** Solon quum interrogarētur,[1] cur nullum supplicium constituisset[8] in eum, qui parentem necasset,[9] respondit, *se id nemĭnem factūrum*[10] *putasse.*[11]

### Theophrastus, the Philosopher.

**129.** Theophrastus ad quendam, qui in convivio prorsus silēbat; "*Si stultus es,*" inquit, "*rem facis sapientem; si sapiens, stultam.*"

### Theocrĭtus, the Poet.

**130.** Miser poēta praelegĕrat Theocrĭto[13] versus suos. Tum interrogābat,[14] quosnam maxĭme approbāret,[15] "*Quos*[16] *omisisti,*" respondit.

---

| | | |
|---|---|---|
| [1] 518, II. | [6] 72, 2. | [11] 545, 3. |
| [2] 396, III. | [7] 520, II. | [12] 234. |
| [3] 367, 3. | [8] 549. | [13] 386, 1. |
| [4] 398, 4, 2). | [9] 525; 481, II. | [14] 460, 2. |
| [5] 112; 75. | [10] 500, 2; 234. | [15] 445, 6. |

### Cornelia.

**131.** Cornelia, Gracchōrum mater, quum Campāna matrōna, apud illam hospĭta,[1] ornamenta sua pulcherrĭma,[2] ipsi ostendĕret,[3] traxit eam sermōne,[4] donec e scholā redīrent[5] libĕri. Tum, " *Et haec,*" inquit, " *mea sunt ornamenta.*"

### Themistocles.

**132.** Memoriam in Themistŏcle fuisse singulārem ferunt. Ităque quum ei Simonĭdes artem memoriae pollicerētur,[6] " *Obliviōnis,*"[7] inquit, " *mallem ;*[8] nam memĭni etiam, quae[9] nolo ; oblivisci non possum, quae volo.*"

**133.** Themistŏcles quum consulerētur,[10] utrum bono viro paupĕri, an minus probāto divĭti filiam collocāret,[11] " *Ego vero,*" inquit, " *malo virum, qui pecuniā[12] egeat,*[13] quam pecuniam, quae viro.*"

**134.** Themistŏcles interroganti,[14] utrum Achilles[15] esse mallet,[16] an Homērus, respondit : " *Tu vero mallesne*[17] *te in Olympĭco certamĭne victōrem*[18] *renuntiāri, an praeco*[19] *esse, qui victōrum nomĭna*[20] *proclāmat.*"

### Diogenes, the Cynic.

**135.** Diogĕnes Cynĭcus Myndum[15] profectus, quum vidēret[16] magnifĭcas[17] portas et urbem exiguam, Mynlios monuit, ut portas claudĕrent,[18] ne urbs egrederĕtur.[19]

---

363.
[2] 163, 1.
[3] 518, II.
[4] 414, 4.
[5] 295, 3 ; 522, II.
[6] 397, 1, (3).
[7] 485, 486, 3.

[8] 445, 6.
[9] 525 : 526, II. 1.
[10] 419, III.
[11] 501, I.
[12] 575 ; 384.
[13] 547, 1.
[14] 525.

[15] 346, II. 1, 1) ; 485.
[16] 546.
[17] 76, 1.
[18] 379.
[19] 164.
[20] 489.

### Thrasybulus.

**136.** Quum quidam Thrasybŭlo, qui civitātem Atheniensium a tyrannōrum dominatiōne liberāvit, dixisset:[1] *" Quantas tibi gratias Athēnae debent ! "* ille respondit: *" Dii faciant,*[2] *ut quantas ipse patriae debeo gratias, tantas ei vidĕar*[3] *retulisse."*

### Xerxes.

**137.** Xerxes refertus donis[4] fortūnae, non equitātu,[5] non pedestribus copiis, non navium multitudĭne, non infinīto pondĕre[6] auri contentus, praemium ei proposuit, qui invenisset[7] novam voluptātem.

### Metellus Pius.

**138.** Metellus Pius, in Hispaniā bellum gerens[8] interrogātus, quid postĕro die[9] factūrus esset ?[10] *" Tunĭcam meam,"* inquit, *" si id*[11] *elŏqui posset, comburĕrem."*[12]

### Publius Rutilius Rufus.

**139.** Publĭus Rutilĭus Rufus quum amīci cujŭsdam injūstae rogatiōni[13] resistĕret,[14] atque is per summam[15] indignatiōnem dixisset, "Quid ergo mihi[16] ŏpus est amicitiā[17] tuā, si, quod[18] rogo, non facis ?" *" Immo,"* inquit, *" quid mihi tuā, si propter te alĭquid injūste factūrus sum ? "*

### Philip.

**140.** Mulier quaedam a Philippo, quum a convivio

---

| | | |
|---|---|---|
| [1] 518, II. | [7] 500, 2. | [12] 510, 1. |
| [2] 487. | [8] 578, I. | [13] 385. |
| [3] 492, 1 ; 549, 4. | [9] 426. | [14] 163, 3. |
| [4] 419, III. | [10] 545. | [15] 419, 3. |
| [5] 419, IV. | [11] 371. | [16] 445, 6. |
| [6] 84, 1. | | |

temulentus recedĕret,[1] damnāta, "*A Philippo*," inquit, "*temulento ad Philippum sobrium provŏco*."

### Titus.

**141.** Titus amor et deliciae genĕris humāni appellātus est. Recordātus quondam super coenam, quod nĭhil cuiquam toto[2] die[3] praestitisset,[4] memorabĭlem illam meritōque laudātam vocem edĭdit: "*Amīci, diem perdĭdi*."

### Xenophon.

**142.** Xenŏphon, quum solemne sacrum facĕret,[1] filium apud Mantinēam in proelio cecidisse[2] cognōvit. Corōnam deposuit, sed, ut audīvit fortissĭme pugnantem interiisse,[3] corōnam capĭti[4] reposuit, numĭna testātus, se[5] majōrem ex virtūte filii voluptātem, quam ex morte dolōrem sentīre.

### Diagoras, the Rhodian.

**143.** Diagŏras Rhodius, quum tres ejus filii in ludis Olympĭcis victōres renuntiāti essent,[1] tanto affectus est gaudio,[2] ut in ipso stadio, inspectante popŭlo,[10] in filiōrum manĭbus[11] anĭmam reddĕret.[12]

### Euripides, the Tragic Poet.

**144.** Athenienses quondam ab Euripĭde postulābant, ut ex tragoediā sententiam quandam tollĕret.[13] Ille autem in scenam progressus dixit, se fabŭlas componĕre solēre,[14] ut popŭlum docēret,[15] non ut a popŭlo discĕret.

---

|  |  |  |
|---|---|---|
| [1] 518, II. | [6] 295, 3. | [11] 118, 1, (1). |
| [2] 151. | [7] 384, II. | [12] 494. |
| [3] 426. | [8] 545. | [13] 492, 3. |
| [4] 554, IV. | [9] 414, 4. | [14] 272, 3. |
| [5] 551, 1. | [10] 431; 431, 2, (1). | [15] 491. |

*Tiberius, the Roman Emperor.*

**145.** Tiberius praesidĭbus[1] onerandas tribūto[3] provincias[3] suadentĭbus[4] rescripsit: *" Boni pastōris[5] est, tondēre[6] pecus, non deglubēre."*

**146.** Tiberius, Iliensium legātis[7] paulo[8] serius[9] de morte filii Drusi consolantĭbus, irrīdens, *se quoque*, respondit, *vicem[10] eōrum dolēre, quod egregium civem Hectŏrem[11] amisissent.[12]* Effluxĕrant autem tum plus quam mille[13] anni a morte Hectŏris.

*Simonides.*

**147.** Quum de Simonĭde[14] quaesivisset[15] tyrannus Hiĕro, quid esset[16] Deus; deliberandi[17] sibi unum diem postulāvit. Quum idem[18] ex eo postridie quaerĕret,[19] bidu̯um petīvit. Quum saepius duplicāret numĕrum diērum, admiransque Hiĕro requirĕret, cur ita facĕret[16]; *" Quia,"* inquit, *" quanto[19] diutius considĕro, tanto mihi res vidētur obscurior."*

---

| | | |
|---|---|---|
| [1] 384 ; 81, 2. | [8] 418. | [14] 374, 3, 4). |
| [2] 419, 2, 1). | [9] 444, 1 & 4. | [15] 518, II. |
| [3] 545. | [10] 133, 1; 371, 3, 1). | [16] 525. |
| [4] 577. | [11] 363. | [17] 563. |
| [5] 401. | [12] 531. | [18] 371. |
| [6] 549. | [13] 178. | [19] 418. |
| [7] 431, 2, (1). | | |

# ROMAN HISTORY.

Note.—It is recommended that, in reading the Roman History, special attention should be given to the *Synopsis of Conjugation* and to the *Formation of the Parts of the Verb.*—213-288.

## Period I.—Italian and Roman Kings.

FROM THE EARLIEST TIMES TO THE BANISHMENT OF TARQUIN, 510 B. C.

### *Early Italian Kings.—Aeneas in Italy.*

**148.** Antiquissĭmis[1] temporĭbus[2] Saturnus in Italiam venisse dicĭtur.[3]    Ibi haud procul a Janicŭlo arcem condĭdit, eamque Saturniam[4] appellāvit.    Hic Itălos primus[5] agricultūram[6] docuit.[7]

**149.** Postea Latīnus in illis regionĭbus imperāvit. Sub hoc rege Troja in Asiā eversa est.    Hinc Aenēas, Anchīsae filius, cum multis Trojānis, quibus[8] ferrum Graecōrum pepercĕrat,[9] aufūgit,[10] et in Italiam pervēnit.[10]    Ibi Latīnus rex ei[11] benigne recepto tiliam Laviniam in matrimonium dedit.[9]    Aenēas urbem condĭdit, quam in honōrem conjŭgis[12] Lavinium appellāvit.

### *Ascanius and the Kings of Alba.*

**150.** Post Aenēae mortem Ascanius, Aenēae filius, regnum accēpit.    Hic sedem regni in alium locum

---

[1] 444, 1.

[2] 426.

[3] 549, 4.

[4] 373.

[5] 442, 1.

[6] 374.

[7] 213, II.

[8] 385.

[9] 273, I. 2.

[10] 273, II. 1.

[11] 384, II.

[12] 96, 3.

transtŭlit,[1] urbemque condĭdit in monte[2] Albāno, eamque Albam Longam nuncupāvit. Eum secūtus est[3]
Silvius, qui post Aenēae mortem a Laviniā genĭtus erat.
Ejus postĕri omnes, usque ad Romam condĭtam,[4] Albae[5]
regnavērunt.

**151.** Silvius Procas, rex Albanōrum, duos filios relī-
quĭt,[6] Numitōrem et Amulium. Horum minor[7] natu,[8]
Amulius, fratri optiōnem dedit, utrum regnum habēre
vellet,[9] an bona,[10] quae pater reliquisset.[11] Numĭtor pa-
terna bona praetŭlit ;[1] Amulius regnum obtinuit.

### Birth of Romulus and Remus.

**152.** Amulius, ut regnum firmissĭme possidēret,[12]
Numitōris filium per insidias interēmit,[13] et filiam fra-
tris, Rheam Silviam, Vestālem virgĭnem fecit.[14] Nam
his Vestae sacerdotĭbus non licet viro[14] nubĕre. Sed
haec a Marte gemĭnos filios, Romŭlum et Remum, pepĕ-
rit.[15] Hoc quum Amulius comperisset,[16] matrem in
vincŭla conjēcit, puĕros autem in Tibĕrim[17] abjĭci
jussit.[18]

**153.** Forte Tibĕris aqua ultra ripam se effudĕrat,[19]
et, quum puĕri in vado essent positi,[19] aqua refluens[20] eos
in sicco relīquit. Ad eōrum vagītum lupa accurrit,[21]
eosque ubĕribus suis aluit. Quod[22] videns Faustŭlus
quidam, pastor illīus regiōnis, puĕros sustŭlit,[1] et uxōri
Accae Laurentiae nutriendos[23] dedit.

---

| | | |
|---|---|---|
| [1] 292, 2. | [9] 525. | [17] 62, II. 2. |
| [2] 110, I. | [10] 411, 1. | [18] 269. |
| [3] 283. | [11] 527. | [19] 518, I. |
| [4] 580. | [12] 491. | [20] 578, II. |
| [5] 421, II. | [13] 214, I. | [21] 255, I. 4. |
| [6] 273, II. 1. | [14] 385, 2. | [22] 453. |
| [7] 165. | [15] 273, I. 1. | [23] 578, V. |
| [8] 129 | [16] 518, II. | |

### Rome founded, 753 B.C.

**154.** Sic Romŭlus et Remus pueritiam inter pastōres transegērunt.[1] Quum adolevissent,[2] et forte comperissent, quis ipsōrum avus, quae mater fuisset,[3] Amuliun interfecērunt, et Numitōri avo regnum restituērunt. Tum urbem condidērunt in monte Aventīno, quam Romŭlus a suo nomĭne Romam vocāvit. Haec quum moenĭbus[4] circumdarētur,[5] Remus occīsus est, dum fratrem irrīdens moenia transiliēbat.

### Seizure of the Sabine Women.

**155.** Romŭlus, ut civium numĕrum augēret,[6] asȳlum patefēcit,[6] ad quod multi ex civitatĭbus suis pulsi accurrērunt. Sed novae urbis civĭbus[7] conjŭges deērant. Ităque festum Neptūni et ludos instĭtuit. Ad hos quum multi[8] ex finitĭmis popŭlis cum mulierĭbus et libĕris venissent,[8] Romāni inter ipsos ludos spectantes[9] virgĭnes rapuērunt.

**156.** Popŭli illi, quorum virgĭnes raptae erant, bellum adversus raptōres suscepērunt. Quum Romae[10] appropinquārent,[8] forte in Tarpēiam virgĭnem incidērunt, quae in arce sacra procurābat. Hanc rogābant, ụt viam in arcem monstrāret,[11] eīque permisērunt, ut munus sibi poscĕret.[12] Illa petiit, ut sibi darent,[13] quod[14] in sinistris manĭbus[14] gerĕrent,[15] annŭlos aureos et armillas signifĭcans. At hostes in arcem ab eā perducti scutis Tarpēiam obruērunt; nam et ea in sinistris manĭbus gerēbant.

---

| | | |
|---|---|---|
| [1] 255, II. | [6] 273, II. 1. | [11] 492, 2. |
| [2] 518, II. | [7] 386, 2. | [12] 273, I. 2. |
| [3] 525. | [8] 441, 1. | [13] 445, 6. |
| [4] 131, 1; 414. | [9] 578, I. | [14] 118, 1. |
| [5] 269; 491. | [10] 386. | [15] 527. |

*The Sabines are received into the City.—Death of Romulus.*

**157.** Tum Romŭlus cum hoste, qui montem Tarpē-
ium tenēbat, pugnam conseruit in eo loco, ubi nunc
forum Romānum est. 'In mediā¹ caede raptae ° processē-
runt, et hinc patres, hinc conjŭges et socĕros complecte-
bantur, et rogābant, ut caedis finem facĕrent.° Utrīque
his precĭbus commōti sunt. Romŭlus foedus icit, et Sabīnos in urbem recēpit.

**158.** Postea civitātem descripsit.⁴ Centum senatōres legit,° eosque quum ob aetātem, tum ob reverentiam
iis debĭtam, Patres appellāvit. Plebem in triginta curias
distribuit, easque raptārum nominĭbus nuncupāvit. Anno regni tricesĭmo septĭmo, quum exercĭtum lustrāret,°
inter tempestātem ortam° repente ocŭlis° homĭnum sub-
ductus est. Hinc alii° eum a senatorĭbus interfectum,
alii ad deos sublātum ¹⁰ esse existimavērunt.

*Numa Pompilius.*

**159.** Post Romŭli mortem unīus anni interregnum
fuit. Quo elapso,¹¹ Numa Pompilius Curĭbus,¹² urbe in
agro Sabinōrum, natus rex creātus est. Hic vir bellum
quidem nullum gessit ; nec minus tamen civitāti° profuit.
Nam et leges dedit, et sacra plurĭma instituit, ut popŭli
barbări et bellicōsi mores mollīret.¹³ Omnia autem,
quae faciēbat, se nymphae Egeriae, conjŭgis suae, mo-
nitu facĕre dicēbat. Morbo decessit,¹⁴ quadragesĭmo
tertio imperii anno.

---

¹ 441, 6.  ⁶ 518, II.  ¹¹ 431, 2.
² 575.  ⁷ 577.  ¹² 421, II.
³ 492, 2.  ⁸ 386.  ¹³ 491.
⁴ 258, I. 3.  ⁹ 459.  ¹⁴ 258, I. 2.
⁵ 255, II.  ¹⁰ 292, 2.

### Tullus Hostilius.

**160.** Numae[1] successit Tullus Hostilius, cujus avus se in bello adversus Sabīnos fortem et strenuum virum praestitĕrat.[2] Rex[3] creātus bellum Albānis indixit, idque trigeminōrum, Horatiōrum et Curiatiōrum, certamĭne finīvit. Albam propter perfidiam Metii Suffetii diruit. Quum triginta duōbus annis[4] regnasset,[5] fulmĭne ictus cum domo suā arsit.[6]

### Ancus Marcius.

**161.** Post hunc Ancus Marcius, Numae ex filiā nepos, suscēpit imperium. Hic vir aequitāte et religiōne avo[7] simĭlis, Latīnos bello domuit,[8] urbem ampliāvit, et nova ei[9] moenia circumdĕdit. Carcĕrem primus[10] aedificāvit. Ad Tibĕris ostia urbem condĭdit, Ostiamque vocāvit. Vicesĭmo quarto anno imperii morbo obiit.[11]

### Lucius Tarquinius Priscus.

**162.** Deinde regnum Lucius Tarquinius Priscus accēpit, Demarāti filius, qui tyrannos patriae Corinthi fugiens in Etruriam venĕrat. Ipse Tarquinius, qui nomen ab urbe Tarquiniis accēpit, aliquando Romam[12] profectus[13] erat.

**163.** Quum Romae[14] commorarētur,[15] Anci regis familiaritātem consecūtus est, qui eum filiōrum suōrum tutōrem[16] relīquit. Sed is pupillis[1] regnum intercēpit. Senatorĭbus, quos Romŭlus creavĕrat, centum alios ad·

---

| | | |
|---|---|---|
| [1] 386. | [6] 269. | [11] 295, 3. |
| [2] 261, 2. | [7] 391. | [12] 379. |
| [3] 362, 3. | [8] 260. | [13] 283. |
| [4] 378, 1. | [9] 384, II. 1. | [14] 421, II. |
| [5] 518, II. | [10] 442, 1. | [15] 373. |

dīdit, qui minōrum gentium sunt appellāti. Plura bella
felicĭter gessit, nec paucos agros, hostĭbus [1] ademptos,
urbis territorio adjunxit. Primus [2] triumphans urbem
intrāvit. Cloācas fecit; [3] Capitolium inchoāvit. Tricesĭmo octāvo imperii anno per Anci filios, [4] quibus [5] regnum eripuĕrat, occīsus est.

### Servius Tullius.

**164.** Post hunc Servius Tullius suscēpit imperium,
genĭtus ex nobĭli femĭnā, captīvā tamen et famŭlā.
Quum adolevisset, [6] rex ei filiam in matrimonium dedit.

**165.** Quum Priscus Tarquinius occīsus esset, Tanăquil de superiōre [7] parte domus popŭlum allocūta est,
dicens: *regem grave quidem, sed non letāle vulnus accepisse; eum petĕre, ut popŭlus, dum convaluisset, [8] Servio Tullio obedīret.* Sic Servius regnāre coepit, sed
bene imperium administrāvit. Montes tres urbi
adjunxit. [9] Primus omnium censum ordināvit. Sub eo
Roma habuit octoginta tria millia civium cum his, qui
in agris erant.

**166.** Hic rex interfectus est scelĕre filiae Tulliae et
Tarquinii Superbi, filii ejus regis, cui [1] Servius successĕ-
rat. Nam ab ipso Tarquinio interfectus est. Tullia in
forum properāvit, et prima conjŭgem regem salutāvit.
Quum domum [11] redīret, aurīgam super patris corpus, in
viā jacens, [12] carpentum agĕre jussit.

### Banishment of Tarquinius Superbus, 510 B. C.

**167.** Tarquinius Superbus cognōmen morĭbus [13] meruit. Bello [14] tamen strenuus plures finitimōrum popu-

---

| | | |
|---|---|---|
| [1] 386. | [6] 518, II. | [11] 370, 3. |
| [2] 442, 1. | [7] 163, 3. | [12] 577. |
| [3] 255, II. | [8] 533, 4. | [13] 414, 4. |
| [4] 414, 5, 1). | [9] 492, 2. | [14] 429. |
| [5] 386, 2. | [10] 258, I. 1. | |

lōrum vicit.' Templum Jovis in Capitolio aedificāvit.
Postea, dum Ardeam oppugnābat,' urbem Latii, imperium perdĭdit.

**168.** Lucius Brutus, Collatīnus, aliīque nonnulli in
exitium regis conjurārunt,' populōque persuasērunt,' ut
ei portas urbis claudĕret.' Exercĭtus quoque, qui civitātem Ardeam cum rege oppugnābat, eum relīquit. Fugit
ităque cum uxōre et libĕris suis. Ita Romae septem reges regnavērunt annos ducentos quadraginta quattuor.

---

### PERIOD II.—ROMAN STRUGGLES AND CONQUESTS.

FROM THE ESTABLISHMENT OF THE COMMONWEALTH TO THE FIRST PUNIC WAR,
264 B. C.

*Consuls at Rome, 509 B. C.—War with Tarquin.*

**169.** Tarquinio expulso,' consŭles coepēre ' pro uno
rege duo creāri, ut, si unus malus esset,' alter eum coër-
cēret.' Annuum iis imperium tribūtum est, ne per
diuturnitātem potestātis insolentiōres redderentur.' Fuērunt igĭtur anno primo, expulsis regĭbus, consŭles Lucius
Junius Brutus, acerrĭmus [10] libertātis vindex, et Tarquinius Collatīnus. Sed Collatīno [11] paulo post dignĭtas
sublāta est.[12] Placuĕrat enim, ne quis ex Tarquiniōrum
familiā Romae manēret.[13] Ergo cum omni patrimonio
suo ex urbe migrāvit, et in ejus locum Valerius Publicŏla consul factus est.[14]

---

| | | |
|---|---|---|
| ¹ 251, 1. | ⁶ 431, 2. | ¹¹ 386. |
| ² 468. | ⁷ 235, 297. | ¹² 202, 2. |
| ³ 234. | ⁸ 509. | ¹³ 492. |
| ⁴ 269, I. | ⁹ 491. | ¹⁴ 294. |
| ⁶ 492, 2. | ¹⁰ 163, 1. | |

**170.** Commŏvit[1] bellum urbi rex Tarquinius. In primā pugnā Brutus consul, et Aruns, Tarquinii filius, sese invĭcem occidērunt. Romāni tamen ex eā pugnā victōres recessērunt.[2] Brutum Romānae matrōnae, quasi commūnem patrem, per annum luxērunt.[3] Valerius Publicŏla Spurium Lucretium, collēgam[4] sibi[5] fecit; quum morbo exstinctus esset,[6] Publicŏla Horatium Pulvillum sibi collēgam sumpsit.[6] Ita primus annus quinque consŭles habuit.

*War with Porsena, 508 B. C.*

**171.** Secundo quoque anno itĕrum Tarquinius bellum Romānis intŭlit,[7] Porsēnā, rege Etruscōrum, auxilium ei ferente.[8] In illo bello Horatius Cocles solus pontem ligueum defendit, et hostes cohibuit, donec pons[9] a tergo ruptus esset.[10] Tum se cum armis in Tibĕrim[11] conjēcit, et ad suos transnāvit.

**172.** Dum Porsĕna urbem obsidēbat, Quintus Mucius Scaevŏla, juvĕnis fortis anĭmi, in castra hostium se contŭlit eo consilio,[12] ut regem occidĕret.[13] At ibi scribam regis pro ipso rege interfēcit. Tum a regiis satcllitĭbus comprehensus et ad regem deductus, quum Porsĕna eum ignĭbus allātis[14] terrēret,[15] dextram arac accensae imposuit, donec flammis consumpta esset.[16] Hoc facĭnus rex mirātus juvĕnem dimīsit[16] incolŭmem. Tum hic, quasi beneficium refĕrens, ait,[17] *trecentos alios juvĕnes in eum conjurasse.*[18] Hac re territus Porsĕna

---

[1] 270, II. 1.
[2] 258, I. 2.
[3] 373.
[4] 384.
  518, II.; 273, II. 1.
[5] 258, I. 4.

[7] 292, 2.
[8] 431, 2.
[9] 110, 1.
[10] 522, II.
[11] 62, II. 2.
[12] 414, 2.

[13] 492.
[14] 580.
[15] 518, II.
[16] 258, I. 2.
[17] 297, II.
[18] 234.

pacem cum Romānis fecit, Tarquinius autem Tuscŭlum[1]
se contŭlit, ibīque privātus consenuit.[*]

### Secession to the Mons Sacer, 494 B. C.

**173.** Sexto decĭmo anno post reges exactos,[2] popŭlus
Romae seditiōnem fecit, questus quod tribūtis et militiā
a senātu exhaurirētur.[4]  Magna pars plebis urbem relīquit, et in montem trans Aniēnem[5] amnem[6] secessit.
Tum patres turbāti Menenium Agrippam misērunt ad
plebem, qui eam senatui conciliāret.[7]  Hic iis inter alia
fabŭlam narrāvit de ventre et membris humāni corpŏris;
quā popŭlus commōtus est, ut in urbem redīret.[8]  Tum
primum tribūni plebis creāti sunt, qui plebem adversum
nobilitātis superbiam defendĕrent.[*]

### Banishment of Coriolanus, 491 B. C.

**174.** Undevicesĭmo anno post exactos reges, Caius
Marcius, Coriolānus dictus ab urbe Volscōrum Coriŏlis,
quam bello cepĕrat, plebi invīsus[9] fiĕri coepit.  Quare
urbe[10] expulsus ad Volscos, acerrĭmos Romanōrum hostes, contendit, et ab iis dux[11] exercĭtus factus Romānos
saepe vicit.  Jam usque ad quintum milliarium urbis
accessĕrat, nec ullis civium suōrum legationĭbus flecti
potĕrat, ut patriae[12] parcĕret.[*]  Denĭque Veturia mater
et Volumnia uxor ex urbe ad eum venērunt;[13] quarum
fletu et precĭbus commōtus est, ut exercĭtum removēret.[*]
Quo facto[14] a Volscis ut proditor occīsus[*] esse dicĭtur.

---

*The Fabii cut off at the Cremĕra,* 477 *B. C.*

**175.** Romăni quum adversum Veientes bellum gerĕrent,[1] familia Fabiōrum sola[2] hoc bellum suscēpit.
Profecti[3] sunt trecenti sex nobilissĭmi homĭnes, duce[4]
Fabio consŭle.[5]  Quum saepe hostes vicissent,[1] apud
Cremēram fluvium castra posuērunt.  Ibi, quum Veientes dolo[6] usi eos in insidias pellexissent, in proelio exorto[7]
omnes periērunt.  Unus superfuit ex tantā familiā, qui
propter aetātem puerīlem duci non potuĕrat ad pugnam.
Hic genus propagāvit ad Quintum Fabium Maxĭmum
illum, qui Hannibălem prudenti cŭnctatiōne debilitāvit.

*Rome taken by the Gauls,* 390 *B. C.*

**176.** Galli Senōnes ad urbem venērunt, Romānos
apud flumen Alliam vicērunt, et urbem etiam occupā-
runt.  Jam nihil praeter Capitolium defendi potuit.  Et
jam praesidium fame[8] laborābat, et in eo erant, ut pacem a Gallis auro[9] emĕrent,[10] quum Camillus cum manu
milĭtum superveniens hostes magno proelio superāvit.

*Valor of Titus Manlius Torquatus,* 361 *B. C.*

**177.** Anno trecentesĭmo nonagesĭmo tertio post urbem condĭtam Galli itĕrum ad urbem accessĕrant, et
quarto milliario[11] trans Aniēnem fluvium consedĕrant.
Contra eos missus est Titus Quinctius.  Ibi Gallus quidam eximiā corpŏris magnitudĭne[12] fortissĭmum Romanōrum ad certāmen singulāre provocāvit.  Titus Manlius,

---

| | | |
|---|---|---|
| [1] 518, II. | [5] 363. | [9] 416. |
| [2] 151. | [6] 419, I. | [10] 494. |
| [3] 283. | [7] 577. | [11] 422, 1, 2). |
| [4] 430, 431. | [8] 414, 2. | [12] 428. |

4

nobilissĭmus juvĕnis, provocatiōnem accepit, Gallum occīdit, eumque torque[1] aureo spoliāvit, qno ornātus erat. Hinc et ipse et postĕri ejus *Torquāti* appellāti sunt. Galli fugam capessivērunt.[2]

*Beginning of Samnite Wars*, 343 B. C.

**178.** Postea Romāni bellum gessērunt[3] cum Samnitĭbus, ad quod Lucius Papirius Cursor cum honōre dictatōris profectus est. Qui[4] quum negotii cujusdam causā Romam redīret,[5] praecēpit Quinto Fabio Rulliāno, magistro equĭtum, quem apud exercĭtum relīquit, ne pugnam cum hoste committĕret.[6] Sed ille occasiōnem nactus[7] felicissĭme dimicāvit, Samnītes delēvit.— Ob hanc rem a dictatōre capĭtis[8] damnātus est. At ille in urbem confūgit,[9] et ingenti favōre[10] milĭtum et popŭli liberātus est; in Papirium autem tanta exorta[11] est seditio, ut paene ipse interficerētur.[12]

*The Roman Army is made to pass under the yoke*, 321 B. C.—*The Samnites are conquered*, 290 B. C.

**179.** Duōbus annis[13] post Titus Veturius et Spurius Postumius consūles bellum adversum Samnītes gerēbant. Hi a Pontio Thelesīno, duce hostium, in insidias inducti sunt. Nam ad Furcŭlas Caudīnas Romānos pellexit[14] in angustias, unde sese expedīre non potĕrant. Ibi Pontius patrem suum Herennium rogāvit, quid faciendum[15] putāret.[16] Ille respondit, *aut omnes occidendos esse, ut*

| | | |
|---|---|---|
| [1] 419, 2, 1). | [7] 283. | [20] 494. |
| [2] 332, I. 2). | [8] 410, 2. | [19] 418. |
| [3] 272, I. | [9] 273, II. | [14] 272, I. 2. |
| [4] 453. | [10] 414, 4. | [15] 545, 3. |
| [5] 518, II. | [11] 283, 2. | [16] 374, 4; 525. |
| [6] 492, 2. | | |

*Romanōrum vires frangerentur,*[1] *aut omnes dimittendos, ut beneficio obligarentur,*[1] Pontius utrumque[2] consilium improbāvit, omnesque sub jugum misit. Samnītes denique post bellum undequinquaginta ănnōrum supe-rāti sunt.

/\ *War with Pyrrhus,* 281 *B. C.*

**180.** Devictis Samnitĭbus,[3] Tarentīnis bellum indictum est, quia legātis Romanōrum injuriam fecissent.[4] Hi Pyrrhum, Epīri regem, contra Romānos auxilium poposcērunt.[3] Is mox in Italiam venit, tumque primum Romāni cum transmarīno hoste pugnavērunt. Missus est contra eum consul Publius Valerius Laevīnus. /Hic, quum exploratōres Pyrrhi cepisset,[2] jussit eos per castra duci, tumque dimitti, ut renuntiārent[1] Pyrrho, quaecunque[1] a Romānis agerentur.[2]

**181.** Pugnā commissā,[1] Pyrrhus auxilio elephantō-rum vicit. Nox proelio finem dedit. Laevīnus tamen per noctem fugit. Pyrrhus Romānos mille octingentos cepit, eosque summo[2] honōre[10] tractāvit. Quum eos, qui in proelio interfecti erant, omnes adversis vulnerĭbus et truci vultu etiam mortuos jacēre vidēret,[2] tulisse ad coelum manus dicĭtur cum hac voce: "*Ego cum talĭbus viris*[11] *brevi orbem*[11] *terrārum subigĕrem.*"[11]

**182.** Postea Pyrrhus Romam perrexit; omnia ferro ignēque vastāvit; Campaniam depopulātus est, atque ad Praeneste[13] venit, milliario[14] ab urbe octāvo decĭmo. Mox terrōre exercĭtus,[15] qui cum consŭle scquebātur, in Campaniam se recēpit. Legāti ad Pyrrhum de captīvis

---

[1] 491.

[2] 151, 4.

[3] 431, 2, (1).

[4] 520, II.

[5] 273, I. 2.

[6] 518, II.

[7] 445, 6.

[8] 527.

[9] 163, 3.

[10] 414, 3.

[11] 503, 2, 2); 510.

[12] 107, 2.

[13] 379, 1.

[14] 422, 1.

[15] 396, II.

redimendis¹ missi² honorifīce ab eo suscepti sunt ; captīvos sine pretio reddĭdit.   Unum ex legātis, Fabricium,
sic admirātus est, ut ei quartam partem regni sui pro-
mittĕret,³ si ad se transīret;⁴ sed a Fabricio contemptus⁵
est.

**183.** Quum jam Pyrrhus ingenti Romanōrum admi-
ratiōne tenerētur,⁶ legātum misit Cineam, praestantissĭ-
mum virum, qui pacem petĕret⁷ eā conditiōne, ut
Pyrrhus eam partem Italiae, quam armis occupavĕrat,
retinēret.⁸ (Romāni respondērunt, eum cum Romānis
pacem habēre non posse, nisi ex Italiā recessisset.⁹ Cineas
quum rediisset, Pyrrho eum interroganti, qualis ipsi
Roma visa esset, ¹⁰ réspondit, *se regum patriam vidisse.*)

**184.** In altĕro proelio Pyrrhus vulnerātus est, ele-
phanti interfecti, viginti millia hostium caesa sunt.
Pyrrhus Tarentum fugit.   Interjecto anno, Fabricius
contra eum missus est.   Ad hunc medĭcus Pyrrhi nocte
venit promittens, se Pyrrhum venēno occisūrum,¹² si
munus sibi darētur.⁴ Hunc Fabricius vinctum redūci
jussit ad domĭnum.   Tunc rex admirātus illum dixisse
fertur : "*Ille est Fabricius, qui difficilius ab honestāte,
quam sol a cursu suo averti potest.*"   Paulo post Pyrrhus, tertio etiam proelio fusus,¹³ a Tarento recessit.

---

| | | |
|---|---|---|
| ¹ 566, II.; 580. | ⁶ 518, II. | ¹⁰ 525. |
| ² 577. | ⁷ 500, 1. | ¹¹ 542, 1. |
| ⁵ 494. | ⁸ 495, 3. | ¹² 545, 3. |
| ⁴ 509. | ⁹ 533, 4. | ¹⁵ 273, II. 2. |
| ⁵ 281. | | |

## Period III.—Roman Triumphs.

**FROM THE FIRST PUNIC WAR TO THE CONQUEST OF GREECE, 146 B. C.**

### First Punic War, 264 B. C.

**185.** Anno quadringentesĭmo nonagesĭmo post urbem
condĭtam Romanōrum exercĭtus primum in Siciliam trajecērunt,[1] regemque Syracusārum Hierōnem, Poenosque,
qui mụltas civitātes in eā insŭlā occupavērant, superavērunt. Quinto anno hujus belli, quod contra Poenos
gerebātur, primum Romāni, Caio Duillio, Cnaeo Cor-
nelio Asīnā consulĭbus,[2] mari[3] dimicavērunt. Duillius
Carthaginienses vicit,[4] triginta naves occupāvit, quattuordĕcim mersit,[5] septem millia hostium cepit, tria millia
occīdit. Nulla victoria Romānis gratior fuit.

### First Punic War, continued.—Invasion of Africa, 256 B. C.

**186.** Paucis annis interjectis, bellum in Afrĭcam
est translātum. Hamĭlcar, Carthaginiensium dux, pugnā navāli superātus est ; nam, perdĭtis sexaginta quattuor
navĭbus, se recēpit ; Romāni viginti duas amisērunt.
Quum in Afrĭcam venissent,[6] Poenos in plurĭbus[7] proeliis vicērunt, magnam vim[8] homĭnum cepērunt, septuaginta quattuor civitātes in fidem accepērunt. Tum victi
Carthaginienses pacem a Romānis petiērunt.[9] Quam[10]
quum Marcus Atilius Regŭlus, Romanōrum dux, dare
nollet[11] nisi durissĭmis conditionĭbus, Carthaginienses
auxilium petiērunt a Lacedaemoniis. Hi Xanthippum

---

[1] 461, 1 ; 260, 2, 1).   [5] 258, I. 1.   [9] 234.
[2] 431.   [6] 518, II.   [10] 453.
[3] 422, 1.   [7] 165, 1.   [11] 518.
[4] 273, II.   [8] 66.

misērunt, qui Rōmānum exercĭtum magno proelio vicit.
Regŭlus ipse captus et in vincŭla conjectus est.

**187.** Non tamen ubīque fortūna Carthaginiensĭbus
favit.[1] Quum alīquot proeliis victi essent,[2] Regŭlum ro-
gavērunt, ut Romam proficiscerētur,[3] et pacem captivo-
rumque permutatiōuem a Rōmānis impetrāret. Ille
quum Romam venisset, inductus in senātum dixit, *se
desiisse[4] Rōmānum esse ex illā die, quā[5] in potestātem
Poenōrum venisset.[6]* Tum Rōmānis suasit,[7] ne pacem
cum Carthaginiensĭbus facĕrent:[8] *illos enim tot casĭbus
fractos spem nullam nisi in pace habēṛe:[9] tanti[10] non
esse, ut tot millia captivōrum propter se unum et paucos,
qui ex Rōmānis capti essent,[6] redderentur.[11]* Haec sententia obtinuit. Regressus igĭtur in Afrĭcam crudelissĭ-
mis suppliciis exstinctus est.[12]

*End of the First Punic War, 241 B. C.*

**188.** Tandem, Caio Luᵥatio Catŭlo, Aulo Postumio
consulĭbus, anno belli Punĭci vicesĭmo tertio magnuin
proeliuin navāle commissum est contra Lilybaeum, promontorium Sicĭliae. In eo proelio septuaginta tres
Carthaginiensium naves captae, centum viginti quinque
demersae,[13] triginta duo millia hostium capta, tredĕcim
millia occīsa sunt. Statim Carthaginienses pacem petiērunt, eisque pax tribūta[14] est. Captīvi Romanōrum,
qui tenebantur a Carthaginiensĭbus, reddĭti sunt. Poeni
Siciliā,[15] Sardiniā, et cetĕris insŭlis, quae inter Italiam
Africamque jacent, decessērunt, omnemque Hispaniam,
quae citra Ibērum est, Rōmānis permisērunt.

---

| | | |
|---|---|---|
| [1] 270. | [6] 531. | [11] 495, 2. |
| [2] 518, II. | [7] 269. | [12] 272, I. |
| [3] 492, 2; 374, 4. | [8] 492, 2. | [13] 272, II. |
| [4] 234. | [9] 530, 1. | [14] 279. |
| [5] 426. | [10] 402, 1. | [15] 434, 1. |

*Siege of Saguntum.—The Second Punic War, 218 B. C.*

**189.** Paulo[1] post Punĭcum bellum renovātum est per Hannibălem, Carthaginiensium ducem, quem pater[2] Hamilcar novem annos[3] natum aris[4] admovĕrat, ut odium perenne in Romănos jurāret.[5] Hic annum agens vicesĭmum aetātis Saguntum, Hispaniae civitātem, Romānis[6] amīcam, oppugnāre aggressus est.[7] Huic Romāni per legātos ḍenuntiavērunt, ut bello[8] abstinēret.[9] Qui quum legātos admittĕre nollet,[10] Romāni Carthagĭnem misērunt, ut mandarētur[8] Hannibăli, ne bellum contra socios popŭli Romāni gerĕret.[11] Dura responsa a Carthaginiensĭbus reddĭta. Saguntīnis interea fame victis, Romāni Carthaginiensĭbus bellum indixērunt.

*Hannibal crosses the Alps, 218 B. C.—Battles of the Ticīnus, Trebia, and Lake Trasimēnus.—Battle of Cannae, 216 B. C.*

**190.** Hannĭbal, fratre Hasdrubăle in Hispaniā relicto,[12] Pyrenaeum et Alpes transiit. Tradĭtur in Italiam octoginta millia pedĭtum, et viginti millia equĭtum, septem et triginta elephantos abduxisse. Interea multi Ligūres et Galli Hannibăli se conjunxērunt. Primus[13] ei occurrit Publius Cornelius Scipio, qui, proelio ad Ticīnum commisso, superātus est, et, vulnĕre accepto,[13] in castra rediit. Tum Sempronius Gracchus conflixit ad Trebiam amnem. Is quoque vincĭtur.[14] Multi popŭli se Hannibăli dedidērunt. Inde in Etruriam progressus Flaminium consulem ad Trasimēnum lacum supĕrat.[14]

---

| | | |
|---|---|---|
| [1] 418. | [6] 391. | [11] 492. |
| [2] 447. | [7] 283. | [12] 431, 2, (3). |
| [3] 378. | [8] 425, 2. | [13] 442, 1. |
| [4] 386. | [9] 492, 2. | [14] 467, III. |
| [5] 491. | [10] 518. | |

Ipse Flaminius interemptus, Romanōrum viginti quinque millia caesa sunt.

**191.** Quingentesĭmo duodequadragesĭmo anno post urbem condĭtam Lucius Aemilius Paulus et Caius Terentius Varro contra Hannibălem mittuntur. Quamquam intellectum erat, Hannibălem non alĭter vinci posse quam morā, Varro tamen, morae[1] impatiens, apud vicum, qui Cannae appellātur, in Apuliā pugnāvit; ambo consŭles victi, Paulus interemptus est. In eā pugnā consulāres aut praetorii viginti, senatōres triginta capti aut occīsi;[2] milĭtum quadraginta millia, equĭtum tria millia et quingenti periērunt. In his tantis malis nemo tamen pacis mentiōnem facĕre dignātus est. Servi, quod[3] nunquam ante factum,[2] manumissi et milĭtes facti sunt.

**192.** Post eam pugnam multae Italiae civitātes, quae Romānis[4] paruĕrant, se ad Hannibălem transtulērunt.[5] Hannĭbal Romānis obtŭlit, ut captīvos redimērent;[6] responsumque est a senātu, *eos cives non esse necessarios, qui armāti capi potuissent.*[7] Hos omnes ille postea variis suppliciis interfēcit, et tres modios aureōrum annulōrum Carthagĭnem misit, quos manĭbus[8] equĭtum Romanōrum et senatōrum detraxĕrat.[9] Interea in Hispaniā frater Hannibălis, Hasdrŭbal, qui ibi remansĕrat[10] cum magno exercĭtu, a duōbus Scipionĭbus vincĭtur,[11] perditque in pugnā triginta quinque millia homĭnum.

**193.** In Siciliā res prospĕre gesta est.[12] Marcellus magnam hujus insŭlae partem cepit, quam Poeni occu-

---

[1] 399, 2.  [5] 292, 2.  [9] 258, I. 1.
[2] 460, 3.  [6] 492.  [10] 269.
[3] 445, 7.  [7] 500, 2.  [11] 467, III.
[4] 385.  [8] 386, 2.  [12] 272, I.

pavĕrant; Syracūsas, nobilissĭmam urbem, expugnāvit, et ingentem inde praedam Romam[1] misit. Laevīnus in Macedoniā cum Philippo et multis Graeciae popŭlis amicitiam fecit; et in Siciliam profectus[2] Ilannōnem, Poenōrum ducem, apud Agrigentuin cepit; quadraginta civitātes in deditiōuem accēpit, viginti sex expugnāvit. Ita omni Siciliā receptā,[3] cum ingenti gloriā Romam regressus est.

**194.** Interea in Hispaniam, ubi duo Scipiōnes ab Hasdrubăle interfecti erant, missus est Publius Cornelius Scipio, vir Romanōrum omnium fere primus.[4] Hic, puer duodeviginti annōrum, in pugnā ad Ticīnum, patrem singulāri virtūte servāvit. Deinde post cladem Cannensem multos nobilissimōrum juvĕnum Italiam deserĕre cupientium,[5] auctoritāte suā ab hoc consilio deterruit. Viginti quattuor annos natus in Hispaniam missus, die,[6] quā venit, Carthagĭnem Novam cepit, in quā omne aurum et argentum et belli apparātum Poeni habēbant, nobilissĭmos quoque obsĭdes,[7] quos ab Hispānis accepĕrant. Hos obsĭdes parentĭbus reddĭdit. Quare omnes fere Hispaniae civitātes ad eum uno anĭmo[8] transiērunt.

**195.** Anno quarto decĭmo postquam in Italiam Hannĭbal venĕrat, Scipio consul creātus, et in Africam missus est. Ibi contra Hannōnem, ducem Carthaginiensium, prospĕre pugnat, totumque ejus exercĭtum delet.[9] Secundo proelio undēcim millia homĭnum occīdit, et castra cepit cum quattuor millĭbus et quingentis militĭbus. Quā[10] re audītā,[5] omnis fere Italia Hannibălem desĕrit. Ipse a Carthaginiensĭbus in Africam redīre jubētur. · Ita Italia liberāta est.

---

1 379.　　　5 577.　　　8 414, 3.

2 283.　　　6 426.　　　9 264.

3 431, 2, (3).　7 81, 2.　　10 453.

4 166.

#### Battle of Zama, 202 B. C.

**196.** Post plures pugnas et pacem plus semel frustra
tentātam, pugna ad Zamam committitur, in quā peritissĭmi duces copias suas ad bellum educēbant. Scipio
victor recēdit; Hannĭbal cum paucis equitĭbus evādit.
Post hoc proelium pax cum Carthaginiensĭbus facta est.
Scipio, quum Romam rediisset,[1] ingenti gloriā triumphāvit, atque Africānus appellātus est. Sic finem accēpit
secundum Punĭcum bellum post annum undevicesĭmum
quam[2] coepĕrat.

#### War with Philip.—Cynoscephalae, 197 B. C.

**197.** Finīto Punĭco bello, secūtum est Macedonĭcum
contra Philippum regem. Superātus est rex a Tito
Quinctio Flaminio apud Cynoscephălas, paxque ei data
est.

#### War with Perseus.—Pydna, 168 B. C.

**198.** Philippo, rege Macedoniae, mortuo, filius ejus
Perseus rebellāvit, ingentĭbus copiis parātis. Dux Romanōrum, Publius Licinius consul, contra eum missus, gravi proelio a rege victus est. Rex tamen pacem
petēbat. Cui[3] Romāni eam praestāre noluērunt, nisi
his conditionĭbus, ut se et suos Romānis dedĕret.[4] Mox
Aemilius Paulus consul regem ad Pydnam superāvit, et
viginti millia pedĭtum ejus occīdit. Equitātus cum rege
fugit. Urbes Macedoniae omnes, quas rex tenuĕrat,
Romānis se dedidērunt. Ipse Perseus ab amīcis desertus .
in Pauli potestātem venit. Hic, multis etiam aliis rebus
gestis,[5] cum ingenti pompā Romam rediit in nave Persei,
inusitātae magnitudĭnis;[6] nam sedĕcim remōrum ordĭnes

---

[1] 518, II.      [3] 453.      [5] 431, 2, (3).
[2] 427, 3.      [4] 495, 3.      [6] 396, IV.

habuisse dicĭtur.   Triumphāvit magnificentissĭme' in
curru aureo, duōbus filiis utrōque latĕre² adstantĭbus.
Ante currum inter captīvos duo regis filii et ipse Perseus
ducti sunt.

### Third Punic War, 149 B. C.

**199.** Tertium deinde bellum contra Carthagĭnem
susceptum est.   Lucius Marcius Censorīnus et Manius
Manlius consŭles in Afrĭcam trajecērunt, et oppugnavē-
runt Carthagĭnem.   Multa ibi praeclāre gesta sunt per
Scipiōnem,³ Scipiōnis Africāni nepōtem, qui tribūnus⁴
in Afrĭcā militābat.

**200.** Quum jam magnum esset⁵ Scipiōnis nomen,
tertio anno postquam Romāni in Afrĭcam trajecērant,
consul est creātus, et contra Carthagĭnem missus.   Is
hanc urbem a civĭbus acerrĭme⁶ defensam' cepit ac diruit.
Ingens ibi praeda facta, plurimăque inventa sunt, quae
multārum civitātum excidiis Carthāgo collegĕrat.   Haec
omnia Scipio civitatĭbus Italiae, Siciliae, Afrĭcae reddĭdit, quae sua recognoscēbant.   Ita Carthāgo septingentesĭmo anno, postquam condĭta erat, delēta est.   Scipio
nomen Africāni juniōris⁸ accēpit.

---

## PERIOD IV.—CIVIL DISSENSIONS.

FROM THE CONQUEST OF GREECE TO THE DISSOLUTION OF THE ROMAN COMMON-
WEALTH, 31 B. C.

*Numantia taken,* 133 *B. C.*

**201.** Deinde bellum exortum est cum Numantīnis,
civitāte Hispaniae. Victus[1] ab his Quintus Pompēius,
et post eum Caius Hostilius Mancīnus consul, qui pacem
cum iis fecit infāmem, quam popŭlus et senātus jussit[2]
infringi, atque ipsum Mancīnum hostĭbus tradi. Tum
Publius Scipio Africānus in Hispaniam missus est. Is
primum militem ignāvum et corruptum correxit;[3] tum
multas Hispaniae civitātes partim bello cepit, partim in
deditiōnem accēpit. Postrēmo ipsam Numantiam fame
ad deditiōnem coēgit, urbemque evertit; relīquam[4] provinciam in fidem accēpit.

*Mithridatic War.—First Civil War.—Marius, Sulla,* 88 *B. C.*

**202.** Anno urbis condĭtae sexcentesĭmo sexagesĭmo
sexto primum Romae bellum civīle exortum est; eōdem
anno etiam Mithridatĭcum. Causam bello civīli Caius
Marius dedit. Nam quum Sullae bellum adversus Mithridātem, regem Ponti, decrētum esset,[5] Marius ei[6] hunc
honōrem eripĕre conātus est. Sed Sulla, qui adhuc cum
legionĭbus suis in Italiā morabātur,[7] cum exercĭtu Romam
venit, et adversarios quum[8] interfēcit, tum fugāvit. Tum
rebus Romae utcunque composĭtis, in Asiam profectus
est, pluribusque proeliis Mithridātem coēgit, ut pacem a

---

| [1] 460, 3.  | [4] 441, 6.   | [7] 468.        |
| [2] 463, 3. | [5] 518, II.  | [8] 587, I. 5. |
| [3] 214, I. | [6] 386, 2.   |                 |

Romānis petĕret,[1] et Asiā, quam invasĕrat, relictā, regni sui finĭbus[2] contentus esset.

### Civil War, continued.

**203.** Sed dum Sulla in Graeciā et Asiā Mithridātem vincit,[3] Marius, qui fugātus fuĕrat, et Cornelius Cinna, unus ex consulĭbus,[4] bellum in Italiā reparārunt,[5] et ingressi Romam nobilissĭmos ex senatu et consulāres viros interfecērunt; multos proscripsērunt; ipsīus Sullae domo eversā, filios et uxōrem ad fugam compulērunt.[6] Universus relĭquus senātus ex urbe fugiens ad Sullam in Graeciam venit, orans ut patriae subvenīret.[7] Sulla in Italiam trajēcit, hostium exercĭtus vicit,[8] mox etiam urbem ingressus est, quam caede[9] et sanguĭne civium replēvit. Quattuor millia inermium,[9] qui se dedidĕrant, interfĭci jussit; duo millia equĭtum et senatōrum proscripsit.[10] Tum de Mithridāte triumphāvit. Duo haec bella funestissĭma, Italĭcum, quod et sociāle dictum est, et civīle, ultra centum et quinquaginta millia homĭnum, viros consulāres viginti quattuor, praetorios septem, aedilitios sexaginta, senatōres fere ducentos consumpsērunt.[11]

### War of the Gladiators.—Spartacus, 73 B. C.

**204.** Anno urbis sexcentesĭmo octogesĭmo primo novum in Italiā bellum commōtum[12] est. Septuaginta enim quattuor gladiatōres, ducĭbus[13] Spartăco, Crixo, et Oenomao, e ludo gladiatorio, qui Capuae[14] erat, effugērunt, et per Italiam vagantes paene non levius bellum,

---

[1] 492, 2.　　　　[6] 273, I. 2.　　　　[11] 258, I. 4.
[2] 419, IV.　　　　[7] 273, II.　　　　　[12] 270, II.
[3] 467, 4.　　　　[8] 419, 2, 1).　　　　[13] 430, 431.
[4] 398, 4.　　　　[9] 441.　　　　　　　[14] 421, II.
[5] 234.　　　　　[10] 258, I. 3.

quam Hannĭbal, movērunt.[1] Nam contraxērunt[2] exercĭtum fere sexaginta millium armatōrum, multosque
duces et duos Romānos consŭles vicērunt. Ipsi victi
sunt in Apuliā a Marco Licinio Crasso proconsŭle, et,
post multas calamitātes Italiae, tertio anno[3] huic bello
finis est imposĭtus.

*Pompey puts down the Pirates, 67 B. C.—Is appointed successor to
Lucullus.—Death of Mithridates, 63 B. C.*

**205.** Per illa tempŏra pirātae omnia maria infestā-
bant ita, ut Romānis,[4] toto orbe[5] terrārum victorĭbus,
sola navigatio tuta non esset.[6] Quare id bellum Cnaeo
Pompēio decrētum est, quod intra paucos menses incre-
dibĭli felicitāte et celeritāte confēcit. Mox ei delātum[7]
bellum contra regem Mithridātem et Tigrānem. Quo[8]
suscepto, Mithridātem in Armeniā Minōre nocturno
proelio vicit, castra diripuit, et quadraginta millĭbus ejus
occīsis, viginti tantum de exercĭtu suo perdĭdit et duos
centuriōnes. Mithridātes fugit[9] cum uxōre et duōbus
comitĭbus,[10] neque[11] multo post, Pharnăcis filii sui sedi-
tiōne coactus,[12] venēnum hausit.[13] Hunc vitae finem
habuit Mithridātes, vir ingentis industriae atque consilii.
Regnāvit annis[14] sexaginta, vixit septuaginta duōbus:
contra Romānos bellum habuit annis quadraginta.

*Victories of Pompey over Tigranes : he takes Jerusalem, 63 B. C.*

**206.** Tigrāni deinde Pompēius bellum intŭlit. Ille
se ei dedĭdit, et in castra Pompēii venit, ac diadēma

---

| | | |
|---|---|---|
| [1] 270. | [6] 494. | [11] 587, I. 2. |
| [2] 272. | [7] 292, 2 ; 460, 3. | [12] 273, II. |
| [3] 426. | [8] 453 ; 431, 2, (3). | [13] 286, I. |
| [4] 391. | [9] 273, II. | [14] 378, 1. |
| [5] 422, 1, 1). | [10] 81. | |

suum in ejus manĭbus collocāvit, quod ei Pompēius reposuit. Parte[1] regni eum multāvit et grandi pecuniā.
Tum alios etiam reges et popŭlos superāvit. Armeniam
Minōrem Deiotăro,[2] Galatiae regi, donāvit, quia auxilium
contra Mithridātem tulĕrat. Seleuciam, vicīnam Antio-
chīae[3] civitātem, libertāte[3] donāvit, quod regem Tigrānem non recepisset.[4] Inde in Judaeam transgressus,
Hierosolўmam, caput gentis, tertio mense cepit, duodĕcim millĭbus Judaeōrum occīsis, cetĕris in fidem receptis.
His[5] gestis finem antiquissĭmo bello imposuit. Ante
triumphantis currum ducti sunt filii Mithridātis, filius
Tigrānis, et Aristobūlus, rex Judaeōrum. Praelāta ingens pecunia, auri atque argenti infinītum pondus. Hoc
tempŏre nullum per orbem terrārum grave bellµm erat.

### Catiline's Conspiracy, 63 B. C.

**207.** Marco Tullio Cicerōne[6] oratōre et Caio Antonio consulĭbus, anno ab urbe condītā[7] sexcentesĭmo nonagesĭmo primo Lucius Sergius Catilīna, nobilissĭmi genĕris
vir, sed ingenii pravissĭmi, ad delendam[8] patriam conjurāvit cum quibusdam claris quidem, sed audacĭbus viris.
A Cicerōne urbe[9] expulsus est, socii ejus deprehensi et
in carcĕre strangulāti sunt. Ab Antonio, altĕro consŭle,
Catilīna ipse proelio victus est et interfectus.

### Caesar Consul, 59 B. C.: in Gaul, 58 B. C.

**208.** Anno urbis.condītae sexcentesĭmo nonagesĭmo
quinto Caius Julius Caesar cum Lucio Bibŭlo consul est
factus. Quum ei Gallia decrēta esset,[10] semper vincendo[11]

---

[1] 425, 2, 2).    [5] 414.    [9] 425.
[2] 384, 1.    [6] 430, 431.    [10] 518, II.
[3] 391.    [7] 580.    [11] 566, L
[4] 520, II.    [8] 565, I.

usque ad Oceănum Britannĭcum processit.[1] Domuit[2] autem annis novem fere omnem Galliam, quae inter Alpes, flumen Rhodănum, Rhenum et Oceănum est. Britannis mox bellum intŭlit,[3] quibus[4] ante eum ne nomeu quidem Romanōrum cognĭtum[5] erat; Germānos quoque trans Rhenum aggressus, ingentĭbus proeliis vicit.

### Civil War of Pompey and Caesar, 49 B. C.

**209.** Bellum civīle successit,[1] quo Romāni nomĭnis fortūna mutāta est. Caesar enim victor e Galliā rediens, absens coepit poscĕre altĕrum consulātum; quem[6] quum multi sine dubitatiōne deferrent,[7] contradictum est a Pompēio et aliis, jussusque est, dimissis exercitĭbus, in urbem redīre. Propter hanc injuriam ab Arimĭno, ubi milĭtes congregātos[8] habēbat, infesto exercĭtu[9] Romam contendit. Consŭles cum Pompēio, senatusque omnis atque universa nobilĭtas ex urbe fugit,[10] et in Graeciam transiit; et, dum senātus bellum contra Caesărem parābat, hic vacuam urbem ingressus dictatōrem se fecit.

### Defeat of Pompey's party in Spain.—Battle of Pharsalia, 48 B. C. —Death of Pompey.

**210.** Inde Hispanias petiit,[11] ibīque Pompēii legiōncs superāvit; tum in Graeciā adversum Pompēium ipsnm dimicāvit. Primo proelio victus est et fugātus; evāsit[12] tamen, quia, nocte interveniente, Pompēius sequi noluit;[13] dixitque Caesar, nec Pompēium scire vincĕre, et illo tantum die se potuisse superāri. Deinde in Thessaliā apud Pharsālum ingentĭbus utrimque copiis[14] com-

---

| | | |
|---|---|---|
| [1] 258, I. 2. | [6] 453. | [11] 234. |
| [2] 260. | [7] 518. | [12] 272, II. |
| [3] 292, 2. | [8] 388, 1, 2). | [13] 293. |
| [4] 391. | [9] 414, 7. | [14] 414. |
| [5] 575. | [10] 463, I. | |

missis dimicavērunt. Nunquam adhuc Romānae copiae majōres neque meliorĭbus ducĭbus[1] convenĕrant. Pugnātum est[2] ingenti contentiōne,[3] victusque ad postrēmum Pompēius, et castra ejus direpta sunt. Ipse fugātus Alexandrīam petiit, ut a rege Aegypti, cui tutor[4] a senātu datus fuĕrat, accipĕret[5] auxilia. At hic fortūnam magis quam amicitiam secūtus,[6] occīdit Pompēium, caput ejus et annŭlum Caesāri misit. Quo[7] conspecto, Caesar lacrĭmas fudisse[8] dicĭtur, tanti viri intuens caput, et genĕri quondam[9] sui.

*Caesar assassinated in the Senate-House, 44 B. C.*

**211.** Quum ad Alexandrīam venisset Caesar, Ptolemaeus ei insidias parāre voluit, quā de causā regi bellum illātum[10] est. Rex victus in Nilo periit, inventumque est corpus ejus cum loricā aureā. Caesar, Alexandriā[11] potītus, regnum Cleopātrae dedit.[12] Tum inde profectus[4] Pompeianārum partium reliquias est persecūtus, bellisque[13] civilĭbus toto terrārum orbe[14] composĭtis, Romam rediit. Ubi quum insolentius[15] agĕre coepisset,[16] conjurātum est in eum a sexaginta vel amplius senatorĭbus, equitibusque Romānis. Praecipui fuĕrunt inter conjurātos[17] Bruti duo ex genĕre illīus Bruti, qui, regĭbus expulsis, primus Romae consul fuĕrat. Ergo Caesar, quum in curiam venisset, viginti tribus vulnerĭbus confossus est.

| | | |
|---|---|---|
| [1] 414, 7. | [7] 453 ; 431, 2, (3). | [13] 431, 2, (3). |
| [2] 301, 1 | [8] 273, II. 2. | [14] 422, 1, 1). |
| [3] 414, 3. | [9] 583,2. | [15] 444, 1 & 4. |
| [4] 362. | [10] 292, 2. | [16] 297. |
| [5] 491. | [11] 419. | [17] 575. |
| [6] 283. | [12] 261. | |

*The Second Triumvirate, Octavius, Antony, and Lepidus,* 43 *B. C.—*
*Death of Cicero.*

**212.** Interfecto Caesăre, annɔ urbis septingentesĭmo
decĭmo bella civilia reparāta sunt.  Senātus favēbat
Caesăris percussorĭbus,[1] Antonius consul a Caesăris par-
tĭbus stabat.  Ergo turbātā re publĭcā, Antonius, multis
scelerĭbus commissis, a senātu hostis[2] judicātus est.
Fusus fugatusque Antonius, amisso exercĭtu, confūgit ad
Lepĭdum, qui Caesări[3] magister equĭtum fuĕrat, et tum
grandes copias milĭtum habēbat; a quo susceptus est.
Mox Octaviānus cum Antonio pacem fecit, et quasi vin-
dicatūrus patris sui mortem, a quo per testamentum
fuĕrat adoptātus, Romam cum exercĭtu profectus extorsit,[4] ut sibi, juvĕni viginti annōrum, consulātus darētur.[5]
Tum junctus cum Antonio et Lepĭdo rem publĭcam armis tenēre coepit, senatumque proscripsit.  Per hos etiam
Cicĕro orātor occīsus est, multīque alii nobīles.[6]

*Battle of Philippi,* 42 *B. C.*

**213.** Interea Brutus et Cassius, interfectōres Caesăris, ingens bellum movērunt.[7]  Profecti[8] contra eos
Caesar Octaviānus, qui postea Augustus est appellātus,
et Marcus Antonius, apud Philippos, Macedoniae urbem,
contra eos pugnavērunt.[9]  Primo proelio victi sunt Antonius et Caesar; periit[10] tamen dux nobilitātis Cassius;
secundo Brutum et infinītam nobilitātem, quae cum illis
bellum suscepĕrat, victam[11] interfecērunt.  Tum victōres rem publĭcam ita inter se divisērunt,[12] ut Octaviā-

[1] 385.
[2] 362.
[3] 390, 2.
[4] 269, II.
[5] 492, 1.
[6] 460, 3.
[7] 270.
[8] 439.
[9] 463, II.
[10] 295, 3.
[11] 579.
[12] 272, II.

nus Caesar Hispanias, Gallias, Italiam tenēret :[1] Antonius Orientem, Lepĭdus Afrĭcam accipĕret.

*Battle of Actium*, 31 *B. C.*

**214.** Paulo[2] post Antonius, repudiātā sorōre Caesāris Octaviāni, Cleopātram, regīnam Aegypti, uxōrem duxit. Ab hac incitātus ingens bellum commōvit, dum Cleopātra cupiditāte muliĕbri optat Romae regnāre. Victus est ab Augusto navāli pugnā clarā et illustri apud Actium, qui[3] locus in Epīro est. Hinc fugit in Aegyptum, et, desperātis rebus, quum omnes ad Augustum transīrent,[4] se ipse interēmit.[5] Cleopātra quoque aspĭdem sibi admīsit, et venēno ejus exstincta[6] est. Ita bellis toto orbe[7] confectis, Octaviānus Augustus Romam rediit anno duodecĭmo postquam consul fuĕrat. Ex eo inde tempŏre rem publĭcam per quadraginta et quattuor annos solus obtinuit. Ante enim duodĕcim annis[8] cum Antonio et Lepĭdo tenuĕrat. Ita ab initio principātus ejus usque ad finem quinquaginta sex anni fuēre.

---

[1] 494.
[2] 418.
[3] 445, 8.
[4] 518.
[5] 273, II.
[6] 281.
[7] 422, 1, 1).
[8] 378, 1.

# GRECIAN HISTORY.

Note.—It is recommended that, in reading the Grecian History, special attention should be given to *Irregular*, *Defective*, and *Impersonal Verbs.*— 289–301.

## PERIOD I.—GRECIAN TRIUMPHS.

FROM THE PERSIAN INVASION, 490 B. C., TO THE PELOPONNESIAN WAR, 431 B. C.

*Darius invades Scythia: prepares to invade Greece.*

**215.** Multis in Asiā felicĭter gestis, Darīus Scythis bellum intŭlit,[1] et armātis septingentis millĭbus[2] homĭnum Scythiam[3] ingressus, quum hostes ei pugnae potestātem non facĕrent,[4] metuens, ne, interrupto ponte Istri, redĭtus sibi intercluderētur,[5] amissis octoginta millĭbus homĭnum, trepĭdus refūgit. Inde Macedoniam domuit: et quum ex Eurōpā in Asiam rediisset,[6] hortantĭbus amīcis ut Graeciam redigĕret[7] in suam potestātem, classem quingentārum navium comparāvit, eīque Datim[8] praefēcit et Artaphernen;[9] hisque ducenta pedĭtum millia, et decem equĭtum dedit.

*Battle of Marathon, 490 B. C.*

**216.** Praefecti regii, classe ad Euboeam appulsā, celerĭter Eretriam cepērunt. Inde ad Attĭcam accessērunt, ac suas copias in Campum Marathōna deduxērunt.

---

| | | |
|---|---|---|
| [1] 292, 2. | [4] 518, II. | [7] 492, 2. |
| [2] 414, 7. | [5] 492, 4. | [8] 62, II. 2. |
| [3] 371, 4. | [6] 295, 3. | [9] 68. |

Is abest ab oppĭdo circĭter millia passuum decem. Hoc in tempŏre nulla civĭtas Atheniensĭbus[1] auxilio fuit, praeter Plataeenses; ea mille[2] misit milĭtum. Ităque horum adventu decem millia armatōrum complēta sunt: quae[3] manus mirabĭli flagrăbat pugnandi cupiditāte. Athenienses copias ex urbe eduxērunt, locōque[4] idoneo castra fecērunt; deinde postĕro die, sub montis radicĭbus proelium commisērunt. Datis etsi non aequum locum vidēbat suis, tămen, fretus numĕro[5] copiārum suārum, confligĕre cupiēbat. Ităque in aciem pedĭtum centum, equĭtum decem millia produxit, proeliumque commīsit. In quo tanto[6] plus virtūte valuērunt Athenienses, ut decemplĭcem numĕrum hostium profligārint;[7] adeōque perterruērunt, ut Persae non castra, sed naves petiĕrint. Quā pugnā nihil est nobilius; nulla enim unquam tam exigua manus tantas opes prostrāvit.

*Xerxes invades Greece*, 480 *B. C.*

**217.** Quum Darīus, bellum instauratūrus, in ipso apparātu decessisset,[8] filius ejus Xerxes Eurōpam[9] cum tantis copiis invāsit, quantas neque antea neque postea habuit quisquam: hujus enim classis mille et ducentārum navium[10] longārum fuit, quam duo millia onerariārum sequebantur: terrestres autem exercĭtus septingentōrum millium pedĭtum, equĭtum quadringentōrum millium fuērunt. Cujus[11] de adventu quum fama in Graeciam esset perlāta, et maxĭme Athenienses peti dicerentur,[12] propter pugnam Marathoniam, misērunt Delphos consultum,[13] quidnam facĕrent[14] de rebus suis.

---

| | | |
|---|---|---|
| [1] 390. | [6] 418. | [11] 453. |
| [2] 178. | [7] 234; 482, 2. | [12] 549, 4. |
| [3] 445, 8. | [8] 518. | [13] 569. |
| [4] 422, 1, 2). | [9] 371, 4. | [14] 525. |
| [5] 419, IV. | [10] 401. | |

Deliberantĭbus Pythia respondit, ut moenĭbus ligneis
se munīrent.[1]  Id responsum quo valēret, quum intelli-
gĕret nemo, Themistŏcles persuāsit, consilium esse Apol-
linis, ut in naves se suăque conferrent:[2] eum enim a deo
significāri murum ligneum.  Tali consilio probāto, ad-
dunt ad superiōres totĭdem naves trirēmes: suăque omnia, quae movēri potĕrant, partim Salamīna,[3] partim
Troezēna, deportant; arcem sacerdotĭbus paucisque majorĭbus natu,[4] ac sacra procuranda[5] tradunt; reliquum
oppĭdum relinquuut.

*Actions at Thermopylae and Artemisium, 480 B. C.*

**218.** Hujus consilium plerisque civitātibus displicēbat, et in terrā dimicāri[6] magis placēbat.  Ităque missi
sunt delecti[7] cum Leonĭdā, Lacedaemoniōrum rege, qui
Thermopȳlas occupārent,[8] longiusque barbăros progrĕdi
non paterentur.  Hi vim[9] hostium non sustinuērunt,
eoque loco omnes interiērunt.[10]  At classis commūnis
Graeciae trecentārum navium,[11] in quā ducentae erant
Atheniensium, primum apud Artemisium, inter Euboeam continentemque terram, cum classiariis regiis conflixit:[12] angustias enim Themistŏcles quaerēbat, ne multitudĭne circumirētur.[13]  Hinc etsi pari proelio[14] discessē-
rant, tamen eōdem loco non sunt ausi[15] manēre, quod
erat pericŭlum, ne, si pars navium adversariōrum Euboeam superasset,[16] ancipĭti premerentur[17] pericŭlo. Quo
factum est, ut ab Artemisio discedĕrent,[18] et exadversum
Athēnas, apud Salamīna, classem suam constitŭerent.

| | | |
|---|---|---|
| [1] 492, 2. | [7] 575. | [13] 491. |
| [2] 495, 3. | [8] 500, 1. | [14] 414, 3. |
| [3] 68. | [9] 66. | [15] 271, 3. |
| [4] 429. | [10] 295, 3. | [16] 509. |
| [5] 578; V. | [11] 397, 2. | [17] 492, 4. |
| [6] 549. | [12] 258, I. ] | [18] 495, 2. |

*Battle of Salamis*, 480 *B. C.*

**219.** At Xerxes, Thermopўlis expugnātis, protĭnus accessit astu,[1] idque, nullis defendentĭbus, interfectis sacerdotĭbus, quos in arce invenĕrat, incendio delēvit. Cujus famā perterrĭti classiarii quum manēre non audērent, et plurĭmi[2] hortarentur, ut domos suas quisque discedĕrent,[3] moenĭbusque se defendĕrent; Themistŏcles unus restĭtit, et, universos pares hostĭbus esse posse[4] aiēbat,[5] dispersos testabātur peritūros, idque Eurybiādi, regi Lacedaemoniōrum, qui tum summae[6] imperii praeĕrat, fore[7] affirmābat. Quem quum minus, quam vellet,[8] movēret,[9] noctu de servis suis, quem habuit fidelissĭmum,[10] ad regem misit, ut ei nuntiāret suis verbis: *adversarios ejus in fugā esse, qui*[11] *si discessissent,*[12] *majŏre cum labōre, et longinquiōre tempŏre bellum confectūrum,*[13] *quum singŭlos consectāri cōgerētur ; quos si statim aggrederētur, brevi universos oppressūrum.* Hoc eo valēbat, ut ingratiis ad depugnandum omnes cogerentur.[14] Hac re audītā, barbărus, nihil doli subesse credens, postridie alienissĭmo sibi[15] loco, contra opportunissĭmo hostĭbus, adeo angusto mari[16] conflixit, ut ejus multitūdo navium explicāri non potuĕrit.[17] Victus ergo est magis consilio Themistŏclis, quam armis Graeciae.

*Xerxes flies back into Asia.*

**220.** Hic etsi male rem gessĕrat, tamen tantas habēbat reliquias copiārum, ut etiamtum his[18] opprimĕre

---

| | | |
|---|---|---|
| [1] 128; 371, 4. | [7] 297, III. 2. | [13] 545, 3. |
| [2] 165, 441. | [8] 527. | [14] 495. |
| [3] 492, 2 ; 461, 3. | [9] 518. | [15] 391. |
| [4] 290. | [10] 453, 5. | [16] 422, 1, 1). |
| [5] 297, II. 1. | [11] 453. | [17] 482, 2. |
| [6] 386. | [12] 509. | [18] 414, 4. |

E

posset hostes. Itĕrum ab eōdem gradu depulsus est. Nam Themistŏcles, verens ne bellāre perseverāret,[1] certiōrem eum fecit, id agi,[2] ut pons,[3] quem ille in Hellesponto fecĕrat, dissolverētur,[4] ac redĭtu in Asiam excluderētur. Ităque in Asiam reversus est, seque a Themistŏcle non superātum,[5] sed conservātum judicāvit. Sic unīus viri prudentiā Graecia liberāta est.

### Battles of Plataea and Mycale, 479 B. C.

**221.** Postĕro anno quam Xerxes in Asiam refugĕrat, Graeci, duce Pausaniā, Mardonium, regis genĕrum, apud Plataeas fudērunt:[6] quo proelio ipse dux cecĭdit,[7] Barbarorumque exercĭtus interfectus est. Eōdem forte die in Asiā, ad montem Mycălen, Persae a Graecis navāli proelio superāti sunt. Jamque omnĭbus pacātis, Athenienses belli damna reparāre coepērunt.[8]

---

### PERIOD II.—CIVIL WARS IN GREECE.

**FROM THE PELOPONNESIAN WAR TO THE ACCESSION OF PHILIP OF MACEDON, 360 B. C.**

### The Peloponnesian War, 431 B. C.—Pericles.

**222.** Hoc bellum, quo[9] nullum aliud florentes Graeciae res gravius afflixit, saepe susceptum et deposĭtum est. Initio Spartāni fines Attĭcae populabantur, hostesque ad proelium provocābant. Sed Athenienses, Perĭclis consilio,[10] ultiōnis tempus exspectantes intra moenia se

---

| | | |
|---|---|---|
| [1] 492, 4. | [5] 545, 3. | [8] 297. |
| [2] 551, 3. | [6] 273, II. | [9] 417. |
| [3] 110, 1. | [7] 273, I. | [10] 414, 2. |
| [4] 495, 3. | | |

continēbant. Deiŋde, paucis diēbus interjectis, naves conscendunt, et, nihil sentientĭbus Lacedaemoniis, totam Laconiam depraedantur. Clara quidem haec Perĭclis expeditĭo est habĭta; sed multo clarior privāti patrimonii contemptus fuit. Nam in populatiōne ceterōrum agrōrum, Perĭclis agros hostes intactos reliquĕrant, ut aut invidiam ei apud cives concitārent,[1] aut in proditiōnis suspiciōnem adducĕrent. Quod intellĭgens, Perĭcles agros rei publĭcae dono dedit. Post haec alĭquot diēbus interjectis, navāli proelio dimicātum est.[2] Victi Lacedaemonii fugērunt. Post plures[3] annos, fessi malis, pacem in annos quinquaginta fecēre, quam sex annos[4] servavērunt.

*Expedition of the Athenians against Sicily, 415 B. C.*

**223.** Bello inter Catinienses et Syracusānos exorto,[5] Athenienses Catiniensĭbus opem ferunt.[6] Classis ingens decernĭtur; creantur duces Nicias, Alcibiădes et Lamăchus; tantaeque vires in Siciliam effūsae sunt, ut iis ipsis terrōri[7] essent, quibus auxilio venĕrant. Nicias et Lamăchus duo proelia pedestria secundo Marte[8] pugnant; munitionibusque urbi Syracusārum[9] circumdătis, incŏlas etiam marīnis commeatĭbus[10] interclūdunt. Quibus rebus fracti[11] Syracusāni, auxilium a Lacedaemoniis petivērunt.[12] Ab his mittĭtur Gylippus, qui auxiliis partim in Graeciā, partim in Siciliā contractis, opportūna bello loca[13] occŭpat. Duōbus deinde proeliis vic-

---

| | | |
|---|---|---|
| [1] 491. | [6] 292; 467, III. | [10] 386, 1. |
| [2] 301, 1. | [7] 390. | [11] 273, II. |
| [3] 165, 1. | [8] 414, 3; 705, II. | [12] 278, 2. |
| [4] 378. | [9] 396, V. | [13] 141. |
| [5] 288, 2. | | |

5

tus, tertio hostes in fugam conjēcit, sociosque obsidiōne⁶ liberāvit. In eo proelio Lamăchus fortĭter pugnans occīsus est.

*Successes of Alcibiades against the Lacedaemonians.*

**224.** Alcibiădes summā curā² classem instruit, atque in bellum adversus Lacedaemonios perrexit. Hac expeditiōne tanta subĭto rerum commutatio facta est,² ut Lacedaemonii, qui paulo ante victōres viguĕrant, perterrĭti pacem petĕrent;⁴ victi enim erant quinque terrestrĭbus proeliis, tribus navalĭbus, in quibus trecentas trirēmes amisĕrant, quae captae in hostium venĕrant potestātem. Alcibiădes simul cum collēgis recepĕrat Ioniam, Hellespontum, multas praeterea urbes Graecas, quae in orā sitae sunt Asiae : quarum expugnavĕrant quam plurĭmas, in his Byzantium ; neque minus multas consilio ad amicitiam adjunxĕrant, quod in captos clementiā⁵ fuĕrant usi. Inde praedā⁶ onusti, locupletāto exercĭtu, maxĭmis rebus gestis, Athēnas venērunt.

*Cyrus favors Lysander and the Lacedaemonians, 407 B. C.*

**225.** Dum haec geruntur, a Lacedaemoniis Lysander classi bellōque praeficĭtur ; et Darīus, rex Persārum, filium suum, Cyrum, Ioniae Lydiaeque praeposuit, qui Lacedaemonios auxiliis opibusque ad spem fortūnae priōris⁷ erexit. Aucti⁸ igĭtur virĭbus⁹ Alcibiădem cum centum navĭbus in Asiam profectum,¹⁰ dum agros populātur, repentīno adventu oppressēre.¹¹ Magnae et inopinātae cladis nuntius quum Athēnas venisset, tanta

| | | |
|---|---|---|
| ¹ 425, 3. | ⁵ 419, I. | ⁹ 429. |
| ² 414, 3. | ⁶ 419, III. | ¹⁰ 283. |
| ³ 294. | ⁷ 166. | ¹¹ 235. |
| ⁴ 494. | ⁸ 269. | |

Atheniensium desperatio fuit, ut statim Conōnem in Alcibiădis locum mittĕrent, ducis se fraude magis quam belli fortūnā victos[1] arbitrantes.

*Fatal defeat of the Athenians at Aegospotamos*, 405 *B. C.*

**226.** Ităque Conon classem maxĭmā industriā adornat ; sed navĭbus[2] exercĭtus deĕrat. Nam, ut numĕrus milĭtum explerētur, senes et puĕri arma capĕre coacti sunt. Plurĭbus ităque proeliis adverso Marte pugnātis, tandem Lysander, Spartanōrum dux, Atheniensium exercĭtum, qui, navĭbus relictis, in terram praedātum[3] exiĕrat,[4] ad Aegos flumen oppressit, eōque impĕtu totum bellum finīvit. Hac enim clade res Atheniensium penĭtus inclināta est.

*Athens surrenders to Lysander*, 404 *B. C.—The Thirty Tyrants.*

**227.** Lysander Athēnas navigāvit, miseramque civitātem, obsidiōne circumdătam, fame[5] urget. Athenienses, multis fame et ferro amissis, pacem petivēre. Quum nonnulli nomen Atheniensium delendum,[1] urbemque incendio consumendam censērent,[2] Spartāni negārunt, se passūros, ut ex duōbus Graeciae ocŭlis alter eruerētur ;[3] pacemque Atheniensĭbus sunt pollicĭti, si longi muri brachia dejicĕrent,[4] navesque tradĕrent ; denĭque si res publĭca triginta rectōres, ex civĭbus deligendos, accipĕret. His legĭbus acceptis, tota civĭtas subĭto mutāri coepit. Triginta rectōres rei publĭcae constituuntur, Lacedaemoniis[5] et Lysandro dedĭti, qui brevi tyrannĭdem in cives exercēre coepērunt.

---

| | | |
|---|---|---|
| [1] 545, 3. | [4] 295, 3. | [7] 495, 1. |
| [2] 386, 2. | [5] 414, 4. | [8] 509. |
| [3] 569. | [6] 518, II. | [9] 384. |

*Thrasybulus occupies Phyle*, 404 *B. C.*

**228.** Quum triginta tyranni, praeposïti a Lacedaemoniis, servitūte oppressas tenērent Athēnas, Thrasybūlus Phylen ' confūgit, quod ' est castellum in Attïcā
munitissïmum, quum non plus secum habēret,' quam
triginta de suis. Hinc, virïbus paulātim auctis, in Pirae-
um transiit,' Munychiamque munīvit. Hanc bis tyranni
oppugnāre sunt adorti, ab eāque turpïter repulsi protïnus
in urbem, armis impedimentisque amissis, refugērunt.
In secundo proelio cecïdit ' Critias, triginta tyrannōrum
acerrïmus.'

*Epaminondas.—Battle of Leuctra*, 371 *B. C.: of Mantinĕa*, 362 *B.C.*

**229.** Epaminondas, dux Thebānus, apud Leuctra
superāvit Lacedaemonios. Idem imperātor apud Mantinēam gravïter vulnerātus concïdit.' Hujus casu aliquantum ' retardāti sunt Boeotii, neque tamen prius
pugnā ' excessērunt, quam '' hostes profligārunt.'' At
Epaminondas quum animadvertěret, mortifěrum se vulnus accepisse, simulque, si ferrum, quod ex hastīli '' in
corpŏre remansěrat, extraxisset,'' anïmam statim emissū-
rum, usque eo retinuit, quoad renuntiātum est, vicisse ''
Boeotios. Id postquam audīvit, " *Satis*," inquit, " *vixi ;
invictus enim morior.*" Tum, ferro extracto, confestim
ĕxanimātus est.

---

| | | |
|---|---|---|
| ' 50, 379. | ' 163, 1. | '' 234. |
| ' 445, 4. | ' 255, I. 4. | '' 63. |
| ' 518, II. | ' 335, 4. | '' 533, 3. |
| ' 295, 3. | ' 434, 1. | '' 549. |
| ' 273, I. | '' 523, 2, 2). | |

## PERIOD III.—GRAECO-MACEDONIAN EMPIRE.

FROM THE ACCESSION OF PHILIP TO THE DEATH OF ALEXANDER, 823 B. C.

*Decline of the Grecian States.—Rise of the Macedonian Power.*

**230.** Post Leuctrĭcam pugnam Lacedaemonii se nunquam refecērunt; et Thebae, quod,[1] quamdiu Epaminondas praefuit rei publĭcae[2] caput fuit totīus Graeciae, post ejus interĭtum perpetuo aliēno paruērunt imperio. Athenienses, non ut olim in classem et exercĭtum, sed in dies festos apparatusque ludōrum redĭtus publĭcos effundēbant, frequentiusque in theātris quam in castris versabantur. Quĭbus rebus effectum est, ut obscūrum antea Macedŏnum nomen emergĕret;[3] et Philippus, obses triennio[4] Thebis habĭtus in Epaminondae domo, hujus praestantissĭmi viri et Pelopĭdae virtutĭbus erudītus, Graeciae servitūtis jugum imponĕret.

*Extension of Philip's power.*

**231.** Philippus, quum magnam gloriam apud omnes natiōnes adeptus esset,[5] Olynthios aggredītur. Hanc urbem antīquam et nobĭlem exscindit, et praedā[6] ingenti fruĭtur. Inde auraria in Thessaliā, argenti metalla in Thraciā occŭpat. His ita gestis, forte evēnit, ut eum fratres duo, reges Thraciae, disceptatiōnum suārum judĭcem[7] eligĕrent.[8] Sed Philippus ad judicium, velut ad bellum, instructo exercĭtu[9] supervēnit, et regno[10] utrumque-spoliāvit.

| | | |
|---|---|---|
| [1] 445, 4. | [4] 378, 1. | [7] 373. |
| [2] 386. | [5] 283. | [8] 414, 7. |
| [3] 495, 2. | [6] 419, L | [9] 419, 2. |

*Battle of Chæronea,* 338 *B. C.*

**232.** Quum, in Scythiam praedandi¹ causā profectus,² Scythas dolo vicisset, diu dissimulātum bellum Atheniensĭbus infert,³ quorum causae Thebāni se junxērunt. Proelio ad Chaeronēam commisso, quum Athenienses longe majōre milĭtum numĕro praestārent,⁴ tamen assiduis bellis⁵ indurātā Macedŏnum virtūte vincuntur. Non tamen immemŏres pristĭnae virtūtis⁶ cecidērunt ; quippe adversis vulnerĭbus⁷ omnes loca, quae tuenda⁸ a ducĭbus accepĕrant, morientes corporĭbus texērunt. Hic dies universae Graeciae et⁹ gloriam dominatiōnis et vetustissĭmam libertātem finīvit.

*Philip prepares to invade Persia.*

**233.** Hujus victoriae callĭde dissimulāta laetitĭa est. Non solĭta¹⁰ sacra Philippus illā die fecit ; non in convivio risit ;¹¹ non corōnas aut unguenta sumpsit ; et, quantum in illo fuit, ita vicit, ut victōrem nemo sentīret.¹² Atheniensĭbus et captīvos gratis remīsit, et bello consumptōrum¹³ corpŏra sepultūrae reddĭdit. Composĭtis in Graeciā rebus, omnium civitātum legātos ad formandum rerum praesentium statum¹⁴ evocāri Corinthum¹⁵ jubet. Ibi pacis leges universae Graeciae pro merĭtis singulārum civitātum statuit, conciliumque omnium, velŭti unum senātum,¹⁶ ex omnĭbus legit. Auxilia deinde singulārum civitātum describuntur ; nec dubium erat, eum Persārum imperium et suis et Graeciae virĭbus impugnatūrum esse.

---

| | | |
|---|---|---|
| ¹ 563. • | ⁶ 399, 2, 2). | ¹¹ 269. |
| ² 283. | ⁷ 428. | ¹² 494. |
| ³ 292, 2. | ⁸ 578, V. | ¹³ 565, 1. |
| ⁴ 518, I. | ⁹ 587, I. 5. | ¹⁴ 379. |
| ⁵ 414, 4. | ¹⁰ 575. | ¹⁵ 303. |

*Death of Philip, 336 B. C.*

**234.** Interea dum auxilia e Graeciă coeunt,[1] nuptias Cleopătrae filiae, et Alexandri, quem regem Epīri fecĕrat, magno apparātu[2] celĕbrat. Ubi quum Philippus ad ludos spectandos, medius inter duos Alexandros, filium et genĕrum, contendĕret,[3] Pausanias, nobĭlis ex Macedonĭbus adolescens, occupātis angustiis, Philippum in transĭtu obtruncat. Hic ab Attălo indīgno modo tractātus, quum saepe querēlam ad Philippum frustra detulisset,[4] et honorātum insŭper adversarium vidēret, iram in ipsum Philippum vertit, ultionemque, quam ab adversario non potĕrat, ab inīquo judĭce exēgit.

*Alexander the Great succeeds to the Macedonian Throne, 336 B.C.*

**235.** Philippo[5] Alexander filius successit, et virtūte[6] et vitiis patre major. Vincendi ratio utrīque[7] diversa. Hic[8] apertā vi, ille artĭbus bella tractābat. Deceptis[9] ille gaudēre[10] hostĭbus,[11] hic palam fusis. Prudentior ille consilio, hic animo magnificentior.[12] Iram pater dissimulāre, plerumque etiam vincĕre; hic ubi exarsisset,[13] nec dilatio ultiōnis, nec modus erat. Vini[14] uterque nimis avĭdus; sed ebrietātis diversa ratio. Pater de convivio in hostem procurrĕre, manum conserĕre, pericŭlis se temĕre offerre; Alexander non in hostem, sed in suos saevīre. Regnāre ille cum amīcis volēbat; hic in amīcos regna exercēbat. Amāri pater malle, hic metui. Litterārum cultus utrīque simĭlis. Sollertiae[15] pater majōris, hic fidei. Verbis atque oratiōne Philippus, hic

---

| | | |
|---|---|---|
| [1] 295, 3. | [5] 429. | [11] 414, 2. |
| [2] 414, 3. | [6] 387. | [12] 164. |
| [3] 518, II. | [7] 450, 2, 1). | [13] 486, 5. |
| [4] 292, 2. | [8] 580. | [14] 399, 2, 2). |
| [5] 386. | [10] 545, 1. | [15] 401, 403. |

rebus moderatior. Parcendi victis[1] filio anĭmus promptior; ille nec sociis[2] abstinēbat. Frugalitāti pater, luxuriae filius magis dedĭtus erat. Quibus[3] artĭbus orbis imperii fundamenta pater jecit, opĕris totīus gloriam filius consummāvit.

### Beginning of Alexander's Reign.

**236.** Imperio suscepto, prima Alexandro cura paternārum exsequiārum fuit; in quibus ante omnia caedis[4] conscios ad tumŭlum patris occīdi jussit. Inter initia regni multas gentes rebellantes compescuit;[5] orientes nonnullas seditiōnes exstinxit. Deinde ad Persĭcum bellum proficiscens, patrimonium omne suum, quod in Macedoniā et Eurōpā habēbat, amīcis divīsit; *sibi*[6] *Asiam sufficĕre* praefātus.[7] Nec exercitui[8] alius quam regi anĭmus fuit. Quippe omnes oblīti conjŭgum[9] liberorumque, et longinquae a domo militiae, nihil cogitābant nisi Orientis opes. Quum delāti[10] in Asiam essent, primus[11] Alexander jacŭlum velut in hostĭlem terram jecit; armatusque de navi[12] trĭpudianti[13] simĭlis prosiluit,[14] atque ita hostias caedit, precātus, ne se regem illae terrae invītae[15] accipiant.[16] In Ilio quoque ad tumŭlos herōum,[17] qui Trojāno bello cecidĕrant, parentāvit.

### Battle of the Granĭcus, 334 B. C.

**237.** Inde hostem petens milĭtes a populatiōne Asiae prohibuit, *parcendum*[18] *suis rebus* praefātus, *nec per-*

---

| | | |
|---|---|---|
| [1] 385, 575. | [7] 297, II. 3. | [13] 575, 391, 1. |
| [2] 425, 2. | [8] 387. | [14] 285. |
| [3] 453. | [9] 406. | [15] 443, 1. |
| [4] 399, 2, 2). | [10] 292, 2. | [16] 492, 3. |
| [5] 275, I. | [11] 442, 1. | [17] 68. |
| [6] 386. | [12] 62, III. | [18] 545, 3. |

*denda ea, quae possessūri*[1] *venĕrint.* In exercĭtu ejus
fuēre pedĭtum triginta duo millia, equĭtum quattuor
millia quingenti, naves centum octoginta duae. Hac
tam parvā manu universum terrārum orbem[2] vincĕre
est aggressus. Quum ad tam periculōsum bellum exercĭtum legĕret,[3] non juvĕnes robustos, sed veterānos, qui
cum patre patruisque militavĕrant, elēgit : ut non tam
milĭtes, quam magistros militiae electos putāres.[4] Prima
cum hoste congressio in campis Adrastīae fuit. In acie
Persārum sexcenta millia milĭtum fuērunt, quae non
minus arte Alexandri quam virtūte Macedŏnum super-
āta, terga vertērunt. Ităque magna caedes Persārum
fuit. De exercĭtu Alexandri novem pedĭtes, centum
viginti equĭtes cecidēre ; quos rex magnifĭce humātos
statuis equestrĭbus donāvit ; cognātis eōrum autem im-
munĭtātes dedit. Post victoriam major[5] pars Asiae ad
eum defēcit. Habuit et plura[6] proelia cum praefectis
Darīi, quos jam non tam armis, quam terrōre nomĭnis
sui vicit.

### Battle of Issus, 333 B. C.

**238.** Interea Darīus cum quadringentis millĭbus
pedĭtum ac centum millĭbus equĭtum in aciem procēdit.
Commisso proelio, Alexander non ducis magis quam
milĭtis munia[7] exsequebātur. Macedŏnes cum rege
ipso in equĭtum agmen irrumpunt. Tum vero simĭlis
ruīnae strages erat. Circa currum Darīi jacēbant nobilissĭmi duces, ante ocŭlos regis egregiā morte[8] defuncti.
Jamque qui Darīum vehēbant equi, confossi hastis et
dolōre efferāti, jugum quatĕre et regem curru[9] excutĕre

---

| | | |
|---|---|---|
| [1] 578, V. | [4] 486, 4. | [7] 131, 4.) |
| [2] 107, 2. | [5] 165. | [8] 419, I. |
| [3] 518, II. | [6] 165, 1. | [9] 434, 1. |

coepĕrant : quum ille, verĭtus ne vivus venīret¹ in hostium potestātem, desĭlit,² et in equnm, qui ad hoc ipsum sequebātur, imponĭtur. Tum vero cetĕri dissipantur metu. Inter captīvos castrōrum mater et uxor et filiae duae Darīi fuēre : in quas Alexander ita se gessit,³ ut omnes ante eum reges et continentiā⁴ et clementiā vincĕret.⁵

*Alexander in Egypt,* 882 *B. C.—He visits the Temple of Jupiter Ammon.*

**239.** Aegyptii, olim Persārum opĭbus infensi, Alexandrum laeti⁶ recepērunt. A Memphi⁷ rex in interiōra⁸ penĕtrat ; compositisque rebus ita, ut nihil ex patrio Aegyptiōrum more mutāret, adīre Jovis Ammōnis oracŭlum⁹ statuit. Quatriduo per vastas solitudĭnes absumpto, tandem ad sedem consecrātam deo¹⁰ ventum est,¹¹ undĭque ambientĭbus ramis contectam. Regem propius adeuntem maxĭmus natu¹² e sacerdotĭbus FILIUM appellat, *hoc nomen illi parentem Jovem reddĕre* affirmans. Ille se vero et accipĕre ait¹³ et agnoscĕre, humānae sortis¹⁴ oblītus. Consŭlit deinde, an totīus orbis imperium sibi destināret¹⁵ PATER. Aeque in adulatiōnem composĭtus, terrārum omnium rectōrem fore ostendit. Post haec instĭtit quaerĕre, an omnes parentis sui interfectōres poenas dedissent. Sacerdos PARENTEM ejus negat ullīus scelĕre posse violāri, PHILIPPI autem omnes luisse supplicia. Sacrificio deinde facto, dona et sacerdotĭbus et deo data,¹⁶ permissumque amīcis, ut ipsi quoque consulĕrent¹⁷ Jovem. Nihil amplius quaesivērunt, quam an

---

¹ 492, 4.       ⁷ 62, II. 2.       ¹³ 297, II. 1.
² 467, III.       ⁸ 441, 1.       ¹⁴ 406, II.
³ 272, I.       ⁹ 371, 4.       ¹⁵ 525.
⁴ 429.       ¹⁰ 384.       ¹⁶ 460, 3.
⁵ 494.       ¹¹ 301, 1.       ¹⁷ 492.
⁶ 443, 1.       ¹² 168, 3.

auctor esset sibi divīnis honorĭbus colendi[1] suum regem.
Hoc quoque acceptum fore Jovi[2] vates respondit. Rex
ex Ammōne rediens[3] elēgit urbi locum, ubi nunc est
Alexandrīa, appellatiōnem trahens ex nomĭne auctōris.

### Darius makes his last proposals of Peace.

**240.** Jam Darīus pervenĕrat Arbēla[4] vicum, nobĭlem suā clade factūrus. Raro in ullo proelio tantum
sanguĭnis[5] fusum est. Tandem Darīi aurīga, qui ante
ipsum sedens equos regēbat, hastā transfixus est; nec
aut Persae aut Macedŏnes dubitavēre, quin ipse rex esset
occīsus.[6] Cedĕre[7] Persae, et laxāre ordĭnes; jamque non
pugna, sed caædes erat, quum Darīus quoque currum
suum in fugam vertit; victōri Alexandro Asiae imperium obtĭgit.[8]

### Disturbances in Greece.

**241.** Dum haec in Asiā gerebantur, Graecia fere
omnis, spe recuperandae libertātis,[1] ad arma concurrĕrat,
auctoritātem Lacedaemoniōrum secūta. Dux hujus belli
Agis, rex Lacedaemoniōrum, fuit. Quem[9] motum Antipăter, dux[10] ab Alexandro in Macedoniā relictus, in ipso
ortu oppressit. Magna tamen utrimque caedes fuit.
Agis rex, quum suos terga dantes vidēret, dimissis satel-
litĭbus[11] ut Alexandro felicitāte, non virtūte inferior
viderētur,[12] tantam stragem hostium edĭdit,[13] ut agmĭna
interdum fugāret. Ad postrēmum, etsi a multitudĭne
victus, gloriā tamen omnes vicit.

---

| | | |
|---|---|---|
| [1] 563. | [6] 498. | [10] 362, 3. |
| [2] 391. | [7] 545, 1. | [11] 81. |
| [3] 295, 3. | [8] 273, I. | [12] 491. |
| [4] 379. | [9] 453. | [13] 273, I. |
| [5] 396, III. | | |

### Alexander invades India.

**242.** Post haec Indiam petit, ut Oceăno finīret imperium. Cui gloriae ut etiam exercĭtus ornamenta convenīrent, phalěras equōrum et arma milĭtum argento
indūcit. Quum ad Nysam urbem venisset, oppidānis¹
non repugnantĭbus parci jussĭt.

### Alexander returns to Babylon, 324 B. C.

**243.** Ab ultĭmis² oris Oceăni Babyloniam reversus,
convivium solemnĭter instituit. Ibi quum totus³ in lae-
titiam effūsus esset, recedentem jam e convivio Medius
Thessălus, instaurātā comissatiōne invītat. Accepto po-
cŭlo, inter bibendum⁴ velŭti telo confixus ingemuit,
elatusque e convivio semianĭmis, tanto dolōre cruciātus
est, ut ferrum in remedia poscĕret.⁵ Venēnum accepisse
credĭtur.

### Death of Alexander, 323 B. C.

**244.** Quartā die Alexander indubitātam mortem
sentiens, *agnoscĕre se fatum domus majōrum suōrum*,
ait, *nam plerosque Aeacidārum intra tricesĭmum annum
defunctos.* Tumultuantes deinde milĭtes, insidiis periisse⁶
regem suspicantes, ipse sedāvit, eosque omnes ad con-
spectum suum admīsit, osculandamque⁷ dextram por-
rexit.⁸ Quum lacrimārent⁹ omnes, ipse non sine lacrĭmis
tantum, verum etiam sine ullo tristiōris mentis argu-
mento fuit. Ad postrēmum corpus suum in Ammōnis
templo condi jubet. Quum deficĕre eum amīci vidērent,
quaerunt, quem imperii faciat herēdem;¹⁰ respondit,

---

¹ 385.  　⁵ 494.  　⁸ 214, I. 1.
² 166.  　⁶ 295, 3.  　⁹ 518, I.
³ 44⁵.  　⁷ 578, V.  　¹⁰ 378.
⁴ 565, 1.

*Dignissĭmum.* Hac voce omnes amīcos suos ad aemŭ-
lam regni cupiditātem accendit. Sextā die, praeclūsā
voce, exemptum digĭto¹ annŭlum Perdiccae. tradĭdit,
quae res gliscentem amicōrum discordiam sedāvit. Nam
etsi non voce nuncupātus heres,³ judicio tamen electus³
esse videbātur.

### Remarks on the character of Alexander.

**245.** Decessit Alexander mensem unum tres et triginta annos⁴ natus, vir supra humānum modum vi⁵ anĭmi praedĭtus. Omĭna quaedam magnitudĭnem ejus in
ipso ortu portendisse existimabantur. Quo die natus
est, pater ejus nuntium duārum victoriārum accēpit;
alterius, belli Illyrĭci, alterius, certamĭnis Olympiăci, in
quod quadrĭgas misĕrat. Puer acerrĭmis litterārum stu-
diis erudītus fuit. Exactā pueritiā, per quinquennium
Aristotĕle, philosŏpho praestantissĭmo, usus est magistro.
Accepto tandem imperio tantam militĭbus suis fiduciam
fecit, ut, illo praesente, nullīus hostis arma timērent.⁶
Ităque cum nullo hoste unquam congressus est, quem
non vicĕrit;⁷ nullam urbem obsēdit, quam non expug-
navĕrit. Victus denĭque est non virtūte hostīli, sed insidiis suōrum et fraude.

---

¹ 434, 1.          ⁴ 378.          ⁶ 494.
³ 362, 3.          ⁵ 419, III.          ⁷ 501, 1.
³ 547.

# SUGGESTIONS TO THE LEARNER.

I. The preparation of a Reading Lesson in Latin involves
1. A knowledge of the Meaning of the Latin.
2. A knowledge of the Structure of the Latin Sentences.
8. A translation into English.

## MEANING OF THE LATIN.

II. Remember that almost every inflected word in a Latin sentence requires the use of both the Dictionary and the Grammar to ascertain its meaning.

The Dictionary gives the meaning of the word without reference to its Grammatical properties of *case, number, mood, tense,* etc., and the Grammar, the meaning of the endings which mark those properties. The Dictionary will give the meaning of *mensa,* a table, but not of *mensārum,* of tables; the Grammar alone will give the force of the ending *arum.*

III. Make yourself so familiar with all the endings of inflection, with their exact form and force, whether in declension or conjugation, that you will not only readily distinguish the different parts of speech from each other, but also the different forms of the same word with their exact and distinctive force.

IV. In taking up a Latin sentence,
1. Notice carefully the endings of the several words, and thus determine which words are *nouns,* which *verbs,* etc.
2. Observe the force of each ending, and thus determine *case, number, voice, mood, tense,* etc.

This will be found to be a very important step toward the mastery of the sentence. By this means you will discover not only the relation of the words to each other, but also an important part of their meaning, that which they derive from their endings.

V. The key to the meaning of any simple sentence (845, I.) will be found in the simple subject and predicate, i. e., in the Nominative and its Verb. Hence in looking out the sentence, observe the following order. Take
1. The Subject, or Nominative.

The ending will in most instances enable you to distinguish this from all other words, except the adjectives which agree with it. These may be looked out at the same time with the subject.

Sometimes the subject is not expressed, but only implied, in the ending of the verb. It may then be readily supplied, as it is always a pronoun of such person and number as the verb indicates; as, *audio*, I hear, the ending *io* showing that the subject is *ego*; *auditis*, you hear, the ending *itis* showing that the subject is *vos*.

### 2. The Verb, with Predicate Noun or Adjective, if any.

This will be readily known by the ending. Now combining this with the Subject, you will have an outline of the sentence. All the other words must now be associated with these two parts.

### 3. The Modifiers of the Subject, i. e., adjectives agreeing with it, nominatives in apposition with it, genitives dependent upon it, etc.

But perhaps some of these have already been looked out in the attempt to ascertain the subject.

In looking out these words, bear in mind the meaning of the subject to which they belong. This will greatly aid you in selecting from the dictionary the true meaning in the passage before you.

### 4. The Modifiers of the Verb, i. e., (1) Oblique cases, Accusatives, Datives, etc., dependent upon it, and (2) Adverbs qualifying it.

Bear in mind all the while the force of the case and the meaning of the verb, that you may be able to select for each word the true meaning in the passage before you.

VI. In complex and compound sentences (345, II., III.), discover first the connectives which unite the several members, and then proceed with each member as with a simple sentence.

VII. In the use of Dictionary and Vocabulary, remember that you are not to look for the particular form which occurs in the sentence, but for the Nom. Sing. of nouns, adjectives, and pronouns, and for the First Pers. Sing. Pres. Indic. Act. of Verbs. Therefore,

1. In Pronouns, make yourself so familiar with their declension, that any oblique case will at once suggest the Nom. Sing.

If *vobis* occurs, you must remember that the Nom. Sing. is *tu*.

2. In Nouns and Adjectives, make yourself so familiar with the case-endings, that you will be able to drop that of the given case, and substitute for it that of the Nom. Sing.

Thus, mens*ibus;* stem *mens*, Nom. Sing. *mensis*, which you will find in the Vocabulary. So duc*em, duc, duce, duce*.

3. In Verbs, change the ending of the given form into that of the First Pers. Sing. of the Pres. Indic. Act.

Thus, am*ā*bat; stem ama, First Pers. Sing. Pres. Indic. Act. amo, which you will find in the Vocabulary. So amaverunt; First Pers. Perf. am*a*vi, Perf. stem amav, Verb stem ama; amo.

To illustrate the steps recommended in the preceding suggestions, we add the following

### Model.

VIII. Themistŏcles imperātor servitūte totam Graeciam liberāvit.

1. Without knowing the meaning of the words, you will discover from their *forms*,

1) That *Themistŏcles* and *imperātor* are probably nouns in the Nom. Sing.

2) That *servitūte* is a noun in the Abl. Sing.

8) That *totam* and *Graeciam* are either nouns or adjectives in the Accus. Sing.

4) That *liberāvit* is a verb in the Act. voice, Indic. mood, Perf. tense, Third Person, Singular number.

2. Now, turning to the Vocabulary for the meaning of the words, you will learn,

1) That *Themistŏcles* is the name of an eminent Athenian general: THEMISTOCLES.

2) That *libĕro*, for which you must look, not for *liberāvit*, means *to liberate*: LIBERATED.

Themistocles liberated.

8) That *imperātor* means *commander*; THE COMMANDER.

Themistocles, the commander, liberated.

4) That *Graeciam* is the name of a country: GREECE.

Themistocles the commander liberated Greece.

5) That *totus* means *the whole, all*: ALL.

Themistocles the commander liberated all Greece.

6) That *servitus* means *servitude*: FROM SERVITUDE.

Themistocles the commander liberated all Greece from servitude.

### STRUCTURE OF THE LATIN SENTENCE.

IX. The structure of a sentence is best shown by *analyzing* it and *parsing* the words which compose it.

### Analysis.

X. Tell whether the sentence is simple, complex, or compound.

XI. In analyzing a Simple sentence (845, I.), name,

1. The Subject and Predicate, (1) in the simple form, and (2) in the complex form (847, 350).

2. The Modifiers of the Subject, (1) in the simple form, and (2) in the complex form (352).

3. The Modifiers of the Predicate, (1) in the simple form, and (2) in the complex form (354–356).

If the Modifiers are complex, the analysis may be continued till all complex elements are explained.

### Model.

XII. In his castris Cluilius, Albānus rex, morĭtur.  *Cluilius, the Alban king, dies in this camp.*

1. This is a simple sentence.

2. *Cluilius* is the simple subject, and *morĭtur,* the simple predicate. *Cluilius Albānus rex,* is the complex subject, and *in his castris morĭtur* is the complex predicate.

3. *Rex* is the simple modifier of the subject *Cluilius,* and *Albānus rex,* the complex modifier, as *rex* is modified by *Albānus.*

4. *In castris* is the simple modifier of the predicate *morĭtur,* showing *where* he dies, and *in his castris* is the complex modifier, as *castris* is modified by *his.*

XIII. In analyzing a Complex sentence (845, II.),

1. Name the sentence, or clause,[1] used as an element in it with its connective (357).

2. Analyze the sentence as a whole, like a simple sentence.

3. Analyze the subordinate clause (345, 2).

### Model.

XIV. Donec eris felix, multos numerābis amĭcos.  *So long as you are prosperous, you will number many friends.*

1. This is a complex sentence.

2. *Donec eris felix,* is a clause introduced as a modifier of *numerābis,* showing *when* you will number.

3. *Tu,* implied in *numerābis,* is the subject; *numerābis* is the simple predicate, *donec eris felix, multos numerābis amĭcos* is the complex predicate.

4. *Amĭcos* is the simple object of the predicate *numerābis,* and *multos amĭcos* the complex object. *Donec eris felix* is the adverbial modifier of the predicate.

5. *Donec eris felix* is a simple sentence, with the connective *donec. Tu,* implied in *eris,* is the subject, and *eris felix,* the predicate, *eris* being the copula (353) and *felix* the predicate adjective.

---

[1] If the sentence is abridged, show wherein (858, 859).

XV. In analyzing a Compound sentence (345, III.),

1. Separate it into its members and name the connectives.[1]

2. Analyze each member as a separate sentence.

## Model.

XVI. Sol ruit et montes umbrantur.
*The sun descends and the mountains are shaded.*

1. This is a compound sentence (345, III.).

2. The members are *sol ruit* and *montes umbrantur*, connected by the conjunction *et*.

3. The members are simple sentences, and are analyzed accordingly.

## Parsing.

XVII. In parsing a word,

1. Name the Part of Speech to which it belongs.

2. Inflect[2] it, if capable of inflection.

3. Give its gender, number, case, voice, mood, tense, person, etc.[3]

4. Give its Syntax and the Rule for it.[4]

## Model.

XVIII. Romāni ab arūtro abduxērunt Cincinnātum, ut dictātor esset, *The Romans took Cincinnatus from the plough, that he might be dictator.*

1. *Romāni* is an adjective : *Romānus, a, um,* STEM, *Romano ;* decline. It is in the *Nom. Plur. Masc.*, is used substantively (441), and is the *subject* of *abduxērunt.* Give Rule III.

2. *Abduxērunt* is an active verb : *ab-dūco, ab-ducĕre, ab-duxi, ab-ductum,* compounded of *ab* and *duco* (313, II.); STEM, *ab-duc,* PERFECT STEM, *ab-dux.* Give *synopsis* of the *mood* (219, I.). Inflect the *tense,* i. e., the Indicative Perf. Act. (209). It is in the *Active* voice, *Indic.* mood, *Perf.* tense, *Third* person, *Plur.* number, and agrees with *Romāni.* Give Rule XXXV.

3. *Cincinnātum* is a Proper noun (39, 1), of the Second Decl. ; STEM

---

[1] If the sentence is abridged, name the compound elements.

[2] Inflect, i. e., decline, compare or conjugate.

[3] That is, such of these properties as it possesses.

[4] No special Rule is deemed necessary for Prepositions, Conjunctions, or Interjections. Prepositions are provided for by the rule for *Cases with Prepositions.* Conjunctions are mere connectives, and are quite fully explained under *Moods.* Interjections are only expressions of emotion, or mere marks of address, explained under *Cases.*

*Cincinnato ;* decline, used only in the singular (130, 1). It is in the *Accus. Sing. Masc.*, and is the *direct object* of *abduxērunt.* Give Rule V.

4. *Ab* is a preposition used with the Abl. *Arātro.*

5. *Arātro* is a noun of the Second Decl.; STEM *aratro ;* decline. It is in the *Abl. Sing. Neut.*, and is used with the Prep. *ab.* Give Rule XXXII.

6. *Ut* is a conjunction of purpose (491), connecting *abduxērunt* and *esset.*

7. *Esset* is an intransitive verb: *sum, esse, fui* (204). Give *synopsis* of the *mood*, and inflect the *tense*, i. e., Subj. Imperf. It is in the *Subj.* mood, *Imperf.* tense, *Third* person, *Sing.* number, and agrees with the pronoun *is*, he, implied in the ending (460, 2). Give Rule XXXV.

8. *Dictātor* is a noun of the Third Decl.; STEM *dictātōr ;* decline (60). It is in the *Nom. Sing. Masc.*, and agrees, as Predicate noun, with the omitted subject of *esset.* Give Rule I.

## TRANSLATION.

XIX. In translating, render as literally as possible without doing violence to the English.

In many important idioms of the Latin, a literal translation would not only fail to do justice to the original, but would also be a gross perversion of the mother-tongue. The following suggestions are intended to aid the pupil in disposing of such cases; but even in these, it is earnestly recommended that he should first construe literally, in order that he may be made to feel the force of the Latin construction before attempting a translation.

## *Participles.*

XX. These are much more extensively used in Latin than in English; hence the frequent necessity, in translating them, of deviating from the Latin construction. They may generally be rendered in some one of the following ways [1] (571–581):

1. Literally :

Pyrrhus proelio fusus a Tarento recessit, *Pyrrhus having been defeated in battle withdrew from Tarentum.*

2. By a Relative Clause :

Omnes aliud agentes, aliud simulantes imprŏbi sunt, *All who do one thing and pretend another are dishonest.*

3. By a Clause with a Conjunction :

---

[1] The pupil must early learn to determine from the context the appropriate rendering in each instance.

1). With a Conjunction of Time,—*while, when, after,* etc.

Uva maturāta dulcescit, *The grape, when it has ripened* (having ripened), *becomes sweet.*

2). With a Conjunction of Cause, Reason, Manner,—*as, for, since,* etc.

Milltes perfidиam verĭti revertērunt, *The soldiers returned, because they feared perfidy.*

3). With a Conjunction of Condition,—*if.*

Accusātus damnabĭtur, *If he is accused, he will be condemned.*

4). With a Conjunction of Concession,—*though, although.*

Urbem acerrĭme defensam cepit, *He took the city, though it was valiantly defended,* or *though valiantly defended.*

4. By a Verbal Noun:

Ad Romam condĭtam, *to the founding of Rome,* lit. *to Rome founded.* Ab urbe condĭtā, *from the founding of the city.* Post reges exactos, *after the expulsion of the kings.*

5. By a Verb:

Rex ei benigne recepto filiam dedit, *The king received him kindly and gave him his daughter,* lit. *gave his daughter to him kindly received.*

XXI. Participles with *non* or *nihil* are sometimes best rendered by *Participial* nouns dependent upon *without:*

Non ridens, *without laughing.*

XXII. Future Participles are sometimes best rendered by *Infinitives,* or by *Participial Nouns* with *for the purpose of:*

Rediit belli casum tentatūrus, *He returned to try* (about to try) *the fortune of war.*

XXIII. The Ablative Absolute is sometimes best rendered (1) by a *Clause* with,—*when, while, after, for, since, if, though,* etc., (2) by a *Noun* with a *Preposition,—in, during, after, by, from, through,* etc., or (3) by an *Active Participle* with its *Object:*

Servio regnante, *while Servius reigned,* or *in the reign of Servius* (lit. *Servius reigning*). Duce Fabio, *under the command of Fabius* (lit. *Fabius being commander*).

Sometimes, as in the last example, a word denoting the *doer* of an action can be best rendered by the word which denotes the *thing done.* Thus, instead of *commander, consul, king,* we have *command, consulship, reign.*

*Subjunctive.*

**XXIV.** This may be rendered as follows:

1. With the *Potential* signs, *may, can, might, could, would, should* (485):

Forsĭtan quaerātis, *Perhaps you may inquire.* Hoc nemo dixĕrit, *No one would say this.*

2. By the English Indicative. This is generally the best ren-dering

1) In clauses denoting Cause, or Time and Cause (517, 521):

Quum vita metus plena sit, *since life is full of fear.* Quum Romam venisset, *when he had come to Rome.*

2) In Indirect Questions (525):

Quaerĭtur, cur dissentiant, *It is asked why they disagree.*

3) In the Subjunctive by Attraction (527):

Vereor, ne, dum minuĕre velim labōrem, augeam, *I fear I shall increase the labor, while I wish to diminish it.*

4) In the Subordinate Clauses of Indirect Discourse (531):

Hippias gloriātus est, annŭlum quem habĕret se suā manu confecisse, *Hippias boasted that he had made with his own hand the ring which he wore (had).*

5) In Relative Clauses defining indefinite antecedents, and sometimes in clauses denoting *result* (501, 494, 495):

Sunt qui putent, *there are some who think.* Ita vixit ut Atheniensĭbus esset carissĭmus, *He so lived, that he was very dear to the Athenians.*

6) Sometimes in Conditional and Concessive clauses, and in clauses with *Quin* and *Quomĭnus* (510, 515, 498, 499):

Dum metuant, *if only* (provided) *they fear.* Si voluisset, dimicasset, *If he had wished, he would have fought.* Ut desint vires, tamen est laudanda voluntas, *Though the strength fails, still the will should be approved.* Adest nemo, quin videat, *There is no one present who does not see.*

3. By the Infinitive. This is often the best rendering

1) In Relative Clauses denoting Result: hence after *dignus, in-dignus, idoneus, aptus*, etc. (501):

Non is sum qui his utar, *I am not such a one as to use* (he who may use) *these things.* Fabŭlae dignae sunt, quae legantur, *The fables are worthy to be read* (which, *or* that they, should be read).

2) Sometimes in Relative Clauses denoting Purpose, and other clauses denoting Result (500, 494):

Decemvīri creāti sunt qui leges scribĕrent, *Decemvirs were appointed to prepare the laws* (who should prepare).

### Infinitive.

XXV. The Infinitive has a much more extensive use in Latin than in English. The following points require notice (539 ff.).

1. The Infinitive with a Subject is rendered by a *Finite* verb with *that*:

Dixit se regem vidisse, *He said that he had seen the king.*

2. The Historical Infinitive (545, 1) is rendered by the Imperfect Indicative:

Iram pater dissimulāre, *The father concealed his anger.*

3. The Infinitive is sometimes best rendered by a *Participial noun* with *of, with*, etc.

Insimulātur mysteria violasse, *He is accused of having violated the mysteries.*

### Miscellaneous Idioms.

XXVI. The following Miscellaneous Idioms are added:

1. *Certiōrem facĕre* should be rendered, *to inform*, and *certior fiĕri, to be informed*:

Caesar certior factus est, *Caesar was informed.*

2. *Inter se*, lit. *between themselves*, is often best rendered, *from each other, to each other, together.*

Omnes inter se diffĕrunt, *They all differ from each other.*

3. *Ne—quidem*, with one or more words between the parts, should be rendered, *not even ;* or *even—not*:

Ne nomen quidem, *not even the name.*

4. When two or more verbs stand together in the same compound tense, the copula (*sum*) is generally expressed only with the last, but in rendering, the copula should be expressed only with the first:

Captus et in vincūla conjectus est, *He was taken and thrown into chains.*

5. *Quanto—tanto*, lit. *by as much as—by so much*, is often best rendered before comparatives, *the—the :*

F

Quanto diutius considĕro, tanto res vidētur obscurior, *the longer* (by as much as the longer) *I consider the subject, the more obscure* (by so much the more obscure) *does it appear.*

6. A Clause with *quomĭnus*, by which, or that, the less, may generally be rendered by a *Clause* with *that*, by the *Infinitive*, or by a *Participial noun* with *from.*

Per eum stetit quomĭnus dimicarētur, *It was owing to him* (stood through him) *that the engagement was not made.* Non recusāvit quomĭnus poenam subīret, *He did not refuse to submit to punishment.* Regem impediit quomĭnus pugnāret, *He prevented the king from fighting.*

# NOTES.

## GRAMMATICAL EXERCISES.

*For Explanation of References, see page* ix.

1. **Ala.** As the Latin has no article, a noun may, according to the **1** connection in which it is used, be translated (1) without the article; as, *ala,* wing; (2) with the indefinite article *a,* or *an ;* as, *ala,* a wing; (3) with the definite article *the ;* as, *ala,* the wing.

4, 23. **Post Romuli mortem.** For the position of the preposition, **3** see 602, II. 3.

7. **Servus bonus.** In Latin the adjective generally follows its noun, as in this example, though sometimes it precedes it, as in English. When emphatic the adjective is placed before its noun; as, *vera amicitia* (7, 25). See Grammar, 598; 598, 2.

11, 18. **Leges . . . sunto,** *let the laws be,* etc. The third person of **5** the Future Imperative is often best rendered by *let,* instead of *shall.*

13, 28. **Omnium.** This agrees with *militum.*

19, 2. **Consul.** See note on " *Consules* " (169).——4. **Vini deus. 9** The ancient Romans recognized a great number of gods and goddesses. Almost every object in nature was under the special care of some one of these fabulous deities. Bacchus presided over the cultivation of the vine, and was the god of festivity.——6. **Testis temporum,** *the witness of times,* i. e. competent to testify in regard to them. Tempŏra, *times,* involves events.——**Habetur,** *is regarded.*——9. **Evaserat ;** from *evado.*

20, 1. **Expulsus est ;** from *expello.*——2. **Regis pater.** *Regis* refers to Tarquinius Priscus, the fifth king of Rome.——6. **Didicit ;** from *disco.*——7. **Dictator.** See note on " *Cum honōre dictatōris* " (178). ——**Voverat ;** from *voveo.*——8. **Interfecerunt ;** from *interficio.*

21, 5. **Malorum.** This depends upon *mater.* **10**

22, 6. **Perdidi ;** from *perdo.*

23, 6. **Fecit,** lit. *made ;* render *composed,* or *wrote.*——8. **Condidit ;** from *condo.*——12. **Vixerunt ;** from *vivo.*——16. **Luxerunt ;** from

**PAGE**

**11** *lugeo.*——20. **Sam praetervectas;** from *praetervĕho.*——21. **Transie-rant;** from *transeo.* See 295, 3.

24, 5. **Nutricem . . . Siciliam.** The ancient Romans annually received large supplies of grain from Sicily. Hence the epithets here applied to it.

25, 3. **Belli;** construe with *artem,* the art of war.——9. **Edoctus fuerat;** from *edoceo.*——10. **Petierunt;** from *peto:* See 234, 278, 2.

**12** ——13. **Iberam tradaxit.** This was at the beginning of the second Punic war, 218 B. C. The Ebro was the boundary between the Roman and the Carthaginian possessions in Spain.——**Tradaxit;** from *tradūco.*——14. **Transdacti sunt;** from *transdūco.*

26, 3. **Bestiolae.** This refers to the insect known as the *ephemeran.*——4. **Natas;** from *nascor.*——6. **Exstruxerunt;** from *exstruo.*——7. **Longos quáterna cubita,** *each four cubits long.* Quaterna is a *distributive.* See 174, 2, 1).

27, 2. **Rediit;** from *redeo,* 295, 8.——3. **Concessit;** from *concēdo.*——4. **Numerum,** *quantity.* The word generally means *number.*——**Misit;** from *mitto.*——8. **Ibo;** from *eo,* 295.

**13** 28, 2. **Nigrantes terga,** literally, *black as to their backs.*——3. **Ietas;** from *ico.*——**Cecidit;** from *cado.*——4. **Incensas est;** from *incendo.*

29, 3. **Videt,** *sees it.* The object is the pronoun understood, referring to *conjuratiōnem.*

30, 9. **Non dat,** *does not allow;* lit. ˙*give.*——10. **Omnes.** This agrees with *nos* implied in *damus.*

**14** 31, 6. **Persuasit;** from *persuadeo.*——8. **Pepercerunt;** from *parco.*

32, 1. **Affuit;** from *adsum.* For the assimilation of *d* before *f,* see 338, 2, *ad.*——2. **Adjunxit;** from *adjungo.*——3. **Singulorum,** *of individuals;* it depends upon *salūti.*——5. **Terrorem injecit,** *he struck terror into,* i. e. inspired with terror; lit. *threw terror into.*——**Injecit;** from *injicio.*——6. **Pugnae . . . . Salaminem.** This was the famous victory gained, 480 B. C., by the Greeks over the Persians.

34, 1. **Caesari erant agenda,** lit. *were to Caesar to be done.*

**15** 36, 10. **Delegerunt;** from *delĭgo.*

37, 2. **Tuae litterae,** *your letter.* This is the common meaning of the plural of this word.——5. **Notas;** Participle from *nosco,* used adjectively, 575.

38, 1. **Esto,** *let there be.*

**16** 39, 4. **Erat,** *it was.*——I. 2. **Sustinuerunt;** from *sustineo.*——4. **Ventorum pater.** Aeŏlus is meant: he was the god of the winds, and ruled them at pleasure.——5. **Singulorum facultates,** *the resources of individuals.* See 441, 1.——IV. 1. **Tarquinius.** Tarquinius Superbus,

**17** the last king of Rome, is meant.——3. **Dederunt;** from *do.*——V. 2.

**Sonat,** lit. *sounds ;* here *expresses, means.*——**Vox voluptatis,** *the word* **17** *pleasure ;* lit. *the word of pleasure.*——**5. Exhorrait ;** from *exhorresco.*

40, 3. **Famae mendacia,** *the falsehoods of report,* i. e. the falsehoods circulated by report.——8. **Nesciam fingit.** Socrates, one of the most eminent philosophers of antiquity, had such a contempt for all pedantry and conceit of knowledge, that he claimed to know only one thing ; viz., *that he knew nothing.*

41, 1. **Poena ;** supply *est,* 460, 2.——3. **Fuit,** *was,* i. e. consisted of. ——4. **Erat somni ;** supply *man* in rendering.——6. **Senescentis ;** sup- **18** ply *aetatis* from the preceding clause.——12. **Ceteri ;** supply *vendunt.*

42, 7. **Suorum,** *his own,* i. e. faults (*vitiōrum*).

43, 9. **Hujus ;** belongs to *gloriae.* **19**

44, I. 1. **Cato ;** supply *magnus habebatur* from preceding clause. ——II. 1. **Res . . . constituit,** *managed the affairs,* etc. He was gov- ernor of the Chersonesus.——III. 7. **Pisces ;** supply *capiuntur.*—— **20** IV. 3. **Sacra,** *sacred rites.* King Numa was the reputed founder of the early religious institutions of Rome.

45, 3. **Viginti talentis,** *twenty talents,* more than $20,000, a high price for an oration, but the purchaser was a wealthy king, and the au- thor one of the most finished of the Attic orators.——**Vendidit ;** from *vendo.*

46, 1. **Aurum ;** supply *vilius est* from the preceding clause.——10. **Adversam ;** supply *fortūnam.*——11. **Virtutis,** *that of virtue.* It de- **21** pends upon *sitis* understood.

47, 2. **Major ;** lit. *greater ;* render *older.*——3. **Caesaris ;** supply *castris.*

48, I. 5. **Functus sum ;** from *fungor.*——III. 9. **Hectora . . . .** **22** **Achilles.** These were the two most eminent warriors in the Trojan war ; the former a Trojan, the latter a Greek.

49, 2. **Gesta sunt ;** from *gero.*——3. **Vixit ;** from *vivo.*——5. **Tra- jecit ;** from *trajicio.*——6. **Fabricius, Aristides.** They were both dis- tinguished for rare integrity and uprightness. The latter was surnamed *the Just.* With *Fabricius* supply *fuit.*——7. **Mortuus est ;** from *morior.* ——12. **Timotheus ;** supply *vixit.*

50, 7. **Destiterant ;** from *desisto.*——11. **Expulsus est ;** from *ex-* **23** *pello.*——13. **Bello Persico,** *in the Persian war,* i. e. the war with Per- sia. Themistocles gained the celebrated victory of Salamis, 480 B. C.

51, 4. **Qua nocte—eadem** = *eādem nocte, quā, on the same night in which.* The antecedent *nocte* is incorporated into the relative clause according to 445, 9.——**Dianae . . . . templum.** This temple of Diana at Ephesus in Ionia was celebrated for its beauty and magnificence.—— 9. **Condita erat ;** from *condo.*

52, 2. **Conjunxit ;** from *conjungo.* **24**

**PAGE**

**24**    53, 1. **Quidam,** *some,* i. e. some persons.——**Non re,** *not in reality.*
——5. **Par;** agrees with *Ancus.*

     54, 1. **Cognite;** from *cognosco.*——4. **Excepta;** from *excipio.*——
6. **Natus est;** from *nascor.*——**Cicerone . . . . consulibus;** XXIII.
See also notes on " *Consules* " (169) and " *Duillio* " (185).

**25**    55, L 1. **Ad summam senectutem,** *till extreme old age.*——5. **Vixit;**
from *vinco.*——6. **Fusae sunt;** from *fundo.*——8. **Erga parentes, pie-
tas**=*justitia erga parentes piëtas dicitur.*——II. 4. **Africanus;** so called
because of his great victory at Zama in Africa.——5. **Ex vire,** i. e. from
the word *vir,* man.——6. **Floruit;** from *floresco,* 282, L.——8. **Dedit;** from *do.*——III. 2. **Divisa est;** from *divido.*——4. **Progressi
sunt;** from *progredior.*——5. **Est,** *there is.*——**Sub pallio sordido,**
*under a soiled coat,* i. e. in the poor man, among the poor.

**26**    56, 5. **Ab omni parte;** lit. *from every part;* render, *in all respects.*
——6. **Condidit;** from *condo.*——9. **Dives.** This is a predicate adjective: *is born rich.*——11. **Dissimillima natura,** *very dissimilar* (things)
*by nature.*

     57, 2. **Ad quas res, in iis**=*in iis rebus, ad quas, in those things for
which.* See note on " *Qua nocte, eädem* " (51, 4).

**27**    58, 2. **Tua;** supply *delectant.*——3. **Amicum,** *a friend,* i. e. my
friend; possessive omitted according to 447.——5. **Consumpsi;** from
*consumo.*

     60, 1. **Deus est,** *there is a God.*——**Temporum,** *of the seasons.*——
**Rerum,** *of events.*——2. **Mala;** construe with *carmina.*——3. **Hones-
tatis;** depends upon *regula* understood, 397, 1, (3).——4. **Dominus;**
supply *erat.*

     62, 1. **Meorum,** *of my friends,* lit. *of my,* or *mine.*——2. **Agnovit;**
from *agnosco.*——3. **Si quisquam;** supply *sapiens fuit.*——5. **Optimum
quidque,** lit. *every best thing;* render, *all the best things, whatever is
best,* or *the best thing ever,* 458, 1.——6. **Perdidit;** from *perdo.*

**28**    63, 3. **Peperi;** from *pario,* 280.——5. **Delati sunt;** from *defëro,*
292, 2.——6. **Exercitum,** *his army.* Observe the omission of the possessive, 447.——7. **Exstinctam est;** from *exstinguo,* to put out, extinguish, applicable to a light. The language is figurative; the beautiful
city of Corinth is represented as a light, *lumen.*

     64, 3. **Victoria;** supply *venit.*

     65, 4. **Consules;** supply *bini creabantur* from the next clause.——
**Bini,** *two by two,* i. e. *two each year,* distributive, 174, 2.

**29**    66, 1. **Perspexere;** from *perspicio.*

     67, 1. **Ubi primum,** *when first,* i. e. as soon as.——2. **Cum Graecis
Latina,** lit. *Latin things with Greek things ;* render, *Latin studies with
Greek studies.*——**Conjunxi;** from *conjungo.*——4. **Lycurgi leges.**
Lycurgus was the great Spartan law-giver. His laws contributed much

to the prosperity and greatness of Sparta.——6. **Aureorum annulorum. 29**
The wearing of gold rings was one of the special privileges of senators
and knights.——**Detraxerat ;** from *detráho.*

68, 3. **Nonnulli,** *not none,* i. e. some, 585, 1.——**Casune ;** *casu* with
the interrogative enclitic *ne* appended.——**Sit effectus ;** from *efficio.*——
4. **Quaesivit ;** from *quaero.*——**Salvusne . . . clipeus.** This was his
question when mortally wounded at Mantinéa. Ancient warriors took
special pride in preserving their shields.——5. **Essent fusi ;** from
*fundo.*——6. **In causis,** *in suits at law.*

69, 3. **Redires ;** from *redeo.*                                        **30**

70, 7. **Tanquam parva,** *as small,* i. e. unimportant.

71, 1. **Abduxerant ;** from *abdüco.*——**Cincinnatum.** Cincinnatus,
who was thus summoned from the plough to the dictatorship in an hour
of great national peril, acted with such remarkable promptness and
energy, that in a few days he conquered the enemy, entered Rome in
triumph, and was rewarded with a golden crown. He then quietly re-
signed his dictatorship and returned to his farm.——**Dictator.** See note
on *" Cum honore dictatöris "* (178).——2. **Patris,** *of his father,* i. e.
the Sun. The story is, that he asked his father, the sun, for the use of
his chariot for a day, but that he found himself unable to manage the
fiery steeds.——5. **Decrevit ;** from *decerno.*——**Ut consul . . . . ne
. . . . caperet.** This was the usual formula by which a Roman citizen
might be clothed with the power of dictator.

72, 1. **Ut . . . diligamus ;** XXIV. 2, 5).——4. **Senserit ;** from **31**
*sentio.*

73, 2. **Quin . . . . abeam ;** XXIV. 2, 6).——4. **Quominus sit ;**
lit. *by which,* or *that, the less God should be ;* render, *that God should
be,* or *God from being,* XXVI. 6.

74, 1. **Qui sustineret,** lit. *who should sustain ;* render, *to sustain,*
XXIV. 3.——4. **Quod . . . possit ;** XXIV. 2, 5).——6. **Inventi sunt ;**
from *invenio.*

75, 1. **Dum metuant ;** XXIV. 2, 6).

77, 4. **Nisi in litteris,** *if not in letters,* i. e. in literary pursuits, stu- **32**
dies.——5. **Non . . . senatum.** Senatus, *senate,* is derived from *senex,*
and meant originally an assembly of *old men.*

78, 2. **Constiterit ;** from *consisto.*——4. **Qui . . . attigissem,** *though
I had commenced* (touched) *Greek studies* (letters); XXIV. 2, 6).——
**Attigissem ;** from *attingo.*

80, 1. **Quum . . . sit ;** XXIV. 2, 1).——2. **Necesse est.** The subject is the clause, *Deum . . . . majöra.* Hence *necesse* is neuter, **33**
438, 3 ; 42, III. 2.——**Deum . . . . habere ;** XXV. 1.——**Haec habere
majora,** lit. *to have these greater,* i. e. in a higher degree.——4. **Suo
tote . . . non viderit.** As the term of the consular office was a year,

**33** this seems a very remarkable statement. But the truth is, Caninius was appointed only to fill a vacancy of a few hours at the very end of the consular year. Hence the remark is only a playful one.

81, 1. **Malorum,** *of evils ;* from *malum.*——**Quod . . . . capiantur ;** XXIV. 2, 1). The Subjunctive implies that the reason is assigned on Plato's authority.——**Pisces ;** supply *capiantur.*——2. **Latine,** *in Latin.*——3. **Redierim ;** from *redeo,* 295, 3.

82, 1. **Dum . . . . convenirent ;** XXIV. 2, 1).——**Ad horam nonam,** *till the ninth hour,* i. e. till 3 P. M. For the divisions of the Roman day, see 711.——2. **Quievere ;** from *quiesco.*——3. **Vocem . . . excitant.** The immense audiences before which the ancient tragedians acted, rendered this precaution quite indispensable.

83, 1. **Quantas . . . . habeat ;** XXIV. 2, 2).——2. **Tantum,** *only.* ——4. **Qui . . . . videant ;** XXIV. 3, 2).——**Quas in partes,** lit. *into what parts ;* render, *in what direction.*——6. **Unus,** *one,* viz. Demos-
**34** thenes.——7. **Est.** The subject is the clause, *qualis res . . . sit,* 555.

84, 1. **Ut . . . servem,** *that I should keep myself neutral,* i. e., in respect to the civil wars.——2. **Quas cognorit.** XXIV. 2, 3).——**Cognorit ;** for *cognoverit,* 234, 2.——3. **Jussit ;** from *jubeo,* 269.——**Quae ;** refers to *naves,* as its antecedent.——5. **Ut—videar ;** XXIV. 2, 5).—— **Vixisse ;** from *vivo.*

85, 1. **Quod scirent ;** XXIV. 2, 4).——2. **Bestiolas.** Reference is here made to the insect known as the *ephemeran.*——3. **Respondit ;** from *respondeo.*——**Sibi, suas.** Here *sibi* refers to Caesar, the subject of the subordinate clause, while *suas* refers to Ariovistus, the subject of the principal clause. See 449, II.——**Vicissent ;** from *vinco.*——4. **Si . . . esset . . . . fuisse.** In the *direct* discourse, this would have the Imperfect Subjunctive in both clauses, the third form of the conditional sentence (510). For changes in the *conclusion,* see 533, 2, 2).—— **Ille,** *he,* i. e. Caesar.——**A se,** *from himself,* i. e. Ariovistus.——5. **Egit ;**
**35** from *ago, treated, argued.*——**Reminisceretur.** In the *direct* discourse, this would have been in the Imperative : hence the Subjunctive here according to 530, II.

86, 2. **Patres conscripti,** *conscript fathers,* often used in addressing the Roman senate.——5. **Dormiunt ;** supply pronoun referring to *virtutes,* they.——6. **Sunto,** *let them be.*——8. **Militiae summum jus,** *the supreme control of military affairs.*——**Parento ;** supply pronoun, referring to *consules.*——9. **Te ;** subject of *esse.*——10. **Quam primum,** *as soon as possible,* 444, 3.

**36** 87, 4. **Positam** esse ; from *pono.*——5. **Traditum est ;** from *trado.* ——7. **Cupidum ;** Acc. Masc. Sing. agreeing with *aliquem,* any one, the omitted subject of *esse.*——9. **Suis rebus ;** *with one's own things. Suis* refers to the omitted subject of *esse.*——**Sunt ;** agrees by attraction with

Pred. Nom. *divitiae,* instead of the subject clause, 462.——11. **Lycurgi 36 temporibus.** This was in the ninth century B. C.——14. **Inventas esse;** from *invenio.*——16. **Amare;** supply *est.*——17. **Minima;** *the smallest,* i. e. the smallest evils (*mala*).

88, 4. **Graece loqui,** *to speak in Greek.*——**Latine;** supply *loqui.*——6. **Didicerunt;** from *disco.*——13. **Esse;** supply *bonus.*

89, 3. **Videre . . . . caperet.** This was the duty, or business, *ne-* **37** *gotium,* assigned to Postumius. The language is the usual form of de-cree by which the Dictator was clothed with extraordinary power, in order to save the state. See note on " *Cum honōre dictatōris* " (178). Postumius was Dictator.——4. **Themistoclem.** This is the subject of the infinitive *sumpsisse,* while the whole clause, *Themistoclem . . . . sumpsisse,* is in apposition with *fama.*——**Sumpsisse;** from *sumo.*

90, 3. **Inter nos;** lit. *between ourselves ;* render, *with each other.*——4. **Accedit quod;** lit. *it is added that,* i. e. there is the additional fact that.

91, 1. **Tu;** subject of *responsūrus sis.*——2. **Pervenissentne;** *per-venissent* and *ne.*——3. **Mei;** subject of *esse* understood.——5. **Inter-fuisset;** from *intersum.*

92, 3. **Discendi;** supply *facultātem,* 397, 1, (8).——4. **Audiendi;** supply *occasio.*——7. **Platonis audiendi,** *of hearing Plato ;* lit. *of Plato* **38** *to be heard.* *Platōnis* depends upon *studiōsus,* while the gerundive *au-diendi* agrees with it, 562.——9. **Quid audierim,** *what I have heard.*

93, 3. **Sacerdotibus creandis;** lit. *to priests to be appointed ;* render, *to the appointment of priests,* 580.——**Adjecit;** from *adjicio.*——6. **Nonnulli,** *some,* 585, 1.

94, 1. **Ad intelligendum;** lit. *to understanding ;* render, *to under-stand.*——**Est natus;** from *nascor,* lit. *has been born ;* render, *is born,* 471, 3.——4. **Ad cognoscendas . . . . leges;** lit. *to the laws to be learned ;* render, *to learn,* or *study the laws,* etc.——**Lycurgi leges.** The laws of Lycurgus, the great law-giver of Sparta, were very famous in antiquity.——6. **Catilina . . . . conjuravit.** This iniquitous con-spiracy was formed during the consulship of the orator Cicero, 63 B. C., by whom it was fortunately discovered and defeated.

95, 1. **Nihil agendo,** *by doing nothing.*

96, 2. **Concessit;** from *concēdo.*——3. **Defensum;** from *defendo.* **39** ——5. **Facies;** the object is *id,* the omitted antecedent of *quod.*——6. **Cognita;** from *cognosco.*——**Oratio;** supply *jucunda est* from the pre-ceding clause.

97, 2. **Hippias.** He had once been tyrant of Athens, but having been driven from the throne, he repaired to the Persian court and espoused the Persian cause.——**Cecidit;** from *cado.*——3. **Pinxit;** from *pingo.*——**Templo . . . . Dianae.** See note on the same, (51, 4).

**39** ——5. **Terra mutata;** lit. *earth,* or *land, having been changed;* render, *change of country,* 580.——6. **Expulsus;** from *expello.*——7. **Factus;** from *facio,* Pass. *fu.*——**Subegit;** from *subigo.*——8. **Vincta;** from *vincio.*——9. **Regibus exactis;** lit. *the kings having been expelled;* render, *when,* or *after, the kings were expelled,* 431, 2, (1). This refers to the overthrow of the regal form of government at Rome by the banishment of Tarquin, 510 B. C. See below (167, 168).——

**40** 12. **Empta;** from *emo.*——13. **Dilapsi sunt;** from *dilabor.*

98, 3. **Secunda;** *prosperous things,* i. e. prosperity.

99, 2. **In bonis rebus;** lit. *in good things;* render, *among good things,* i. e. as blessings.——4. **Eripi, surripi.** *Eripio* means *to tear away forcibly; surripio, to take away stealthily.*

---

# FABLES.

**41** 100. **Praetereunti;** Dative Sing. Part. of *praetereo,* 295, 3.——**Inquit;** the object is the clause, or sentence, "*Non .... maledixit,*" 357, I.

101. **Orto;** from *orior.*——**Quantum boni,** lit. *how much of a good thing;* render, *how much good,* 396, 2, 3). Both adjectives are here used *substantively,* 441, 2.

**42** 102. **Coepit,** *she* (the woman) *began.*——**Illam,** *that she,* i. e. the hen.——**Minores;** supply *divitias.*——**Perdidit;** from *perdo.*

103. **Deprehensus;** from *deprehendo.*——**Mehercule;** lit. *by Hercules;* render, *indeed,* 589, 590.

104. **Subsiliit;** from *subsilio.*——**Si .... posset;** *if perchance she might be able,* i. e. to ascertain whether she might, a dependent question, 525, 1.——**Acerbae sunt;** *they are sour,* agreeing with *uvae* understood. ——**Repertas;** from *reperio.*——**Quae;** depends upon *assequi.*—— **Quae .... desperent;** XXIV. 2, 5).

105. **Inhaeserat;** from *inhaereo.*——**Qui extrahat;** lit. *who may remove it;* render, *that he may remove it,* or *to remove it,* XXIV. 3, 2). ——**Hoc,** *this,* i. e. the removal of the bone.——**Quum .... postularet;**

**43** XXIV. 2, 1).——**Videtur;** the subject is the clause, *quod .... extraxisti.*——**Extraxisti;** from *extraho.*

106. **Propter hoc ipsum,** *on account of this very thing,* or *for this very reason.*——**Quum,** *though.*——**Eos;** supply *esse puniendos.*

107. **Quum .... sentiret;** XXIV. 2, 1).——**Ut fieri solet,** *as is wont to happen. Solet* is used impersonally.——**Quibus allatis,** *which*

*having been brought,* i. e. when these were brought, 431, 2.——**Quibus ;** **43**
see 453.——**Allatis ;** from *affĕro,* 292, 2.——**Quod ;** *which,* or *this,* i. e.
the breaking of the bundle of rods ; it refers to the clause, *ut . . . . frangĕrent.*——**Imbecillis ;** supply *res esset* from the preceding clause.

108. **Quomodo,** *how,* i. e. to determine *how.*——**Proposuitis ;** from
*propōno.*——**Posse ;** depends upon a verb of saying understood ; *for* **44**
*thus,* they said, *they would be able,* etc., 530, 1.——**Nemo repertus est,**
*no one was found,* i. e. who would do it.——**Repertus est ;** from *reperio.*

109. **Unus ;** supply *residēbat.*——**Orta ;** from *orior.*——**Quum . . . .**
**desperarent,** *while all despaired,* etc., 518, II.——**Interrogat.** The two
objects are *gubernatōrem,* and the clause, *utram . . . . existimāret,* 374, 4.
——**Submersum iri ;** Fut. Pass. Infin. of *submergo, would be submerged,*
*would go down.*——**Proram.** The full form would be : *Proram prius*
*submersum iri existĭmo.*——**Ille ;** supply *dixit,* 367, 3.——**Quum . . . .**
**sim ;** XXIV. 2, 1).——**Adspecturus sim ;** from *adspicio.*

110. **Illa,** *she,* i. e. the tortoise.——**Se voluerem facere,** *to make her*
*winged,* i. e. to teach her to fly.——**Arreptam ;** from *arripio,* agrees
with *illam : the eagle carried her, seized in his talons*=seized her in his
talons and carried her ; XX. 5 ; 579.——**Sustulit ;** from *tollo.*——**In**
**sublime,** *on high.*

111. **Junxerant ;** from *jungo.*——**Ovis ;** supply *et* before this word. **45**
**Prima ;** supply *pars.*——**Quartam ;** supply *partem,* the object of *arro-*
*gāre.*——**Habiturum ;** supply *esse,* 545, 3.

---

# ANECDOTES.

112. **Sciebam . . . . mortalem ;** object of *dixisse,* 357, I.——**Gen-**
**uisse ;** from *gigno.*——**Mortalem ;** agrees with *eum* understood.

113. **Quod,** *that which.* The full form would be, *Deus est id*
*quod,* etc.

114. **Se ipsum nosse ;** supply *difficile est.*——**Nosse ;** for *novisse.*

115. **Spes ;** supply *commūnis est,* etc.——**Qui ;** supply *habent.*

116. **Deus ;** supply *est,* etc.

117. **In pompa.** In the sacred processions, so common at the reli- **46**
gious festivals at Athens, the consecrated vessels of gold and silver
were often displayed.

118. **Scire . . . . nihil.** See note on " *Nescium fingit* " (40, 8).

119. **Scipio Africanus.** This is the celebrated Roman general who
conquered Hannibal at Zama. See below (196) and note on " *Africa-*
*nus* " (196).——**Antequam . . . . precatus esset ;** XXIV. 2, 1).

**46**    120. **Gentis Corneliae.** This was the *gens* to which Scipio belonged.
——**Jussit;** from *jubeo.*——**Res gestas,** lit. *things done,* i. e. deeds,
achievements. *Gestas,* participle from *gero.*

121. **Plus esse,** *that it,* i. e. the talent, *was more.*——**Qued,** *that
which ;* supply *id.*

122. **Se . . . . habere,** *that he had thirty years,* i. e. was thirty
years old.

123. **Quae conarentur;** XXIV. 2, 4).——**Quaesiverunt;** from
*quaéro.*

**47**    124. **Scripsisset;** from *scribo.*——**Cape;** supply *ea,* them, i. e.
arms (*arma*).

125. **Quum . . . . dixisset;** XXIV. 2, 1).——**Nos;** supply *sumus.*

126. **Prae . . . . multitudine,** *because of the multitude.*

127. **Est propositum;** from *propóno.*

128. **Solon;** the great law-giver of Athens.——**Cur . . . . constituisset;** XXIV. 2, 2).

129. **Sapientem;** this agrees with *rem,* and *stultam,* with *rem* understood.——**Sapiens;** supply *es.*

130. **Quos;** *those which ;* supply *eos.*

**48**    131. **Ipsi;** refers to Cornelia.——**Traxit;** from *traho ; detained.*
——**Donec . . . . redirent;** XXIV. 2, 1).——**Haec,** *these,* i. e. the children. It is attracted from *hi* to *haec,* to agree with the Pred. Noun,
*ornamenta,* 445, 4.

132. **Ferunt,** *they report, say.* For the omission of the subject, see
460, 2.——**Oblivionis;** supply *artem.*——**Quae,** *those things which ;*
supply *ea.*

133. **Bono viro pauperi,** lit. *to a good poor man ;* render, *to a good
man who was poor,* 442.——**Minus probato diviti;** *to one less upright,
who was rich.*——**Filiam;** *a daughter,* not *his* daughter.——**Virum.**
*Vir* means *man* in the noblest sense of the word, *the true man.*——
**Quae;** supply *egeat.*

134. **Achilles, Homerus.** The former is the hero of the *Iliad,* the
latter, its author.——**Olympico certamine,** *the Olympic contest.* The
Olympic Games were celebrated once in four years at Olympia in Elis,
and were the most famous games in Greece. To be crowned victor at
these games was a coveted honor, while the herald had but an humble
office.

135. **Profectus;** from *proficiscor.*——**Quum videret;** XXIV. 2, 1).
——**Egrederetur;** from *egredior.*

**49**    136. **Tyrannorum dominatione.** This refers to the oppressive rule
of the *Thirty Tyrants* appointed over Athens by the Spartans. See
below (228). The city was liberated from them by the heroism of
Thrasybulus.——**Quantas gratias, tantas**=*tantas gratias, quantas.*

137. **Proposuit;** from *propōno.*——**Qui invenisset,** *who should* **49** *discover.* The Pluperfect is explained by the fact that the discovery must *precede* the giving of the reward.

138. **Id,** *that,* i. e. what he intended to do.

139. **Is,** *he,* i. e. the friend.——**Per ... indignationem,** *with* (lit. *through*) *the greatest indignation.*——**Quid mihi tua;** supply *opus est amicitiā* from the preceding question. *Tuā* agrees with *amicitiā* to be thus supplied.

140. **Philippo.** This is Philip, king of Macedonia.

141. **Titus amor ... humani.** Titus was the most beloved of the **50** Roman Emperors.——**Quod nihil praestitisset,** *that he had rendered no service.* The Subjunctive implies that this fact was the reason which the writer would give *on the authority of Titus* for the exclamation, *Amici .... perdidi.* See 520, II.——**Praestitisset;** from *praesto.*—— **Edidit;** from *edo.*

142. **Cecidisse;** from *cado.*——**Cognovit;** from *cognosco.*——**Coro-nam.** Crowns, or wreaths, were often worn by the ancient Romans on sacred and festive occasions.——**Deposuit;** from *depōno.*——**Volupta-tem;** depends upon *sentīre.*

143. **In lud. Ol. Victores.** See note on "*Olympĭco certamĭne*" (134).——**Affectus est;** from *afficio.*——**Stadio,** *race-course.* Races formed a prominent feature in the Olympic contests.

144. **Progressus;** from *progredior.*——**Fabulas,** *fables;* here *tra-gedies.*——**Ut ... doceret.** This implies that he aimed to *instruct,* rather than to *please* the people.

145. **Praesidibus,** *the presidents,* or *governors,* i. e. of the provinces. **51** *Praesidĭbus* depends upon *rescripsit.*——**Onerandas;** supply *esse.*

146. **Vicem eorum,** *their fate.*——**Hectorem,** *Hector,* the most fa-mous Trojan warrior.——**Effluxerant;** this agrees with *anni.*——**Plus quam mille,** *more than a thousand years.* *Plus,* when thus introduced, has no effect upon the construction; otherwise we might expect the verb *effluxĕrant* to be put in the singular. See 417, 3.

147. **Quaesivisset;** from *quaero.*——**Idem,** *the same thing,* i. e. the same question.——**Petivit,** *he,* i. e. Simonides, *asked. Duplicāret* be-low has the same subject.——**Quanto diutius—tanto obscurior,** *the longer—the more obscure.* Quanto—tanto, lit. *by as much as—by so much,* is often best rendered before comparatives, *the—the,* XXVI. 5.

# ROMAN HISTORY.

**52**    148. **In Italiam.** What construction would be used with the name
of a town? 379.——**Janiculo:** a hill on the west side of the Tiber,
not one of the *seven* hills of Rome, though included within the wall
built by Aurelian in the third century.

149. **Troja ... eversa est.** This refers to the famous Trojan war,
said to have taken place in the twelfth century B. C.——**Eversa est;**
from *everto*.——**Hinc,** *hence,* i. e. from Troy.——**Pepercerat;** from
*parco*.——**Ei benigne recepto ... dedit,** lit. *gave to him kindly received :* render, *received him kindly and gave,* 579.——**Lavinium;** a
town in Latium a few miles south of Rome.

**53**    150. **Monte Albano.** Mount Albanus is about 16 miles southeast of
Rome.——**Eum,** *him,* i. e. Ascanius.——**Genitus erat;** from *gigno*.——
**Ejus.** For whom does this pronoun stand?

151. **Minor natu;** lit. *smaller in respect to birth,* or *age:* render,
*younger*.——**Bona,** lit. *good things=goods, property.*

152. **Vestalem virginem.** The *Vestal Virgins* were the priestesses
of the goddess Vesta : they ministered in her temple, and, by turns,
watched the perpetual fire upon her altars night and day.    They were
bound by an oath of chastity, whose violation was punished by death.
——**Viro;** indirect object after *nubĕre,* to marry=*to veil one's self
for,* in allusion to the custom of the bride's wearing the veil at the
marriage ceremony.——**Peperit;** from *pario*.——**Hoc,** *this,* i. e. the
fact spoken of in the preceding sentence.——**Quum .... comperisset.**
XXIV. 2, 1).——**Comperisset;** from *comperio.*

153. **Effuderat;** from *effundo*.——**Quum .... essent positi;**
XXIV. 2, 1).——**Essent positi;** from *pono*.——**Sicco;** supply *loco*.

**54**    154. **Sic,** *thus,* i. e. as explained above.——**Transegerunt;** from
*transigo*.——**Quum adolevissent ... comperissent;** XXIV. 2, 1).——
**Adolevissent;** from *adolesco*.——**Quis;** subject of *fuisset* understood.
——**Quae .... fuisset;** XXIV. 2, 2).——**Aventino;** one of the seven
hills of Rome.    According to the best authority, Romulus founded his
city not on the *Aventine* as here stated, but on the *Palatine,* which
stands a little to the north of it.——**Quum .... circumdaretur,**
XXIV. 2, 1).

155. **Asylum.** This was a place of refuge where exiles and even
criminals might obtain shelter and protection.——**Quum .... venissent;** XXIV. 2, 1).——**Inter ipsos ludos,** *in the midst of the very games.*

156. **Quum . . . appropinquarent ;** XXIV. 2, 1).——**In Tarpeism 54** . . . **inciderunt.** *They fell in with,* or *met Tarpeia,* etc.——**Annulos . . . . armillas.** Rings and bracelets were often awarded to soldiers who had distinguished themselves in battle.

157. **Tarpeium.** This was one of the seven hills of Rome: it was **55** also called *Capitolinus.* The Capitol was built upon it.——**Forum Romanum.** This was an open space in the form of an irregular quad-rangle between the Palatine and Capitoline Hills. In this were held the great public meetings of the Roman people.——**In media caede,** *in the midst of the slaughter,* 441, 6.——**Raptae ;** supply *mulieres.*—— **Hinc . . . . hinc,** *on the one side . . . . on the other.*——**Foedus icit,** *made a compact. Ico,* lit. *to strike,* has reference to striking and slaying the victim in ratification of treaties, compacts, etc.——**In urbem recepit,** lit. *received into the city:* the meaning is, *he received them into full citizenship.*

158. **Descripsit ;** from *describo.*——**Quum . . . . tam,** *not only . . . . but also.*——**Quum . . . . lustraret ;** XXIV. 2, 1). *Lustraret,* reviewed, lit. *purified,* as there were certain ceremonies appointed for the review of a Roman army.——**Ortam ;** from *orior.*——**Interfectum ;** from *interficio.* Supply *esse.*

159. **Interregnum.** This was the interval between the death of one king and the accession of his successor to the throne. In this instance the government was administered by the senate.——**Elapso ;** from *elabor.*——**Natus ;** from *nascor.*——**Gessit ;** from *gero.*——**Egeriae monita . . . dicebat.** This was the device of Numa to give sanctity to his institutions, as Egeria was a goddess.——**Morbo decessit,** lit. *died from disease,* i. e. died a natural death.

160. **Successit ;** from *succedo.*——**Praestiterat ;** from *praesto.*—— **56** **Horatiorum et Curiatiorum.** After the necessary preparations for hostilities had been made both by the Albans and the Romans, and the two armies were already drawn up face to face, it was agreed to decide the question of supremacy by a combat between the three brothers, the Horatii, on the part of the Romans, and the three Curiatii, also brothers, on the part of the Albans. The Curiatii were all slain ; one of the Horatii survived ; his victory therefore decided the question in favor of Rome. See *Schmitz's Hist. Rome.*——**Perfidiam Metii Suffetii.** Metius Suffetius, dictator of the Albans, having been summoned by the Romans to aid them against the Veientines, drew off his forces at the very moment of battle, and awaited the issue of the engagement. For this perfidy he was put to death, and Alba was razed to the ground. See *Schmitz's Hist. Rome.*——**Annis.** What is the common construction for duration of time ? 378.

161. **Nova et moenia circumdedit.** The same thought may be ex-

**56** pressed thus: *Novis eam moenibus circumdĕdit ;* in which *eam* is the *direct object,* and *mocnibus,* the ablative of *means.* 384, II. 1.——
**Morbo oblit.** Compare *morbo decessit* (159).

162. **Qui .... Tarquiniis accepit.** He was called *Tarquinius* from the city *Tarquinii* in Etruria, where he lived many years.

**57** 163. **Minorum gentium,** supply *patres,* or *senatŏres.*——**Nec paucas,** lit. *nor a few ;* render, *and not a few.*——**Ademptes,** from *adĭmo.*——
**Triumphans,** *triumphing=in triumph.* The honor of entering Rome with an imposing triumphal procession was, in later times, often award-ed to victorious generals.——**Capitolium.** The term Capitol was some-times applied to the temple of Jupiter, and sometimes to the whole Capitoline Hill, including both the temple and the citadel.——**Per Anci filos.** What is the usual construction for the agent after passive verbs ? 414, 5.

164. **Genitus ;** from *gigno.*——**Adolevisset ;** from *adolesco.*

165. **Tanaquil ... dicens, regem ... obediret.** This was the de-vice which Tanaquil, the widow of the murdered Tarquin, employed to place her son-in-law, Servius Tullius, upon the throne. Her success was complete.——**Dicens.** What is the direct object of this transitive par-ticiple ? 550.——**Convaluisset ;** from *convalesco.*——**Montes tres.** The *Viminal, Esquiline,* and *Coelian* Hills are undoubtedly meant, though the *Coelian* was probably added under the reign of Ancus Marcius. The other *four* of the *seven* hills, the *Palatine, Capitoline, Quirinal,* and *Aventine,* were already occupied.——**Censum.** The *census* was taken every five years for the purpose of ascertaining the number of citizens, the amount of property, etc.——**In agris,** *in the fields,* i. e. in the coun-try, or territory about Rome.

166. **Interfectus est ;** from *interficio.*——**Quum ... rediret ;** XXIV. 2, 1).

167. **Cognomen .. meruit ;** he was called *Superbus,* because his character deserved the title.——**Moribus ;** observe the difference of meaning between the singular and the plural, 132.

**58** 168. **In exitium,** lit. *into the destruction ;* render, *for the destruc-tion.* What cases does *in* admit, and with what significations ? 435, 1. Ei, *against him,* indirect object.

169. **Consules.** The consuls were joint presidents of the Roman Commonwealth, with all the power and most of the insignia of office which the kings had assumed.——**Annuum,** *for one year.*——**Placuerat,** lit. *it had pleased, seemed good ;* render, *it had been determined.*——
**Tarquiniorum familia.** Collatinus belonged to this family. He was accordingly deprived of his office and went into exile.——**In ejus locum,** lit. *into his place :* here, by a difference of idiom, it must be rendered, *in his place.*

170. **Sese invicem,** lit. *themselves in turn ;* render, *each other.*—— **59**
**Luxerant;** from *lugeo.*——**Quinque consules.** One consul had been
deprived of his office during the year, one had been slain in battle, and
another had died.

171. **Horatius .... esset.** This achievement of Horatius Cocles,
and that of Mucius Scaevola, mentioned below (172), became famous in
the annals of Rome. They have been celebrated in prose and verse.
See Macaulay's Lays of Ancient Rome.——**Donec . . . raptus esset,**
XXIV. 2, 1).——**Ad suos,** *to his friends, companions.*

172. **Castra;** observe difference of meaning between the singular and the plural. 132.——**Scribam pro rege.** He mistook the secre-
tary for the king.——**Terreret,** *endeavored to terrify.* 469, 1.——
**Donec .... consumpta esset.** XXIV. 2, 1).——**Consenuit;** from **60**
*consenesco.*

173. **Exactos;** from *exigo.*——**Questus;** from *queror.*——**Quod**
**.... exhauriretur;** XXIV. 2, 1).——**Secessit;** from *secedo.*——**Pa-**
**tres,** *senators,* see above (158).——**Qui .... conciliaret;** XXIV. 3, 2).
——**Tribuni plebis.** The tribunes were at first two in number, then
five, and finally ten. Their persons were sacred and they were clothed
with great power. They might at any time, by their power of *veto,* arrest the action of the magistrates, or even of the senate.

174. **Milliarium urbis,** lit. *milestone of the city ;* render, *milestone*
*from the city.* The Roman roads were furnished with milestones mark-
ing the distance from the city.

175. **Duce Fabio consule,** lit. *Fabius the consul* (being) *leader ;* **61**
render, *under the command of Fabius the consul.*——**Quum .... vi-**
**cissent,** XXIV. 2, 1).——**Pellexissent;** from *pellicio.*——**Exorto;** from
*exorior.*——**Perierant;** from *pereo.*——**Potuerat;** from *possum.*——
**Prudenti cunctatione,** *by prudent delay.* Fabius, in the second Punic
war, deliberately adopted the policy of weakening Hannibal by *delay,* i. e.
by not allowing him an engagement. His policy was entirely successful.

176. **In eo erant, ut .... emerent,** *they were in this,* i. e. in such
a condition, *that they would purchase ;* the meaning is, *they were on the*
*point of purchasing.*

177. **Magnitudine.** What other case might have been used ? 396, IV.
——**Provocavit,** *challenged.*——**Hinc,** *hence,* i. e. from the fact of taking **62**
the *torquis* and adorning himself with it. *Torquati* is derived from
*torquis.*

178. **Cum honore dictatoris,** *with the rank of dictator.* The dictator
was appointed only in times of great danger, and was invested with almost unlimited power for a period of six months.——**Magistro equitum.**
This is the title of an officer always appointed in connection with the
dictator, or by him.——**Occasionem nactus,** *taking advantage of a fa-*

**PAGE**

**62** *vorable opportunity.*——**Nactus ;** from *nanciscor.*——**Capitis,** lit. *of the head ;* render, *to death.*

179. **Post,** *afterwards.*——**Quid . . . . putaret ;** XXIV. 2, 2).——

**63 Respondit.** What is the direct object? 550.——**Dimittendos ;** supply *esse.*——**Sub jugum.** The yoke was thus used as the symbol of submission and servitude ; it consisted of a spear supported horizontally by two others placed in an upright position.

180. **Quia . . . . fecissent.** If this reason had been given on the authority of the narrator, the indicative would have been used. The subjunctive implies that this was the reason then alleged for waging the war. See 520, II.——**Primum . . . transmarino hoste.** Their previous wars had been waged with various nations in Italy and Gaul.—— **Quum . . . . cepisset ;** XXIV. 2, 1).——**Quaecunque . . . . agerentur ;** XXIV. 2, 3).

181. **Auxilio elephantorum.** The Romans had never before met elephants in battle, and indeed were unacquainted with the animal. The battle was fought in Lucania ; accordingly the Romans called the elephants Lucanian oxen, *boves Lucae.*——**Per noctem,** *during the night.* ——**Adversis vulneribus,** *with wounds in front:* it was a disgrace to receive a wound in the back.——**Etiam mortuos,** *even in death.*——**Ego . . . . subigerem ;** in apposition with *voce.*

182. **Perrexit ;** from *pergo.*——**Octavo decimo.** What other form **64** of this numeral is common? 174.——**De captivis redimendis ;** lit. *concerning captives to be ransomed:* the meaning is, *to treat concerning the ransoming of captives.*——**Fabricium.** Fabricius was celebrated for his integrity. See note on "*Fabricius*" above (49, 6).——**Ut . . . . promitteret ;** XXIV. 2, 5).——**Contemptus est ;** from *contemno.*

183. **Quum . . . . teneretur ;** XXIV. 2, 1).——**Qui . . . preteret,** lit. *who should seek :* render, *that he might ask,* or *to ask ;* XXIV. 3, 2).——**Ut Pyrrhus . . . . obtineret.** This clause expresses the condition on which Cineas was to ask peace, and may accordingly be regarded as in apposition with *conditiöne.* 495, 3.——**Ex Italia.** What construction would be used, if the name of a *town* should be substituted here ? 421, II.——**Redisset ;** from *redeo,* 295, 3.——**Pyrrho ;** indirect object of *respondit ;* the *direct* object is the clause, *se regum patriam vidisse.* 550.——**Qualis . . . . visa esset.** XXIV. 2, 2).

184. **Altero,** *second.*——**Interfecti ;** supply *sunt.*——**Vinctum ;** from *vincio,* bound, or *in chains.*——"**Ille . . . ab honestate . . . potest.**" This entire sentence, as a direct quotation, is the object of *dixisse,* 357, I. ——**Ille est Fabricius qui.** *Fabricius is that one who,* i. e. the man, who.——**Honestate ;** supply *averti potest.*——**A Tarento.** What is the common construction ? 423, I. ; 423, 1:——**Recessit ;** from *recēdo.*

**65**          185. **Post urbem conditam,** lit. *after the city built ;* render, *after the*

PAGE

*building of the city*, 580.   Rome, the city here spoken of, is said to **65** have been founded 753 B. C.——**Primum . . . dimicaverunt.** This was the first naval engagement of the Romans. Their previous wars had been waged only on land.——**Duillio . . . consulibus.** The date of an event was generally denoted by the names of the two *consuls* for that year ; *in the consulship of Duillius and Asina*, lit. *Duillius, Asina, consuls*, or *being consuls.* These names are thus put in the *Ablative Absolute*, generally without the connective *et.*——**Mersit ;** from *mergo.*

186. **Paucis . . . interjectis,** lit. *a few years having been thrown between ;* render, *after a few years had intervened*, or *after an interval of a few years*, 431, 2.——**Est translatum ;** from *transfero.*——**Sexaginta quattuor.** May *quattuor* stand before *sexaginta ?* If so, would *et* be expressed, or omitted ? 174, foot-note.——**Viginti duas ;** supply *naves.*——**Amiserunt ;** from *amitto.*——**Quum . . . venisset ;** XXIV. 2, 1).——**In fidem acceperant,** *received under their protection*, though as subject states.——**Captus ;** supply *est* from next clause. See also **66** XXVI. 4.——**Conjectus est ;** from *conjicio.*

187. **Favit.** How is the Perfect of this verb formed ? 270. How is the Perfect regularly formed in the second conjugation ? 213, II.—— **Quum victi essent ;** XXIV. 2, 1).——**Ut . . . proficisceretur . . . et impetraret.** Verbs of *asking* take two Accusatives, or Objects : these clauses may accordingly be treated as one of the objects of *rogaverunt,* while at the same time they express the *purpose* of the request. 492, 2 ; 374, 4.——**Dixit.** Give the direct object of this verb, 550.——**Desiisse ;** from *desino.*——**Illa die.** What is the usual gender of *dies ?* 121.—— **Illos,** *that they*, i. e. the Carthaginians.——**Illos . . . . habere.** This infinitive-clause does not strictly depend upon *suasit,* but upon a verb, or participle, signifying *to say*, involved in it. 530, 1.——**Fractos ;** from *frango.*——**Tanti non esse,** *that it was not of so much importance*= *worth the while.*

188. **Punici,** *Punic,* i. e. Carthaginian. The word is derived from *Poeni.*——**Captae, demersae, capta ;** supply *sunt* from *occisa sunt.*—— **Demersae ;** from *demergo.*——**Citra Iberum,** *on this side of the Ebro,* i. e. on the side toward Rome, the northern side.——**Decesserunt ;** from *decido.*

189. **Novem annos natum,** lit. *having been born nine years :* render, **67** *when he was nine years old ;* XX. 3.——**Hic . . . aetatis,** *he living*, or *passing the twentieth year of his age ;* render, *he when in his twentieth year ;* XX. 3.——**Qui quum,** *when he,* i. e. Hannibal, 453.——**Miserunt.** The object is *legatos* understood, though it is scarcely necessary to supply it in translating.——**Socios,** *the allies,* meaning the citizens of Saguntum.——**Reddita ;** supply *sunt.*

190. **Fratre . . . relicto.** Hannibal left his brother in Spain to

**67** take care of that province in his absence.——**Transiit;** from *transeo.* 295, 3.——**Traditur,** *he,* i. e. Hannibal, *is said.*——**Se conjunxerat.** Why is *se* here used, rather than *eos* or *illos?* 449, I.——**Dediderant** ,
**68** from *dedo.*——**Progressus;** from *progredior.*——**Interemptus;** from *interimo;* supply *est.*

191. **Quingentesimo duodequadragesimo.** For combination of numerals, see 174.——**Intellectum erat;** from *intelligo.* The infinitive-clause, *Hannibălem . . . posse,* is the subject.——**Mora.** The Roman general, Fabius, had adopted with great success the policy of weakening Hannibal by *delay,* i. c. by not allowing him an engagement. See above (175).——**Victi, capti, occisi;** supply *sunt* with each participle.——**Perierunt;** from *pereo.*——**Quod.** This relative does not relate to any particular word as its antecedent, but to the leading proposition, or the fact mentioned in it; the relative is accordingly neuter, as clauses used substantively uniformly take that gender, 42, III. 2.——**Factum;** supply *erat.*

192. **Obtulit;** from *offĕro.* Here *obtŭlit* takes *Romănis* as its *in-direct* object, while the *direct* object appears in the form of a clause, viz. *ut captīvos redimĕrent.* This is plainly the *offer* made to the Romans; but this clause also states the *purpose* of the offer, viz. *that they might ransom the prisoners.* Hence the subjunctive *redimĕrent.* 492.
——**Qui . . . potuissent,** *who had been able ;* XXIV. 2, 5).——**Armati.** The senate regarded it as a disgrace, that any should be captured so long as they had arms to defend themselves.——**Aureorum annulorum.** See note on the same (67, 6).——**Hos omnes.** Observe position at the beginning of the sentence to mark emphasis. 594, I.——**Detraxerat;** from *detrăho.* How is the Perfect formed? 258, I. 1.——**Hasdrubal . . . . exercitu.** See above (190, line 1).——**Remanserat;** from *re-maneo.*——**Duobus Scipionibus.** These were Cnaeus Cornelius Scipio and Publius Cornelius Scipio, the latter the father of Publius Cornelius Scipio Africanus, who defeated Hannibal at Zama. See below (196).

193. **Res prospere gesta est,** *a successful battle was fought.* In a military sense, *rem gero* frequently has this meaning.——**Magnam hujus**
**69** **insulae partem.** For arrangement of words, see 598, 3.——**Inde,** *thence,* i. e. from Syracuse.——**In Macedonia.** What construction would have been used, if this had been the name of a *town* instead of that of a country? 421, II.——**In deditionem accepit,** lit. *received into surrender ;* the meaning is, *accepted the terms of a surrender.*——**Re-gressus est;** from *regredior.*

194. **Duo Scipiones.** See *duobus Scipionibus* (192) and note on the same. They were both slain in battle within a month of each other, in the year 212 B. C.——**Hic, puer duodeviginti annorum,** *he when a boy eighteen years of age,* 363, 3.——**Post cladem Cannensem,** *after the*

*defeat at Cannae* (191).——**Viginti quattuor . . . . natus,** lit. *having* **69** *been born twenty-four years ;* render, *when twenty-four years of age.*
——**Carthaginem Novam,** *New Carthage,* a city in Spain, founded soon after the first Punic war by Hasdrubal, brother-in-law of Hannibal. It was named after Carthage in Africa ; its present name is *Carthagena.*
——**Parentibus,** *to their parents.*——**Transierunt ;** from *transeo.*

195. **Creatus ;** supply *est.*——**Millibus . . . militibus.** When is *millia* followed by the Genitive and when by its own case ? 178.——**Qua re audita,** lit. *which thing having been heard ;* render, *having heard this,* or *on hearing this,* 431, 2, 3).

196. **Plus semel**=*plus quam semel, more than once.*——**Ad Zamam,** **70** *near Zama.*——**Peritissimi duces,** Hannibal and Scipio are meant.——
**Scipio victor recedit,** lit. *withdrew victor ;* render, *left the field as victor,* or simply *was victorious.*——**Ingenti gloria triumphavit.** Compare *cum ingenti gloria . . . regressus est* (193).——**Africanus.** This title was conferred upon Scipio in commemoration of his victories in *Africa.* See also *nomen Africani junioris* (200).

197. **Finite Punico bello.** Which Punic war is meant ? (185 and 189).——**Macedonicum ;** supply *bellum.*——**Contra Philippum.** This limits *bellum* understood, *the war against Philip,* 352, II.——**Regem.** Philip was king of Macedonia.

198. **Rebellavit,** *rebelled,* i. e. renewed the war against Rome.——
**Rex.** What king ?——**Dederet, dediderunt ;** from *dedo.*——**Remorum ordines,** *banks of oars.* These were arranged, one above another, so that the oars belonging to the highest *ordo,* or *bank,* were much longer than those belonging to the lowest. War-vessels generally had three banks, and were accordingly called *triremes* (*tres, remi*), but it was no uncommon thing to see vessels with four or five banks, and some are said to have had thirty or forty.——**Ante currum,** *before the chariot,* **71** i. e. of the conqueror. In the triumphal procession, the captives and spoils preceded the chariot of the victor, while the victorious army followed it.

199. **Susceptum est ;** from *suscipio.*——**Ibi,** *there,* i. e. in Africa.——
**Per Scipionem.** What is the common construction for the *Agent* of passive verbs ? 414, 5.——**Tribunus,** *tribune,* an officer in the army commanding a part of a legion. The number of tribunes to each legion was at first three or four, afterward six.——**Nepotem,** *grandson,* but only by adoption. He was the son of Aemilius Paulus, the celebrated general, who conquered Macedonia. See above (198).

200. **Quum . . . esset . . . nomen,** *when now the name of Scipio was* (or, *had become*) *great ;* XXIV. 2, 1).——**Missus ;** supply *est.*——**Acerrime defensam,** lit. *most valiantly defended ;* render, *though* (it was) *most valiantly defended.*——**Facta ;** supply *est.*——**Plurima,** *very many*

**71** *things*, referring especially to the works of art, statues and votive offerings, which the Carthaginians had taken from the temples of the conquered cities in Sicily.

**72**   201. **Exortum est;** from *exorior.*——**Civitate.** Logically this is in apposition with *Numantia* implied in *Numantinis.*——**Victus;** supply *est.*——**Pacem infamem.** The terms were that Numantia should remain free and independent.——**Tradi;** depends upon *jussit* in the line above.——**Militem;** lit. *soldier*, the individual representing the class; render, *soldiery.*——**Correxit;** from *corrigo.*——**Partim—partim;** lit. *partly—partly;* render, *either—or.* These words may, however, be often best rendered by *some—others*, followed by *of.* Thus, *he captured some of the many cities of Spain and accepted others*, etc.—— **In deditionem accepit.** See note on the same (193).

  202. **Anno urbis conditae . . . sexto,** *in the six hundred and sixty-sixth year from,* or *after* (lit. *of*) *the founding of the city.* *Urbis conditae* is here equivalent to *post urbem conditam* (185), or *ab urbe condita* (207).——**Romae.** What case would have been used, if this had been a noun of the third declension ? 421, II.——**Mithridaticum;** supply *bellum.*——**Marius, Sullae.** These generals were the leaders of rival political parties. Marius was supported by the common people and Sulla by the nobles.——**Adversus Mithridatem.** This limits *bellum*, 398, 4.——**Quum . . . decretum esset;** the meaning is : *when the management of the war had been entrusted to him by a decree of the Senate.* The Subjunctive is here rendered according to XXIV. 2, 1).——**Decretum esset;** from *decerno.*——**Ei,** i. e. *Sullae.*——**Quum—tum.** Usual meaning, *not only—but also ; both—and,* etc. ; render here *either —or.*——**Compositis;** from *compono.*——**Profectus est;** from *proficis-*

**73** *cor.*——**Asia, quam invaserat.** Not all Asia, but that portion of it which he had invaded, referring especially to those portions of Asia Minor west of his own dominions.

  203. **In Graecia et Asia.** Mithridates, emboldened by his success in Asia Minor, had sent an army into Greece. Athens and Thebes were at this time in his possession.——**Fugatus fuerat.** Marius had been for some time in concealment.——**Unus ex,** *one of ;* lit. *one from.* ——**Ingressi;** from *ingredior.*——**Multos proscripserunt,** *proscribed many.* In the civil wars, Sulla caused lists of the names of those persons whom he wished to have killed to be exposed to public inspection. Those whose names were on these lists were outlawed or proscribed, and any one might slay them and claim a reward; their property was confiscated, and their descendants were excluded from all offices of honor and trust. See *Smith's Dict. of G. and R. Antiquities ;* also *Schmitz's Hist. of Rome.*——**Compulerunt;** from *compello.*——**Sanguine.** Gender ?   **Civium.** Genitive plural, how formed ? 65, 3, 1).

——**De,** lit. *concerning ;* render in this instance, *over.*——**Itallcum, 73 civile ;** supply *bellum.*——**Sociale dictum est ;** this is the predicate of the relative clause.——**Viros consulares,** *men who had been consuls,* i. e. men of consular rank or dignity=*ex-consuls.* The consuls, it will be remembered, were two in number, were elected for one year, and had all the powers of king. See note on *" Consŭles "* (169).——**Praetorios,** *those who had been praetors.* When the office of praetor was first instituted, only one was appointed, who was to act as a kind of third consul with the leading part in the administration of justice ; about a century later a second was added, called *praetor peregrinus,* to administer justice among foreigners and strangers resident at Rome. The number of praetors was increased from time to time, until at the beginning of the civil wars of Sulla and Marius, it was six ; and in the dictatorship of Sulla it was raised to eight. See *Smith's Dict. of G. and R. Antiquities,* and *Schmitz's Hist. Rome.*——**Aedilitios,** *those who had been aediles.* The *aediles* (from *aedes*) were Roman magistrates who had charge of the public buildings, highways, etc., and acted as city police. They were at first two in number, afterwards more. See *Smith's Dict.*—— **Senatores.** The Roman senate (from *senex*) was regarded as a body of *elders* or *fathers* (patres). The number was at first 100 (see 158), then 200 (see 163), and finally 300, which continued to be the number until the time of the civil wars between Sulla and Marius. The number was then increased to 500 or 600 by the election of a large body of Roman knights. See *Smith's Dict.*

204. **Commotum est ;** from *commoveo.*——**Gladiatores.** Gladiators were men who fought for the amusement of the Roman people. They consisted mostly of prisoners, slaves, and malefactors ; they were trained in the skilful use of weapons at schools established for the purpose (*ludo gladiatorio*).——**Capuae,** *at Capua.*——**Hannibal ;** subject **74** of *movit* understood.——**Contraxerunt ;** from *contrǎho :* explain formation of the Perfect ; 258, I. 1.——**Vicerunt ;** from *vinco.*——**Proconsule.** The *proconsul,* as the name implies, was one who acted with the power of a consul. Those who had been consuls (*viri consulāres*) were often allowed to assume the government of provinces, and to exercise in these provinces all the powers of a consul ; they were then called *proconsuls.*——**Italiae.** Is this genitive *objective,* or *subjective ?* 396, II.

205. **Per illa tempora.** How could *tempŏra* be governed without the preposition ? 378. *Per* makes the idea of duration more prominent, *throughout those times.*——**Maria.** What is the ending of the stem ? 63.——**Id bellum,** *this war,* i. e. that against the pirates.——**Decretum est ;** from *decerno.* For the meaning see note on "*Quum . . . . decrātum esset*" (202).——**Menses ;** give gender, 107, 2.——**Contra**

**PAGE**

**74 regem.** This limits *bellum.*——**Quo suscepto,** lit. *which having been undertaken;* render, *having undertaken this;* 431, 2, (3).——**Tantum,** *only.*——**Coactus;** from *cogo.*——**Hausit;** from *haurio.*——**Hunc vitae finem.** For the order of these words, see 598, 3, and for their position at the beginning of the sentence, see 594, I.

206. **Ille se ei.** What nouns are represented by these pronouns ?

**75** ——**Dedidit;** from *dedo.*——**Grandi pecunia,** *a large sum of money,* according to Plutarch, 6,000 talents, more than $6,000,000.——**Seleuciam libertate donavit.** What two constructions occur ? 384, 1.—— **Quia ... tulerat; quod ... recepisset.** These are both causal clauses. The first, with the *Indicative,* states the reason as a *fact,* while the second, with the *Subjunctive,* implies that the reason was assigned *by Pompey.* 520.——**Occisis;** from *occido.*——**His gestis,** lit. *by means of these things done,* i. e. *by these achievements,* Abl. of Means, 414, 4. ——**Antiquissimo bello.** This war continued nearly thirty years.—— **Ante triumphantis currum,** lit. *before the chariot of* (him) *triumphing;* render, *before his chariot, as he triumphed,* referring to the triumphal procession.——**Filii Mithridatis.** They were five in number.——**Infinitum pondus.** According to Plutarch, this amounted to 20,000 talents, more than $20,000,000.——**Orbem terrarum,** strictly *the world,* but sometimes used by the Romans with special reference to the *Roman Empire.*

207. **Cicerone et Antonio consulibus,** lit. *Cicero and Antony* (being) *consuls:* render, *when Cicero and Antony were consuls,* or, *in the consulship of Cicero,* etc.——**Deprehensi;** from *deprehendo.* Supply *sunt* from the next clause.

208. **Quum .... decreta esset,** *when Gaul had been assigned to him by decree,* i. e. as a military province; XXIV, 2, 1).——**Vincendo processit,** *proceeded by conquering,* i. e. advanced victoriously.——**Oceanum 76 Britannicum,** *British Ocean,* i. e. the English Channel.——**Omnem Galliam quae,** etc. Not all Gaul, but that portion which is bounded as described.——**Ne nomen quidem,** *not even the name;* 602, III. 2.—— **Cognitum;** from *cognosco.*

209. **Absens.** It was unlawful for a general, while in command of an army, to offer himself as a candidate for the consulship, and indeed for any one to do so while absent from Rome. Caesar was both absent from Rome and in command of an army.——**Quem quum ... deferrent, contradictum est,** etc., *when many would confer this,* etc., *opposition* (or, objection) *was made.*——**Dimissis;** from *dimitto.*——**Transiit;** from *transeo.*——**Dictatorem.** See note on "*Dictatoris*" (178).

210. **Inde,** *thence,* i. e. from Rome.——**Hispanias,** *Spain.* The plural is often used, as the country was divided into two parts, viz. *citerior,* on this side of the Ebro, i. e. on the side toward Rome, and

*ulterior*, beyond the Ebro.——**Nec .... superari.** This entire clause **76** is the object of *dixit.* 550.——**Nec**, *and not*, 587, I. 2.——**Vincere.** This is the object of *scire ;* Caesar said that Pompey did not know (what ?) *to conquer*, or *how to conquer.*——**Ingentibus .... commissis,** *with great forces engaged on both sides.*——**Pugnatum est**, *the battle was* **77** *fought.*——**Direpta sunt ;** from *diripio.*——**A rege Aegypti.** This king was the last of the Ptolemies and the brother of Cleopatra.——**Occidit ;** *slew*, though not with his own hands. He employed men to do it.—— **Generi.** Pompey had married Julia, the daughter of Caesar ; while she lived, she was, of course, a strong bond of union between the two, but she had died six years before the battle of Pharsalia.

211. **Qua de causa**, *for which cause.* For the order of words, see 602, II. 1.——**Pompeianarum .... reliquias**, *the remnant of Pompey's party.* —— **Insolentius agere.** He allowed himself to be proclaimed consul for ten years, imperator and dictator for life. This was a virtual overthrow of the Roman Republic.——**Conjuratum est ;** *a conspiracy was formed.*——**Sexaginta vel amplius**, *sixty or more.*——**Inter conjuratos ;** lit. *among the having conspired*, i. e. among the conspirators. ——**Bruti duo ;** viz. *Marcus* and *Decimus.*——**Illius Bruti.** See above (169).——**Regibus expulsis**, lit. *the kings having been banished ;* render, *after the banishment of the kings.*——**Quum ... venisset ;** XXIV. 2, 1).——**Confossus est ;** from *confodio.*

212. **Interfecto ;** from *interficio.*——**A Caesaris partibus stabat**, **78** *favored the party of Caesar* (stood by the party, etc.).——**Magister equitum.** See note on " *Magistro equitum* " (178).——**Susceptus est ;** from *suscipio.*——**Octavianus.** He was the son of Octavius, but was adopted by Julius Caesar, with the name *Octaviänus Caesar.*——**Patris sui**, i. e. his father by adoption, *Julius Caesar.*——**Extorsit ;** from *extorqueo.*——**Ut ... daretur.** This clause expresses both the *direct object* of *extorsit* and the *purpose* of the action : *Caesar extorted* (what ?) *that the consulship should be given*, and (for what purpose ?) *in order that it might be given.* See 492, 1.——**Viginti annorum.** The age required by law was forty-three.——**Junctus ;** from *jungo.*——**Proscripsit.** See note on " *Proscripsërunt* " (203).——**Per hos.** By whom ?

213. **Profecti.** This is in the plural to agree with *Octaviänus et Antonius.*——**Secundo ;** supply *proelio.*——**Infinitam nobilitatem**, **quae**, lit. *the infinite nobility, which ;* render, *the countless nobles, who.*—— **Victam interfecerant**, lit. *they slew* (them) *being conquered ;* render, *they conquered and slew.* See 579.——**Hispanias.** See note on this word (210).——**Gallias.** The plural is used because the Romans divided **79** the country into two parts, viz. *Gallia ulterior* or *Transalpina*, or *Gaul beyond the Alps ;* and *Gallia citerior* or *Cisalpina*, or *Gaul on this side of the Alps ;* i. e. on the side toward Rome.

G .

**79**   214. **Repudiata sorore.** Antony had married Octavia, the sister of
Octaviānus.——**Uxorem duxit,** *married,* lit. *lead as wife.* The language
is explained by the fact that the bride was usually conducted to her
new home by her husband and friends. See note on " *Nubĕre* " (152).
——**Qui locus.** The relative here has only the force of an adjective.
——**Desperatis rebus,** lit. *things having been despaired of ;* render, *as
his cause was desperate* (or *hopeless*).——**Interemit ;** from *interĭmo.*——
**Ex eo inde tempore,** *from this time,* or *from this time forth. Inde*
need not be translated.——**Ante ;** Adverb, *before,* or *previously.*

# GRECIAN HISTORY.

**80**   215. **Pugnae . . . . facerent,** *did not give him an opportunity of
coming to an engagement.* XXIV. 2, 1).——**Ponte Istri,** *the bridge
over the Ister,* i. e. the Danube; lit. *the bridge of the Ister.*——**Quum
rediisset ;** XXIV. 2, 1); 518, II.——**Eique.** *Ei* refers to the fleet.

   216. **Praefecti regii,** *the royal commanders,* i. e. Datis and Artaphernes.——**Appulsa ;** from *appello.*——**In Campum Marathona,** *into*
**81** *the plain of Marathon.* For ending *a,* see 68, 1.——**Ab oppido,** *from
the city,* i. e. from Athens.——**Circiter . . . . decem.** The distance by
any suitable road was somewhat greater than this.——**Ea, this,** i. e. this
state ; supply *civĭtas.*——**Decem . . . . completa sunt,** *the number of ten
thousand armed men was completed,* or *filled up.* Thus there were 9000
Athenians and 1000 Plataeans.——**Sub montis radicibus,** *at the base of
the mountain.*——**Commiserant ;** from *committo.*——**Suis,** *for his men,*
441, 1.——**Tanto plus,** *so much more.* .

   217. **Quum Darius decessisset,** *when Darius had died;* XXIV.
2, 1).——**Decessisset ;** from *decēdo.*——**In ipso apparatu,** *in the midst
of his very preparations,* i. e. while actually engaged in preparing for a
second invasion.——**Hujus classis,** *the fleet of this one,* i. e. Xerxes ;
render *his fleet.*——**Navium longarum,** *ships of war,* called *longae,* because they were built much longer than the ships of burden (*onerariārum*).——**Navium . . . . fuit,** *was of . . . . ships,* i. e. *consisted of,* etc.
——**De adventu.** This is an attributive modifier of *fama,*—the report
of his approach.——**Peti,** *to be aimed at.*——**Miserunt Delphos,** *they
sent to Delphi ;* object omitted, *sent messengers.* The Delphic oracle
was the most famous in Greece.——**De rebus suis,** lit. *concerning their*
**82** *things,* i. e. *for their safety.*——**Id . . . . valeret,** what this answer
meant.——**Ut . . . . conferrent.** This clause is the predicate after *esse,*

as it states what the design was.——**Eum—ligneum,** *for that that* **82**
*wooden wall was meant,* etc., i. e. that that was the wooden wall meant,
etc.——**Triremes.** See note on "*Remorum ordines*" (198).——**Majoribus natu,** *old or aged men, elders.*

218. **Hujus consilium,** *the plan of this one,* i. e. Themistocles.——
**Delecti,** *picked men.*——**Qui .... occuparent;** XXIV. 3, 2.——**Thermopylas.** Thermopylae is a narrow pass between Locris and Thessaly,
immortalized as the scene of one of the most remarkable instances of
heroic daring and self-sacrifice recorded in history, that of Leonidas and
his three hundred Spartans, here mentioned.——**Barbares,** Barbarians,
i. e. the Persians. The term was applied to all who were not Greeks.
——**Non sustinuerunt.** They were unable to resist the overwhelming
force brought against them, but they performed prodigies of valor unsurpassed in the annals of war.——**Classis .... navium,** *the common
fleet of Greece* (i. e. the fleet of all Greece), *consisting of,* etc.——**Angustias.** The narrow channel, *Euripus,* between Boeotia and Euboea,
is here meant.——**Ancipiti periculo,** *by a double danger,* i. e. by being
confined in the channel with one foe in front and another in the rear.
——**Exadversum Athenas,** *over against Athens. Exadversum,* like *adversum,* admits the Accus., 433.

219. **Thermopylis;** see above (218).——**Astu,** *the city,* i. e. Athens. **83**
The word is often thus applied.——**Idque,** *and this,* i. e. the city of
Athens.——**Cujus,** *of this,* i. e. of the burning of the city.——**Themistocles unus restitit,** *Themistocles alone stood firm, objected.*——**Universos,** *all together, united.*——**Idque .... affirmabat,** lit. *he affirmed to
Eurybiades that this would be,* etc., i. e. he assured him that this would
be the result.——**Summae,** dative depending upon *praeёrat.* 386.——
**De servis suis, quem,** etc., *one of his servants, whom,* etc.——**Suis verbis,** *in his words,* i. e. *in his name, from him.*——**Nuntiaret.** This
verb has *ei* as its *indirect* object, and all the rest of the sentence after
*verbis* as its *direct* object. 550.——**Confecturum;** supply *eum,* referring to the king.——**Oppressurum;** from *opprimo.*——**Hoc eo valebat,**
*the object of this was.*——**Barbarus,** *barbarian,* meaning Xerxes.——
**Contra,** *on the contrary, on the other hand.*——**Explicari,** *to be unfolded,* i. e. to be brought into successful action.

220. **Hic etsi .... gesserat,** *although he* (Xerxes) *had fought an
unsuccessful battle;* 516, III.——**Ut .... posset hostes;** XXIV.
2, 5).——**Ab eodem,** *by the same one,* i. e. Themistocles: *eōdem,* it **84**
must be observed, does not belong to *gradu.*——**Gradu,** *from his position.*——**Certiorem fecit;** XXVI. 1.——**Id agi,** lit. *that it was doing;*
render, *was in contemplation.*——**In Hellesponto,** *over the Hellespont.*
——**Reversus est;** from *reverto, revertor,* Dep. in certain forms. See
273, III. *verto.*——**Unius viri,** *of one man,* i. e. Themistocles.

**PAGE**

**84** 221. **Quam**—*postquam ;* 427, 3.——**Interfectus est,** *destroyed, cut in pieces.*

222. **Pericles.** Pericles, a distinguished orator and statesman of Athens, directed the counsels of state for many years. The period in which he lived is famous in Grecian history as the "*Age of Pericles.*"

**85** ——**Interjectis ;** from *interjicio.*——**Clara ;** observe its position ; 594, I.——**Patrimonii contemptus,** *disregard of patrimony,* referring to the fact that he gave his ancestral estates to the republic, as explained below.——**Hostes ;** subject of *reliquerant.*——**In suspicionem adducerent ;** supply *eum ; that they might bring him into suspicion of treachery.*——**Navali . . . . dimicatum est,** lit. *it was fought,* etc. ; render, *a naval battle was fought.*——**In annos quinquaginta,** lit. *into fifty years ;* render, *for fifty years.*

223. **Decernitur,** *is decreed,* or *authorized.*——**Effusae sunt ;** from *effundo.*——**Ut . . . essent ;** XXIV. 2, 5).——**Iis, quibus ;** i. e. to the Catinienses.——**Secundo Marte pugnant,** lit. *they fight, Mars being propitious ;* render, *they fight a successful battle,* or *successfully.*——**Ab his,** *by these,* i. e. the Lacedaemonians.——**Contractis ;** from *contraho.*

**86** 224. **Triremes.** See note on "*Remorum ordines*" (198).——**In hostium potestatem,** *into the power of the enemy. In* is construed with *potestatem.* Observe separation, 602, II. 3.——**Simul cum,** *at the same time with,* or simply *with.*——**Sitae sunt ;** from *sino.*——**Quam plurimas.** *Quam* before a superlative is intensive, and is often best rendered by *possible ;* as, *quam plurimas, the greatest possible number, as many as possible,* or sometimes *very many.*——**Neque minus multas,** lit. *nor less many=and not less many=and as many more.*

225. **Darius.** This was *Darius the Second,* and not the one spoken **87** of above (215).——**Ut . . . . mitterent ;** XXIV. 2, 5).——**In . . . . locum,** lit. *into the place of ;* render, *to take the place of, to succeed.*

226. **Ut numerus . . . . expleretur,** *that the number . . . . might be filled,* i. e. to raise the required number of soldiers.——**Coacti sunt ;** from *cogo.*——**Proeliis adverso Marte pugnatis,** lit. *battles fought, Mars being adverse ;* render, *having lost battles,* or *having fought unsuccessfully.*——**Res . . . . inclinata est.** The power of the Athenians was utterly overthrown by this defeat. The figure involved in the verb *inclino,* to incline, fall, is that of a building leaning and ready to fall.

227. **Nomen Atheniensium,** *the Athenian name=the Athenian state* or *nation.*——**Negarunt . . . . passuros,** lit. *denied that they would permit ;* render, *said that they would not permit.*——**Passuros.** What is the object ? 554, III.——**Duobus oculis,** *the two eyes,* these were *Athens* and *Sparta.*——**Longi muri brachia.** Reference is here made to the long walls which connected Athens with its ports.——**Triginta**

**rectores.** These are known in history as " *The Thirty Tyrants*."—— **87 Dediti,** *devoted to,* i. e. to the interests of.

228. **Thrasybulus.** See note on " *Thrasybūlo* " (136).——**Quod. 88** This relative, it will be observed, does not agree with its antecedent *Phylen,* but with the Predicate noun *castellum ;* 445, 4.——**Triginta de suis,** lit. *thirty from* (of) *his ;* render, *thirty of his associates,* or *thirty associates.'*

229. **Idem imperator,** *the same,* i. e. Epaminondas, *when commander,* 3G3, 3.——**Boeotii,** *the Boeotians.* They were the inhabitants of Boeotia, north of Attica, of which Thebes was the chief city.——**Ex hastili,** *from the spear.* The iron point, separated from the shaft, had remained in the flesh.——**Extraxisset;** from *extrăho.*——**Vidisse Boeotios,** *that the Boeotians* (his own men) *had conquered.*

230. **Leuctricam pugnam,** *the battle of Leuctra.* This battle des- **89** troyed the power of Sparta and made Thebes the leading state in Greece, but Thebes speedily lost the supremacy after the death of Epaminondas.——**Athenienses, non ut olim.** Formerly Athens had been eminent in war and had been for many years the leading state in Greece, but of late the sterner virtues had disappeared from the Athenian character, and the love of ease, luxury, and festivity had taken their places. Thus Athens, Sparta, and Thebes, each of which had been in turn the leading state in Greece, had now become weak and degenerate. This state of things enabled Macedonia to rise to power, as mentioned in the next sentence.——**Obses . . . . Thebis.** In the year 369 B. C., when the power of Thebes was supreme in Greece, Amyntas, king of Macedonia, had been obliged to send his son Philip as a hostage to that powerful capital.

231. **Auraria;** supply *metalla* from the next clause.——**Argenti . . . . Thracia.** There were also *gold* mines in Thrace near Philippi.

232. **Diu dissimulatum.** He had long intended to make war upon **90** Athens, but had from policy concealed that intention.——**Quorum causae . . . . junxerunt,** *to whose cause the Thebans had joined themselves,* i. e. with whom they had allied themselves.——**Quum,** *though ;* 516, II.——**Assiduis bellis indurata,** *hardened,* or *strengthened by continual wars.* Philip had a well-disciplined army of veterans, long accustomed to severe and constant service.——**Adversis vulneribus.** See note on the same (181).——**Ille dies . . . . finivit.** The battle of Chaeronea reduced Greece to a Macedonian province.

233. **Hujus victoriae . . . . laetitia,** lit. *joy of this victory ;* render, *joy on account of this victory.*——**Coronas, unguenta.** The Greeks often made use of *crowns, garlands, ointments,* and *perfumes* on joyous and festive occasions.——**Quantum . . . . fuit,** lit. *as much as was in him ;* render, *as far as was in his power.*——**Ut . . . . victorem**

**PAGE**

**90** . . . . **sentiret**, *that no one would recognize the victor*, i. e. the fact that he was such.——**Bello consumptorum**, *of those slain in war*, or *battle. Consumptorum* is used substantively; 575.——**Ad formandum** . . . . **statum**, lit. *to form the state of present things;* the meaning is, *to adjust* or *settle the posture of affairs.*——**Auxilia**, *the quotas*, i. e. the quotas which the several states were to furnish.——**Erat;** the subject is the clause, *cum* . . . . *esse;* 549.——**Suis;** supply *viribus.*

**91**　　234. **Medius inter duos**, *in the middle between the two*, or simply, *between the two. Medius* is explained by *inter duos.*——**Occupatis angustiis.** He had deliberately placed himself in a narrow passage with the determination to slay the king as he passed.——**Ab Attalo**, *by Attalus*, one of Philip's generals.——**Adversarium**, *his adversary*, meaning Attalus.——**Non poterat;** supply *exigere.*——**Ab iniquo judice**, *from the unjust judge*, meaning Philip.

235. **Deceptis hostibus**, lit. *in the deceived enemy;* render, *in deceiving the enemy.* 580.——**Gaudere**, *rejoiced*, Historical Infinitive, of which several other examples occur in this paragraph.——**Hic;** supply *gaudere.*——**Fusis;** supply *hostibus.*——**Hic** . . . . **exercebat**, *the latter was wont to exercise his royal power upon*, or *against, his friends.* ——**Amari;** depends upon *malle.*——**Metui;** supply *malle.*——**Soller-**

**92** **tiae pater;** supply *erat.*——**Ille** . . . . **abstinebat**, *he did not abstain from* (i. e. from óppressing or annoying) *even his allies.*——**Nec**=*et non*, is here rendered *not even.*——**Quibus artibus**, *by these arts*, referring to the enumeration just given of the characteristics of the father and son, Philip and Alexander.

236. **Caedis conscios** . . . . **occidi jussit.** It was a common custom in antiquity thus to slay murderers and assassins upon the graves of their victims, to appease the shades, or spirits, of the dead. In the same way, in war, prisoners were often slain over the graves of fallen heroes.——**Sibi** . . . . **praefatus.** There is no little ostentation in this statement. It was of course made for *effect.*——**Opes.** Object of *cogitabant* understood; construed literally, the passage would read thus: *they thought of nothing if not the riches*, i. e. *if they did not think of the riches*, etc. ; render, *they thought of nothing except the*, etc.—— **In Ilio**, *in Ilium*, i. e. in the *district*, not in the *city;* hence the Ablative with *in*, not the Genitive, as in the rames of towns.——**Tumulos heroum.** In the vicinity of Troy, mounds are still pointed out as the burial places of heroes, who three thousand years since fell in the Trojan war.

237. **Parcendum suis rebus.** Alexander thus inspires his soldiers with courage and confidence. He speaks of the country as already

**93** *his* and *theirs.*——**In exercitu** . . . . **duae.** Observe that the *copulative connectives* are omitted between the several subjects.——**Veteranos,**

*veterans*, used substantively, 441.——**Electos ;** supply *esse.*——**In cam- 93 pis Adrastiae,** *in the plains of Adrastia*, in the vicinity of the river Granicus, from which the battle took its name : *battle of the Granicus.*

238. **Defuncti ;** from *defungor.*——**Confossi ;** from *confodio.*—— **Ad hoc ipsum,** *for this very purpose.*——**Omnes ante eum reges,** lit. *all* **94** *before him kings,* i. e. all the kings before him, or before his time.

239. **Nihil ex . . . . Aegyptiorum more.** Alexander was careful not to give offence by disregarding the customs of the country.——**Jovis Ammonis oraculum.** The oracle of Jupiter Ammon was one of the most celebrated in the world.——**Sedem consecratam deo.** This was situated in a beautiful oasis of the Libyan desert.——**Parentem Jovem,** *parent* or *father Jupiter,* i. e. *his* father Jupiter. Thus the priest, per- ceiving his ambitious vanity, flattered him with the title—*son of Ju- piter.*——**Parentem ejus,** *his parent,* i. e. Jupiter. The priest still continues his flattery.——**An auctor . . . . colendi . . . . regem,** lit. *whe-* **95** *ther he,* i. e. Jupiter, *would be to them the author of worshipping the king with divine honors,* i. e. whether he would authorize them to wor- ship their king with divine honors.

240. **Nobilem,** *famous.*——**Quin . . . . esset occisus,** *that the king himself was slain ;* XXVI. 6.

241. **Spe . . . . libertatis.** Greece, it will be remembered, lost its independence by the battle of Chaeronea. See above (232).

242. **Cui gloriae,** *this glory,* i. e. that of conquest and empire. **96**

243. **Recedentem ;** supply *eum.*——**Invitat,** *invites,* i. e. invites him to drink with him.——**Ut . . . . posceret ;** XXIV. 2, 5).——**Inter bibendum,** *while drinking.*

244. **Aeacidarum.** Alexander was, by his mother, a lineal descend- ant of Aeacus, the grandfather of Achilles.——**Sine ullo . . . . argu- mento,** *without any mark of a more sad mind,* i. e. without any indica- tion of unusual sadness.——**Dignissimum.** Adjective used substan- **97** tively ; object of *facere* understood.——**Judicio,** *by a tacit decision,* opposed to *voce.*

245. **Quo die**=*die, quo, the day, on which.* Here the relative must not be rendered according to 453.——**Alterius—alterius,** *the one—the other.*——**Belli Illyrici,** *that of the Illyrian war,* i. e. the victory gained in it.——**Certaminis Olympiaci.** See note on " *Olympico certamine* " (134).——**Puer,** *when a boy ;* 363, 3.——**Quadrigas.** Chariots and horses were often sent to the Olympic games to contend for the prizes.——**Aristotele . . . . magistro.** Philip placed the youthful Alex- ander under the special instruction of Aristotle, the celebrated philo- sopher of Athens. Both teacher and pupil have left names famous in the annals of the world.——**Tantam . . . . fiduciam fecit,** *he inspired his soldiers with such confidence.*

# LATIN-ENGLISH VOCABULARY.

*For Explanation of References and Abbreviations, see page* ix.

## A

**A.** An abbreviation of *Aulus.*

*A, ab, abs,* prep. with abl. From, by.

*Ab-dūco, ĕre, duxi, ductum.* To lead away, take away, remove.

*Ab-eo, īre, īvi,* or *ii, ītum.* To go away, depart, withdraw from. 295.

*Ab-hinc,* adv. Henceforth, from this time, before, ago, since.

*Abjicio, ĕre, jĕci, jectum,* (ab, jacio). To throw away, throw, reject; prostrate, humble.

*Abripio, ĕre, ripui, reptum,* (ab, rapio). To take away, carry off.

*Ab-rumpo, ĕre, rūpi, ruptum.* To break off *or* away, rend, sever.

*Absens, entis,* part. (absum). Absent.

*Abstineo, ēre, tinui, tentum,* (abs, teneo). To keep *or* hold back, abstain from.

*Ab-sum, esse, fui.* To be absent *or* away, to be distant from. 204, 290.

*Ab-sūmo, ĕre, sumpsi, sumptum.* To take from *or* away; destroy, consume.

*Ab-undo, āre, āvi, ātum.* To abound, abound in, superabound, have an abundance.

*Ab-ūtor, ūti, ūsus sum,* dep. To use up, consume, abuse.

*Ac,* a shortened form of *atque.* And. *Ac si,* as if.

*Acca, ae,* f. Acca, a Roman name. *Acca Laurentia, ae,* f. Acca Laurentia, the wife of Faustulus, and nurse of Romulus and Remus, (153).

*Accēdo, ĕre, cessi, cessum,* (ad, cedo). To approach, come to, accede to; be added to. *Accēdit,* impers., it is added, there is the additional fact that.

*Accendo, ĕre, cendi, censum,* (ad, candeo). To set on fire, kindle; to excite, inflame.

*Acceptus, a, um,* part. (accipio). Accepted; acceptable, pleasing.

*Accipio, ĕre, cēpi, ceptum,* (ad, capio). To accept, receive.

*Accurro, ĕre, curri, (cucurri* rare), *cursum,* (ad, curro). To run to, hasten to.

*Accūsō, āre, āvi, ātum,* (ad, causa). To call to account, to accuse.

*Acer, acris, acre.* Sharp; powerful, valiant; diligent, intense, severe. 163, 1.

*Acerbus, a, um,* (acer). Sour, unripe, morose, disagreeable.

*Achaia, ae,* f. Achaia, an important

province in the northern part of
the Peloponnesus.

*Achilles, is,* m. Achilles, the most
celebrated Grecian hero in the
Trojan war, son of Peleus and
Thetis, (134).

*Acies, ēi,* f. The order of battle,
battle array; line of soldiers; army in battle array.

*Acquiesco, ĕre, quiēvi, quiētum* (ad,
quiesco). To become quiet, to repose; to acquiesce in.

*Acrĭter, acrius, acerrĭme,* adv. (accr).
Vehemently, valiantly. 305.

*Actium, ii,* n. Actium, a promontory
and town at the entrance of the
Ambracian Gulf on the western
coast of Greece, celebrated for the
victory of Augustus over Antony
and Cleopatra, (214).

*Acuo, ĕre, ui, ūtum.* To sharpen,
quicken; stimulate.

*Acūtus, a, um,* part. (acuo). Sharp-
ened, pointed, sharp, acute, intel-
ligent, clear-sighted.

*Ad,* prep. with acc. To, towards;
until; at, near.

*Ad-do, ĕre, dĭdi, dĭtum.* To add,
carry to, appoint to.

*Ad-dūco, ĕre, duxi, ductum.* To lead
to, conduct, bring, induce.

*Ad-eo,* adv. So, to such an extent.

*Ad-eo, īre, īvi* or *ii, ĭtum.* To go
to, approach, visit; encounter.
295.

*Ad-huc,* adv. Thus far, as yet, even
yet; still.

*Adĭmo, ĕre, ēmi, emptum,* (ad, emo).
To take from, deprive of.

*Adipiscor, ci, adeptus sum,* dep. (ad,
apiscor). To obtain, get possession of.

*Adjicio, ĕre, jēci, jectum,* (ad, jacio).
To throw or cast to or against, add
to; anĭmum adjicĕre, to direct or
give attention to.

*Ad-jungo, ĕre, junxi, junctum.* To
join to, unite with.

*Adjūtor, ōris,* m. (adjuvo). Aid,
helper, assistant.

*Ad-jŭvo, āre, jŭvi, jūtum.* To help,
assist, support.

*Ad-ministro, āre, āvi, ātum.* To administer, manage.

*Ad-mirabĭlis, e.* Admirable, wonderful.

*Ad-mirātio, ōnis,* f. (admiror). Ad-
miration, respect.

*Admiror, āri, ātus sum,* dep. (ad,
miror). To admire, wonder at.

*Ad-mitto, ĕre, mĭsi, missum.* To send
to or forward, to admit, receive.

*Admŏdum,* adv. (ad, modus). Very,
exceedingly.

*Ad-moneo, ĕre, ui, ĭtum.* To admonish, warn.

*Admonĭtus, us,* m. (admoneo). Warning, advice; instigation.

*Ad-moveo, ĕre, mŏvi, mōtum.* To
move to, apply to, bring to.

*Adolescens, entis,* adj. and subs., m.
and f. (adolesco). Young, growing; a young man, a youth.

*Adolescentia, ae,* f. (adolescens).
Youth.

*Ad-olesco, ĕre, olēvi, ultum.* To grow,
grow up, increase.

*Ad-opto, āre, āvi, ātum.* To choose,
adopt; take for a son, daughter,
etc.

*Ad-orior, īri, ortus sum,* dep. To attack, attempt, strive; begin. 288, 2.

*Ad-orno, āre, āvi, ātum.* To adorn,
furnish, equip.

*Adrastia, ae,* f.  Adrastia, a district and city of Mysia, (237).

*Adspicio, ĕre, spexi, spectum,* (ad, specio).  To see, look at, behold.

*Ad-sto, āre, stĭti, stătum.*  To stand near, stand by.

*Ad-sum, esse, fui.*  To be present *or* at hand, assist, stand by. 204, 290.

\ *Adulatio, ŏnis,* f.  Adulation, flattery.

*Advectus, a, um,* part. (advĕho).  Brought, carried to.

*Ad-vĕho, ĕre, vexi, vectum.*  To conduct, convey, import.

*Ad-venio, īre, vĕni, ventum.*  To come to, arrive.

*Adventus, us,* m. (advenio).  Arrival, approach.

*Adversarius, a, um.* adj. (adversus).  Opposite, opposing.

*Adversarius, ii,* m. subs. (adversus).  Adversary, opponent, antagonist.

*Adversus, a, um,* part. (adverto).  Opposite, over against, adverse, hostile; fronting, in front.

*Adversus,* or *adversum,* adv., and prep. with acc. (adverto).  Against, towards, opposite to.

*Aeacīdes, ae,* m.  A patronymic denoting a descendant of Aeacus, who was the grandfather of Achilles.  The name is often applied to Achilles; Alexander the Great also claimed it for himself, (244).

*Aedes,* or *aedis, is,* f.  Temple *in the sing. ; but in the plur.* dwelling, habitation, house. 132.

*Aedifico, āre, āvi, ātum,* (aedes, facio).  To build.

*Aedilitius,* or *aedilicius, a, . um,* (aedes).  Pertaining to the aediles.

*Aedilitius, i,* m., one who has been aedile.  The aediles were Roman magistrates who had charge of the public buildings, highways, &c., and acted as city police.

*Aegina, ae,* f.  Aegina, an island near Attica, (55).

*Aegos flumen.*  Aegospotamos, a river and town in the Thracian Chersonesus, noted for the defeat of the Athenians by Lysander, (226).

*Aegrōtus, a, um.*  Sick, ill, diseased.

*Aegyptus, i,* f.  Egypt, (210).

*Aegyptius, a, um,* Egyptian ; subs. *Aegyptius, i,* m., an Egyptian, (239).

*Aemilius, ii,* m.  The family name of several distinguished Romans.  *Lucius Aemilius,* surnamed *Paulus,* fell in the battle of Cannae, (101).  Another of the same name conquered Perseus and reduced Macedonia to a Roman province, (198).

*Aemŭlus, a, um.*  Emulous ; *often used substantively, as,* rival, competitor.

*Aenēas, ae,* m.  Aeneas, a Trojan prince who after the destruction of Troy is said to have fled into Italy and formed a settlement, (149).

*Aequālis, e.*  Equal, like.

*Aeque, aequius, aequissĭme,* adv. (aequus).  Equally, similarly.

*Aequipăro, āre, āvi, ātum.*  To equal, make equal.

*Aequĭtas, ātis,* f. (aequus).  Equality, equity, justice.

*Aequus, a, um.*  Equal, similar ; just, fair ; favorable, propitious.

Aër, aëris, m. The air, atmosphere.

Aestĭmo, āre, āvi, ātum. To value, estimate. Parvi aestimāre, to think little of, esteem lightly.

Aestuo, āre, āvi, ātum. To be in agitation; to be warm, endure heat.

Aetas, ātis, f. Age, time of life, life.

Affĕro, ferre, attŭli, allātum, (ad, fero). To bring, carry to, report.

Afficio, ĕre, fēci, fectum (ad, facio). To affect, influence.

Affīgo, ĕre, fixi, fixum, (ad, fīgo). To affix, fasten to.

Affirmo, āre, āvi, ātum, (ad, firmo). To affirm, confirm, ratify.

Afflictus, a, um, part. (affīgo). Afflicted, troubled, prostrated.

Afflīgo, ĕre, flixi, flictum, (ad, flīgo). To afflict, trouble, overthrow.

Affluo, ĕre, fluxi, fluxum, (ad, fluo). To flow toward; overflow, abound in.

Afrĭca, ae, f. Africa, (200).

Africānus, a, um, (Afrĭca). African. Also the surname given to the two most distinguished Scipios for their achievements in Africa during the Punic wars, (196, 200).

Ager, agri, m. Field, land, territory.

Agesilāus, i, m. Agesilaus, a Spartan king, (96).

Agger, ĕris, m. Mound, rampart, wall.

Aggredior, i, gressus sum, dep. (ad, gradior). To approach, attack, attempt.

Agis, ĭdis, m. Agis, king of the Lacedaemonians in the time of Alexander the Great, (241).

Agitātus, a, um, part. (agĭto). Agitated, troubled.

Agĭto, āre, āvi, ātum. To harass, trouble, think of.

Agmen, ĭnis, n. (ago). An army, generally on the march, band of soldiers, troop.

Agnosco, ĕre, nōvi, nĭtum, (ad, (g)nosco). To recognize.

Ago, ĕre, ēgi, actum. To conduct, drive, do, act, execute, treat, argue; annum vicesĭmum agĕre, to be in his (or her) twentieth year.

Agricŏla, ae, m. (ager, colo). Husbandman, farmer.

Agricultūra, ae, f. Agriculture.

Agrigentum, i, n. Agrigentum, a large and wealthy town in Sicily.

Agrippa, ae, m. A family name among the Romans. Menenius Agrippa induced the people who had revolted at Rome and taken up their quarters upon Mons Sacer to return into the city, (173).

Aio, ais, ait, etc., defect. To say, affirm. 297, II. 1.

Ala, ae, f. Wing.

Alăcer, cris, cre. Active, prompt, joyful.

Alba, ae, f.; or Alba Longa, ae, f. A city of Latium founded by Ascanius, (150).

Albānus, a, um. Alban. Mons Albānus, a rocky mountain sixteen miles southeast of Rome, (150).

Albānus, i, m. An Alban, a citizen of Alba, (151).

Albus, a, um. White.

Alcibiădes, is, m. Alcibiades, an Athenian general in the Peloponnesian war, (223–225).

Alexander, dri, m. Alexander. The

most distinguished of this name was the son and successor of Philip, king of Macedonia, (235–245). A second of the same name was king of Epirus and son-in-law of Philip, (234).

*Alexandria, ae,* f.　Alexandria, a celebrated city of Egypt, built by Alexander the Great; (239).

*Algeo, ēre, alsi.*　To be cold, to feel cold, endure cold.

*Alias.*　Otherwise, at another time; *non alias,* on no other occasion.

*Aliēnus, a, um,* (alius).　Belonging to another, foreign; unfavorable.

*Aliquando.*　At some time, once, formerly, finally, now at last.

*Aliquantum,* adv.　Somewhat, in some degree.

*Aliquis, qua, quod,* and *quid,* (alius, quis).　Some one, some.

*Aliquot,* indecl. pl. adj.　Several, some.

*Aliter,* adv. (alius).　Otherwise.

*Alius, a, ud,* (gen. alīus, etc.) Other, another; *alius — alius,* one — another: *alii—alii,* some—others, (151).

*Allia, ae,* f.　The river Allia, a few miles north of Rome, (176).

*Allŏquor, lŏqui, cūtus sum,* dep. (ad, loquor).　To speak to, address.

*Alo, ĕre, alui, alĭtum* or *altum.*　To support, keep, nourish, strengthen, feed.

*Alpes, ium,* f.　The Alps, a high range of mountains north of Italy.

*Alte, ius, issĭme,* adv. (altus).　On high, high.

*Alter, ĕra, ĕrum,* (gen. alterius). One

of two, the other; *alter—alter,* the one — the other; *alter* as numeral = *second.* 151, 2.

*Altus, a, um.*　High, noble, great; deep, profound; *altum* substantively, the sea, the deep.

*Amabĭlis, e,* (amo).　Lovely, amiable.

*Ambio, īre, īvi* or *ii, ītum,* (amb, or ambi, eo).　To surround, encompass. 295, 3.

*Ambitio, ōnis,* f. (ambio).　Canvassing, flattery, ambition.

*Ambo, ae, o.*　Both. 175, 2.

*Amentia, ae,* f. (amens).　Folly, want of reason.

*Amicitia, ae,* f. (amīcus).　Friendship.

*Amīcus, i,* m.　Friend.

*Amīcus, a, um.*　Friendly, kind.

*A-mitto, ĕre, mīsi, missum.*　To send away, to lose.

*Ammon,* or *Hammon, ōnis,* m.　An appellation of Jupiter as worshipped in Africa, (239).

*Amnis, is,* m.　River.

*Amo, āre, āvi, ātum.*　To love.

*Amor, ōris,* m. (amo).　Love, affection, desire; a loved object, darling.

*Amphitheātrum, i,* n.　Amphitheatre, *in Rome* a circular or oval building used for public spectacles.

*Ample, ius, issĭme,* adv. (amplus).　Abundantly, amply.

*Amplio, āre, āvi, ātum,* (amplus).　To enlarge.

*Amplius,* adv. (comp. of *ample*).　More, further.

*Amplus, a, um.*　Ample, spacious, large.

*Amulius, ii,* m. Amulius, son of Procas king of Alba ; he was the brother of Numitor, (152).

*An,* interrog. particle. Or, whether. 346, II, 2.

*Anaxagŏras, ae,* m. Anaxagoras, a distinguished Greek philosopher of Clazomenae, (112).

*Anaxarchus, i,* m. Anaxarchus, a philosopher of Abdera, who accompanied Alexander into Asia.

*Anceps, ancipĭtis.* Twofold, double.

*Anchīses, ae,* m. Anchises, the father of Aeneas. 50.

*Ancus, i,* m. ; or *Ancus Martius, ii,* m. The fourth king of Rome, (161).

*Angor, ōris,* m. Anxiety, care, anguish.

*Angustia, ae,* f. (angustus), used mostly in pl. Narrow pass, difficulty ; straits, channel.

*Angustus, a, um.* Narrow, confined, contracted, small.

*Anĭma, ae,* f. Breath, life.

*Animadverto, ĕrc, verti, versum* (anĭmus, adverto). To notice, observe, perceive.

*Anĭmal, ālis,* n. Animal.

*Anĭmus, i,* m. Mind, soul, courage.

*Anio, Aniēnis,* m. The Anio, a small river of Italy, a tributary of the Tiber, (173).

*Annecto, ĕre, nexui, nexum,* (ad, necto). To tie to, annex, fasten to.

*Annŭlus,* or *anŭlus, i,* m. Ring.

*Annus, i,* m. Year.

*Annuus, a, um,* (annus). Lasting a year, for a year, annual.

*Ante,* adv., and prep. with acc. Before, *in respect to place or time ;* formerly.

*Antea,* adv. (ante, ea). Formerly, hitherto.

*Ante-pōno, ĕre, posui, posĭtum.* To place before ; to prefer.

*Antĕ-quam,* adv. Before, before that.

*Antigŏnus, i,* m. Antigonus, king of Macedonia, (121).

*Antiochīa, ae,* f. Antioch, the chief city of Syria, founded by Seleucus, and named by him in honor of his father Antiochus, (206).

*Antiŏchus, i,* m. 1. Antiochus the Great, king of Syria. 2. Antiochus, the Academic philosopher and teacher of Cicero, (80).

*Antipăter, tri,* m. Antipater, one of Alexander's generals ; after the death of Alexander he received the government of Greece and Macedonia, (241).

*Antīquus, a, um.* Ancient, early.

*Antistes, ĭtis,* m. and f. President ; priest, priestess.

*Antonius, ii,* m. Antony ; *Marcus Antonius* formed a triumvirato with Octavianus and Lepidus, (212). *Caius Antonius* was the colleague of Cicero in the consulship, (207).

*Anxiĕtas, ătis,* f. Anxiety, solicitude.

*Apelles, is,* m. Apelles, a distinguished Greek painter in the time of Alexander the Great, (97).

*Aperte, ius, issĭme,* adv. (apertus). Openly, publicly.

*Apertus, a, um,* part. (aperio). Opened ; open, free, clear, manifest.

*Apollo, ĭnis,* m. Apollo, the god of divination.

*Apparātus, us,* m. Preparation, equipment.

*Apparātus, a, um,* part. (appăro). Prepared, ready, equipped.

*Appellatio, ōnis,* f. (appello). Name, title.

*Appello, āre, āvi, ātum,* (ad, pello). To call, name.

*Appello, ĕre, pŭli, pulsum,* (ad, pello). To drive to, bring to, induce.

*Appĕto, ĕre, petīvi, petii, petītum,* (ad, peto). To long for, strive after; assail: *appĕtens, entis,* desiring, desirous of.

*Appius, ii,* m. Appius, a Roman name. *Appius Claudius, ii,* m., one of the Decemviri, (26).

*Approbo, āre, āvi, ātum,* (ad, probo). To approve, favor.

*Appropinquo, āre, āvi, ātum,* (ad, propinquo). To approach, come near.

*Aptus, a, um.* Fitted, adapted, suited, proper.

*Apud,* prep. with acc. At, near, among, at the house of, in the works of (*applied to authors*).

*Apulia, ae,* f. Apulia, a province in southern Italy, (204).

*Aqua, ae,* f. Water.

*Aquila, ae,* f. Eagle.

*Ara, ae,* f. Altar.

*Arabs, ăbis.* Arabian; *subs.* an Arabian, inhabitant of Arabia in Asia, (26).

*Arātrum, i,* n. Plough.

*Arbēla, ōrum,* n. Arbela, a town in Assyria, famous for the victory of Alexander over Darius, (240).

*Arbĭtror, āri, ātus sum,* dep. To think, judge, regard.

*Arcĕo, arcēre, arcui.* To inclose, restrain, keep from.

*Ardea, ae,* f. Ardea, a city of La-

tium, a few miles south of Rome, (167).

*Ardeo, ēre, arsi, arsum.* To be on fire, burn.

*Ardesco, ēre, arsi.* To take fire, kindle.

*Aresco, ēre, arui.* To become dry, to dry.

*Arethūsa, ae,* f. Arethusa, a celebrated fountain in Sicily, near Syracuse.

*Argenteus, a, um,* (argentum). Made of silver, of silver.

*Argentum, i,* n. Silver.

*Argos,* n. (only in nom. and acc.), or *Argi, ōrum,* m. pl. Argos, the capital of the province of Argolis in the Peloponnesus; the name was often applied to the province itself and poetically to all Greece, (96).

*Argumentum, i,* n. Argument, sign, mark.

*Arimīnum, i,* n. Ariminum, a town in Umbria on the Adriatic, (209).

*Ariovistus, i,* m. Ariovistus, king of a German tribe in the time of Caesar, (47).

*Aristīdes, is,* m. Aristides, an Athenian general and statesman, renowned for his integrity, (49).

*Aristobūlus, i,* m. A king of Judea, who was taken by Pompey and carried as prisoner to Rome, (206).

*Aristotēles, is,* m. A distinguished philosopher, and the teacher of Alexander the Great, (85, 245).

*Arma, ōrum,* n. pl. Arms, force of arms.

*Armātus, a, um,* part. (armo). Armed.

*Armenia, ae,* f. Armenia, a country of Asia, divided by the river Euphrates into two unequal parts, viz.: the eastern, called *Armenia Major*, and the western, called *Armenia Minor*, (205).

*Armilla, ae,* f. Bracelet.

*Armo, āre, āvi, ātum,* (arma). To arm.

*Arripio, ĕre, ripui, reptum,* (ad, rapio). To seize upon, seize.

*Arrŏgans, antis,* part. (arrŏgo). Proud, arrogant.

*Arrŏgantia, ae,* f. (arrŏgans). Arrogance, pride.

*Arrŏgo, āre, āvi, ātum,* (ad, rogo). To claim, arrogate.

*Ars, artis,* f. Art, skill.

*Artaphernes, is,* m. Artaphernes, nephew of Darius, (215).

*Artemisium, ii,* n. Artemisium, a promontory and town on the island of Euboea, (218).

*Artus, us,* m.; sing. rare. Joint, limb.

*Aruns, Aruntis,* m. 1. Aruns, the brother of Tarquin the Proud, (39, iv.). 2. Aruns, the son of Tarquin, (170).

*Arx, arcis,* f. Citadel.

*Ascanius, ii,* m. Ascanius, the son of Aeneas, (150).

*Asia, ae,* f. Asia, (16).

*Asina, ae,* m. Asina, a surname of Cnaeus Cornelius, who was the colleague of Duillius in the consulship in the early part of the first Punic war, (185).

*Aspis, ĭdis,* f. Asp.

*Asporto, āre, āvi, ātum,* (abs, porto). To bear or carry away.

*Assĕquor, sĕqui, sĕcūtus sum,* dep. (ad, sequor). To overtake, obtain.

*Asseveratio, ōnis,* f. Declaration, assertion.

*Assĭduus, a, um.* Assiduous; frequent; continual, incessant, constant.

*Assigno, āre, āvi, ātum,* (ad, signo). Assign, bestow.

*Asto,* for *ad-sto.*

*Astrum, i,* n. Star, constellation.

*Astu,* n, indec. City, *generally applied to* Athens.

*Asŷlum, i,* n. Asylum, place of refuge.

*At,* conj. But, yet.

*Ater, tra, trum.* Dark, black, gloomy.

*Athēnae, ārum,* f. pl. Athens, the capital of Attica, (227).

*Atheniensis, e,* adj. (Athēnae). Athenian; subs. *Atheniensis, is,* m., an Athenian, (216).

*Atilius, ii,* m. Atilius, a Roman name. See *Regŭlus.*

*Atque,* conj. And, and also, and besides; *atque—atque,* both—and.

*Attălus, i,* m. Attalus, one of Philip's generals, (234).

*Attĭca, ae,* f. An important state in Greece, (216).

*Attĭcus, a, um,* (Attĭca). Attic, Athenian; subs. *Attĭcus, i,* m. An inhabitant or citizen of Attica, (36).

*Attĭcus, i,* m. Atticus, a surname of the Roman, Titus Pomponius, (99).

*Attingo, ĕre, tĭgi, tactum,* (ad, tango). To attain, touch, enter upon, undertake, commence.

*Attius, ii,* m. Attius, a Roman name, (89).

*Attribuo, ĕre, tribui, tribūtum,* (ad, tribuo). To attribute to, ascribe to, to bestow, to assign, or impute to.

*Auctor, ōris,* m. (augeo). Author, founder, approver, adviser, authority.

*Auctorītas, ātis,* f. (auctor). Authority, influence.

*Audacia, ae,* f. (audax). Boldness, insolence, audacity.

*Audax, audācis,* (audeo). Bold, audacious, desperate.

*Audeo, ēre, ausus sum.* To dare, attempt. 271, 3.

*Audio, īre, īvi or ii, ītum.* To hear, listen to.

*Aufugio, ēre, fūgi, fugītum,* (ab, fugio). To flee from; run away from. 338, 1, *ab.*

*Augeo, ēre, auxi, auctum.* To enlarge, increase.

*Augūror, āri, ātus sum,* dep. To augur, predict, foretell.

*Augustus, i,* m. Augustus, surname of Octavius Caesar, the first of the Roman Emperors. This surname was also often applied to the Emperors generally, (213).

*Aulus, i,* m. Aulus, a Roman praenomen.

*Aurarius, a, um,* (aurum). Pertaining to gold; *auraria metalla,* gold mines.

*Aureus, a, um,* (aurum). Made of gold, golden.        [driver.

*Aurīga, ae,* m. and f.   Charioteer,

*Auris, is,* f.  Ear.

*Aurum, i,* n.  Gold.

*Aut,* conj.  Or; *aut—aut,* either—or, partly—partly.

*Autem,* conj.  But, moreover.

*Auxilium, ii,* n. (augeo.) Aid; *plur.* auxiliaries.

*Avaritia, ae,* f. (avārus). Avarice.

*Avārus, a, um.*  Avaricious.

*Aventīnus, i,* m.   The Aventine, one of the seven hills of Rome, (154).

*Averto, ēre, verti, versum,* (ab, verto). To avert, turn from, remove.

*Avīdus, a, um.*  Desirous, eager.

*Avis, is,* f.  Bird.

*Avus, i,* m.  Grandfather.

### B.

*Babylonia, ae,* f.  Babylonia, a province of Syria: also Babylon, the capital of Babylonia, (243).

*Bacchantes, ium,* pl. (bacchor). Votaries of Bacchus.

*Bacchor, āri, ātus sum,* dep. (Bacchus). To celebrate the festival of Bacchus, to revel.  *Bacchans, antis,* part. revelling.

*Bacchus, i,* m.  The god of wine, (19).

*Barba, ae,* f.  Beard.

*Barbārus, a, um.*  Foreign, barbarous, rude.

*Barbārus, i,* m.  Foreigner, barbarian.

*Beāte, ius, issīme,* adv. (beātus). Happily.

*Beātus, a, um.*  Happy.

*Belgae, ārum.*  The Belgians, a warlike people in the north of Gaul, (25).

*Bellicōsus, a, um,* (bellum). Warlike.

*Bello, āre, āvi, ātum,* (bellum). To carry on war.

*Bellum, i,* n.  War.

*Bene, melius, optīme,* adv.  Well. 305, 2.

*Beneficium, ii,* n. (beneficus, *from* bene, facio). Benefit, favor, kindness.

*Benevolentia, ae,* f. (benevŏlens,

*from* bene, volo). Kindness, benevolence.

*Benigne, ius, issime,* adv. (benignus). Kindly.

*Benignus, a, um.* Kind, good, benignant.

*Bestia, ae,* f. A beast.

*Bestiöla, ae,* f. (bestia). A small animal, insect.

*Bibo, ĕre, bibi, bibĭtum.* To drink.

*Bibŭlus, i,* m. Bibulus, a Roman name; *Lucius Bibŭlus* was Caesar's colleague in the consulship, (208).

*Biduum, i,* n. (biduus). A period of two days.

*Biduus, a, um,* (bis, dies). Continuing two days.

*Biennium, ii,* n. (bis, annus). A period of two years, two years.

*Biformis, e,* (bis, forma). Having two forms, biformed.

*Bini, ae, a,* distributo. Two by two, two and two. 174, 2.

*Bis,* adv. Twice.

*Boeotius, ii,* m. (Boeotia). A Boeotian, inhabitant of Boeotia in central Greece, (229).

*Bolētus, i,* m. Mushroom.

*Bonĭtas, ātis,* f. (bonus). Goodness, excellence.

*Bonum, i,* n. (bonus). Blessing, prosperity, any good; pl. *bona,* goods, property.

*Bonus, a, um ; melior, optĭmus.* Good, noble, brave. 165.

*Bos, Bovis,* m. and f. Ox, cow. 43, 2; 66.

*Brachium,* i, n. Arm, fore-arm.

*Brevis, e.* Short, brief; *brevi* (tempŏre), in a short time, shortly.

*Britannĭcus, a, um,* (Britannia, Great Britain). British, English, (208).

*Britannus, i,* m. (Britannia). A Briton, (208).

*Brutus, i,* m. Brutus, a Roman name. *Lucius Junius Brutus* was one of the first consuls of Rome, (168). *Marcus Junius Brutus* and *Decĭmus Junius Brutus* acted prominent parts in the assassination of Caesar, (211).

*Byzantium, ii,* n. Byzantium, a city on the Bosphorus, now Constantinople.

## C.

*C.* An abbreviation of *Caius ; Cn.* of *Cnaeus.*

*Cado, ĕre, cecĭdi, casum.* To fall, fall in battle, perish.

*Caecus, a, um.* Blind.

*Caedes, is,* f. (caedo). Slaughter, bloodshed.

*Caedo, ĕre, cecidi, caesum.* To cut, kill, slay.

*Caesar, ăris,* m. Caesar, a surname of the Julian family ; *Caius Julius Caesar,* a distinguished general and statesman. The title, or surname, *Caesar,* was also applied generally to denote the Roman emperors, (208).

*Caius, ii,* m. Caius, a Roman name. See *Caesar.*

*Calamĭtas, ātis,* f. Loss, calamity, disaster.

*Callĭde, ius, issĭme,* adv. (callĭdus). Shrewdly, skilfully.

*Camillus, i,* m. Camillus, a distinguished Roman general, (176).

*Campania, ae,* f. Campania, a province in Central Italy, (182).

*Campānus, a, um,* (Campania). Campanian, of Campania. *Subs.* a Campanian, (44, 131).

*Campus, i,* m.  A plain, field of battle.

*Candidus, a, um.*  White, clear, bright, light.

*Caninius, ii,* m.  Caninius, a Roman consul, (80).

*Cannae, ārum,* f. plur.  Cannae, a village in Apulia, famous for the great victory of Hannibal over the Romans, (191).

*Cannensis, e,* adj. (Cannae). Belonging to Cannae, of Cannae, (194).

*Cano, ĕre, cecĭni, cantum.*  To sing, sound, crow.

*Canto, āre, āvi, ātum,* (cano).  To sing, play.

*Cantus, ūs,* m. (cano).  Singing, song, melody.

*Capax, ācis,* (capio).  Capacious, large, comprehensive, able.

*Capesso, ĕre, īvi, ītum,* (capio).  To take, seize; *fugam capessĕre,* to resort to flight, betake one's self to flight.  332, 4.

*Capillus, i,* m.  Hair.

*Capio, ĕre, cēpi, captum.*  To take, take possession of, hold, receive.

*Capitālis, e,* (caput).  Deadly, mortal, *capitāle crimen,* a capital crime or offence.

*Capitolium, ii,* n.  Capitol.  This term is applied sometimes to the temple of Jupiter, and sometimes to the whole Capitoline Hill, including both the temple and the citadel of Rome.

*Capra, ae,* f.  A she-goat.

*Captivĭtas, ātis,* f. (captivus.)  Captivity, bondage.

*Captivus, a, um,* (capio).  Captive, enslaved; *substantively,* a prisoner, a captive.

*Captus, a, um,* part. (capio).  Captured, taken.

*Capua, ae,* f.  Capua, the chief city of Campania, (204).

*Caput, ĭtis,* n.  Head, capital; *capĭtis damnāre,* to condemn to death.

*Carcer, ĕris,* m.  Prison.

*Careo, ēre, carui, carĭtum.*  To be destitute, be free from, be without.

*Carmen, ĭnis,* n.  A song, poem; poetry.

*Caro, carnis,* f.  Flesh.

*Carpentum, i,* n.  Chariot, carriage.

*Carthāgo, ĭnis,* f.  Carthage, an ancient city in Northern Africa, (189).  *Carthāgo Nova.*  New Carthage, a town in Spain; now *Carthagena,* (194).

*Carthaginiensis, e,* adj. (Carthāgo). Carthaginian; subs. *Carthaginiensis, is,* m. a Carthaginian, (185).

*Carus, a, um.*  Dear.

*Cassius, ii,* m.  Cassius, a Roman name.  *Lucius Cassius,* one of the accomplices of Catiline, (97, 15).  *Caius Cassius,* one of the conspirators against Caesar, (213).

*Caste, ius, issĭme,* adv. (castus). Virtuously, chastely.

*Castus, a, um.*  Chaste, pure.

*Castellum, i,* n. dimin. (castrum). Castle, fortress.  315, 3.

*Castor, ŏris,* m.  Castor, son of Tyndarus and brother of Pollux, (63, 9).

*Castra*, *ŏrum*, n. (pl. of *castrum*, a castle). Camp. 132.

*Casus*, *us*, m. (cado). Fall, misfortune, chance, accident.

*Catilīna*, *ae*, m. Catiline. *Lucius Sergius Catilīna*, the notorious conspirator against the Roman government, (207).

*Catinensis* or *Catiniensis*, *is*, m. A Catinean, a citizen of Catina, a city in Sicily, (223).

*Cato*, *ŏnis*, m. Cato, the name of several distinguished Romans. The most celebrated was *Marcus Porcius Cato*, the *Censor*, (88, 13).

*Catŭlus*, *i*, m. Catulus, surname of *Caius Lutatius*, a Roman consul at the close of the first Punic war, (188).

*Caudīnus*, *a*, *um*. Caudine; *Furcŭlae Caudīnae*, the Caudine Forks, a narrow defile near Caudium, in Italy, (179).

*Causa*, *ae*, f. Cause, purpose, business, suit at law.

*Causidīcus*, *i*, m. (causa, dico). Pleader, advocate; speaker.

*Caules*, *is*, f. A crag, cliff, rock.

*Caveo*, *ēre*, *cāvi*, *cautum*. To shun, avoid, guard against; *sibi ab aliquo cavēre*, to protect one's self from any one.

*Cedo*, *ĕre*, *cessi*, *cessum*. To give place to, yield to, withdraw, depart.

*Celĕber*, *bris*, *bre*. Renowned, celebrated.

*Celĕbro*, *āre*, *āvi*, *ātum*, (celĕber). To celebrate, solemnize.

*Celer*, *celĕris*. Swift. 163, 1.

*Celerĭtas*, *ātis*, f. (celer). Celerity, swiftness.

*Celerĭter*, *ius*, *rĭme*, adv. (celer). Swiftly, quickly. 305, 2.

*Cella*, *ae*, f. Store-room, store-house; *cella penaria*, granary.

*Celo*, *āre*, *āvi*, *ātum*. To hide, conceal.

*Censeo*, *ēre*, *censui*, *censum*. To think, judge, decree.

*Censorīnus*, *i*, m. Censorinus, surname of *Lucius Marcius*, a Roman consul in the third Punic war, (199).

*Census*, *us*, m. Census.

*Centum*, indec. Hundred.

*Centurio*, *ŏnis*, m. (centum). Centurion.

*Cerno*, *ĕre*, *crēvi*, *crētum*. To perceive, see, discern.

*Certāmen*, *ĭnis*, n. (certo). Contest, game, engagement.

*Certātim*, adv. (certātus, *from* certo). Earnestly, eagerly.

*Certo*, *āre*, *āvi*, *ātum*. To fight, struggle, contend, endeavor.

*Certus*, *a*, *um*. Sure, certain; *certiŏrem facĕre*, to inform.

*Cesso*, *āre*, *āvi*, *ātum*, (cedo). To cease, pause.

*Cetĕrus*, *a*, *um*, nom. sing. m. not used. The other, the rest.

*Chaeronēa*, *ae*, f. Chaeronea, a town in Boeotia, the birth-place of Plutarch, (232).

*Chersonēsus*, *i*, f. The Chersonesus, a peninsula in Thracia, west of the Hellespont.

*Christiānus*, *a*, *um*. Christian, *often used substantively*.

*Cicātrix*, *īcis*, f. Scar.

*Cicĕro*, *ŏnis*, m. Cicero, the celebrated Roman orator, (207).

*Cincinnātus*, *i*, m. Cincinnatus, a

renowned Roman citizen and dictator, (71).

*Cineas, ae,* m. A friend and favorite minister of Pyrrhus.

*Cingo, ĕre, cinxi, cinctum.* To surround, encompass; crown; invest.

*Cinna, ae,* m. Cinna, a surname among the Romans. *Lucius Cornelius Cinna,* confederate of Marius in the civil war, (203).

*Circa,* prep. with acc. About, around, among.

*Circĭter,* prep. with acc. About, near.

*Circum* = circa.

*Circum-do, dăre, dĕdi, dătum.* To place around, surround, invest.

*Circum-eo, ĭre, ĭvi* or *ii, ĭtum.* To go around, surround, encompass, 295.

*Circumspicio, ĕre, spexi, spectum.* (circum, specio). To look round, look for, seek.

*Circum-venio, ĭre, vēni, ventum.* Tu come around, encompass, surround, circumvent, deceive.

*Cis,* prep. with acc. On this side of, within.

*Cito, āre, āvi, ātum.* To excite, urge, hasten; *citāto equo,* at full gallop *or* speed.

*Cito, citius, citissĭme,* adv. (citus). Soon, quickly.

*Citra,* adv., and prep. with acc. On this side.

*Citus, a, um.* Quick, swift, rapid.

*Civĭlis, e,* (civis). Civil, domestic.

*Civilĭtas, ātis,* f. (civĭlis). Civility, politeness.

*Civis, is,* m. and f. Citizen.

*Civĭtas, ātis,* f. (civis). City, state, citizenship.

*Clades, is,* f. Loss, slaughter, destruction, defeat.

*Clam,* adv., and prep. with acc. *or* abl. Secretly, without the knowledge of.

*Clarus, a, um.* Splendid, renowned, illustrious, clear.

*Classiarius, ii,* m. (classis). A marine, *pl.* naval forces.

*Classis, is,* f. A fleet.

*Claudius, ii,* m. The fourth Roman emperor, (41). *Appius Claudius,* one of the decemviri, (26).

*Claudo, claudĕre, clausi, clausum.* To close, shut.

*Claudus, a, um.* Lame.

*Clemens, entis.* Mild, gentle, clement.

*Clementia, ae,* f. (clemens). Mildness, clemency.

*Cleopatra, ae,* f. Cleopatra, queen of Egypt, (211). Another of the same name was the daughter of Philip of Macedon, (234).

*Clipeus,* or *clypeus, i,* m. Shield.

*Cloaca, ae,* f. Sewer, drain.

*Cnacus,* or *Cneus, i,* m. Cnaeus, a Roman name; as *Cnaeus Pompeius.*

*Coarguo, ĕre, coargui,* (cum, arguo). To arraign, accuse, indict; convict.

*Cocles, ĭtis,* m. Cocles, a Roman surname. *Horatius Cocles,* a Roman, distinguished in the war with Porsĕna, (171).

*Coelum, i,* n. The heavens, sky, weather.

*Coena, ae,* f. Principal meal of the Romans, supper, dinner.

*Coeo, ĭre, ĭvi* or *ii, ĭtum,* (cum, eo) To collect, assemble. 295.

*Coepi, isi, it, def.* To begin. 297.

*Coerceo, ercēre, ercui, ercitum,* (cum, arceo). To check, confine, restrain.

*Cogito, āre, āvi, ātum.* To think, ponder.

*Cognātus, a, um.* Related, *subs.* a relative.

*Cognitus, a, um,* part. (cognosco). Ascertained, known.

*Cognōmen, inis,* n. (cum, nomen *or* gnomen). Surname.

*Cognomino, āre, āvi, ātum,* (cognōmen). To surname, call, name.

*Cognosco, ĕre, nōvi, nitum,* (cum, nosco *or* gnosco). To ascertain, learn, recognize.

*Cogo, ĕre, coēgi, coactum.* To collect, force, compel.

*Cohibeo, ĕre, ui, itum,* (cum, habeo). To hold, check, confine.

*Cohors, cohortis,* f. Cohort, tenth part of a legion.

*Collatīnus, i,* m. Collatinus, surname of Tarquinius, the colleague of Brutus in the consulship, (169).

*Collēga, ae,* m. Colleague.

*Colligo, ĕre, lēgi, lectum,* (cum, lego). To collect, bring together.

*Collŏco, āre, āvi, ātum,* (cum, loco). To place, set, erect; to give in marriage.

*Colloquium, ii,* n. (collŏquor). Conversation, interview.

*Collŏquor, lŏqui, locūtus sum,* dep. (cum, loquor). To converse, talk with.

*Collum, i,* n. Neck.

*Colo, ĕre, colui, cultum.* To cultivate; honor, worship.

*Color, ōris,* m. Color, complexion.

*Combūro, ĕre, bussi, bustum,* (cum, buro = uro, *to burn*). To burn, consume.

*Comes, itis,* m. and f. Companion.

*Comissatio, ōnis,* f. Revelling.

*Commeātus, us,* m. Supplies.

*Commemŏro, āre, āvi, ātum,* (cum, memŏro). To recall, remember, commemorate, mention.

*Commentor, āri, ātus sum,* dep. To meditate, muse upon, consider, think, devise, invent.

*Commigro, āre, āvi, ātum,* (cum, migro). To migrate.

*Comminuo, ĕre, minui, minūtum,* (cum, minuo). To dash in pieces, crush; lessen; weaken.

*Committo, ĕre, misi, missum,* (cum, mitto). To bring together, unite, intrust, commit; *pugnam committĕre,* to engage in battle.

*Commŏdum, i,* n. Advantage, benefit.

*Commŏdus, a, um,* (cum, modus). Suitable, fit, proper, convenient.

*Commŏnefacio, ĕre, fēci, factum,* (cum, moneo, facio). To put in mind, remind, impress earnestly.

*Commŏror, āri, ātus sum,* (cum, moror). To tarry, delay.

*Commoveo, ĕre, mōvi, mōtum,* (cum, moveo). To move, excite.

*Commūnis, e.* Common.

*Communiter,* adv. (commūnis). In common, conjointly.

*Commutatio, ōnis,* f. Change.

*Compăro, āre, āvi, ātum,* (cum, paro). To prepare, make, procure, compare.

*Compello, āre, āvi, ātum,* (cum, pello). To address, call.

*Compello, ĕre, pŭli, pulsum,* (cum,

pello). To thrust together, to force, compel, impel.

*Compensatio, ōnis, f.* Compensation, exchange, barter.

*Comperio, īre, pĕri, pertum.* To find, find out.

*Compes, ĕdis, f.* (cum, pes). Fetter, chain.

*Compesco, ĕre, cui.* To confine, check.

*Complector, ti, plexus sum,* (cum, plector). To embrace, encompass.

*Compleo, ēre, ēvi, ētum,* (cum, pleo). To fill, complete.

*Complūres, a.* More than one; several, very many.

*Compōno, ĕre, posui, posĭtum,* (cum, pono). To settle, adjust, adapt, compose.

*Comporto, āre, āvi, ātum,* (cum, porto). To carry, bear, collect.

*Compos, ōtis,* (cum, potis). Having the mastery or control over anything; sharing in, partaking of.

*Comprehendo, ĕre, di, sum,* (cum, prehendo). To seize, arrest, comprehend.

*Concēdo, ĕre, cessi, cessum,* (cum, cedo). To concede, grant; to depart, withdraw; *pass. impers.,* it is conceded.

*Concĭdo, ĕre, cĭdi,* (cum, cado). To fall, perish.

*Concilio, āre, āvi, ātum,* (concilium). To unite, conciliate, procure, win.

*Concilium, ii, n.* Council, meeting.

*Concio, ōnis, f.* Public assembly.

*Concĭto, āre, āvi, ātum,* (cum, cito). To raise; excite, excite rebellion.

*Concordia, ae, f.* (concors, *harmonious*). Concord, harmony.

*Corcurro, ĕre, curri (cucurri), cur-*

sum, (cum, curro). To meet, assemble; engage, fight; rush to.

*Conditio, ōnis, f.* (condo). Condition, terms.

*Condo, ĕre, dĭdi, dĭtum,* (cum, do). To found; conceal, hide; place, bury.

*Condūco, ĕre, duxi, ductum,* (cum, duco). To conduct, collect; hire, contract for.

*Confĕro, conferre, contŭli, collātum,* (cum, fero). To collect, confer, compare; engage battle; *se conferre,* to betake one's self.

*Confestim, adv.* Immediately.

*Conficio, ĕre, fēci, fectum,* (cum, facio). To finish, accomplish, make, produce, wear out.

*Confīdo, ĕre, fisus sum,* (cum, fido). To trust, confide in.

*Confīgo, ĕre, fixi, fixum,* (cum, figo.) To transfix, fasten together.

*Confingo, ĕre, finxi, fictum,* (cum, fingo). To form, feign, pretend.

*Confirmo, āre, āvi, ātum,* (cum, firmo). To make firm, strengthen; encourage; corroborate.

*Confīsus, a, um, part.* (confīdo). Trusting, relying upon.

*Conflīgo, ĕre, flixi, flictum,* (cum, fligo). To engage, fight.

*Confodio, ĕre, fōdi, fossum,* (cum, fodio). To pierce, wound.

*Confugio, ĕre, fūgi, fugĭtum,* (cum, fugio). To flee for refuge.

*Congredior, grĕdi, gressus sum, dep.* (cum, gradior). To encounter, fight.

*Congrĕgo, āre, āvi, ātum,* (cum, grego). To collect, congregate.

*Congressio, ōnis, f.* (congredior). Engagement, battle.

*Conjicio, ĕre, jĕci, jectum,* (cum, jacio). To discharge, hurl, throw, drive.

*Conjungo, ĕre, junxi, junctum,* (cum, jungo). To join, combine.

*Conjuratio, ōnis,* f. (conjūro). Conspiracy.'

*Conjurātus, a, um,* part. (conjūro). Having conspired.

*Conjūro, āre, āvi, ātum,* (cum, juro) To conspire.

*Conjux, ūgis,* m. and f. (conjungo). Husband, wife.

*Conon, ōnis,* m. Conon, a celebrated Athenian general, (39, 111).

*Conor, āri, ātus sum,* dep. To endeavor, attempt.

*Conscendo, ĕre, scendi, scensum,* (cum, scando). To ascend, embark.

*Conscius, a, um.* Privy to; conscious of; *subs.* accomplice, confidant.

*Conscrībo, ĕre, scripsi, scriptum* (cum, scribo). To summon; to enrol, arrange, order; compose.

*Conscriptus, a, um,* part. (conscrībo). Enrolled, assembled. *Patres conscripti,* conscript fathers, i. c. senators.

*Consĕcro, āre, āvi, ātum* (cum, sacro). To consecrate.

*Consector, āri, ātus sum,* dep. (cum, sector). To follow, pursue.

*Consenesco, ĕre, senui* (cum, senesco). To grow old.

*Consĕquor, sĕqui, secūtus sum,* (cum, sequor). To succeed, follow, pursue; secure, obtain.

*Consĕro, ĕre, ui, tum,* (cum, scro). To join together; *manum* or *pug-*

*nam conserĕre,* to join battle, engage in battle.

*Conservo, āre, āvi, ātum,* (cum, servo). To preserve, watch over, rescue.

*Considĕro, āre, āvi, ātum.* To inspect, examine.

*Consīdo, ĕre, sēdi, sessum,* (cum, sido). To encamp, settle.

*Consilium, ii,* n. Counsel, advice, wisdom, intention, design, council.

*Consisto, ĕre, stĭti, stĭtum,* (cum, sisto). To place or station one's self, to stand.

*Consōlor, āri, ātus sum,* dep. (cum, solor). To comfort, console.

*Conspectus, us,* m. (conspicio). Sight, presence.

*Conspicio, ĕre, spexi, spectum,* (cum, specio). To see, observe.

*Conspĭcor, āri, ātus sum,* dep. (conspicio). To behold, see.

*Conspiratio, ōnis,* f. (conspīro). Union, conspiracy.

*Constanter, ius, issĭme,* adv. (consto). Consistently.

*Constantia, ae,* f. (consto). Constancy, firmness.

*Constat,* impers.(consto). It is known, is an admitted fact.

*Constĭtuo, ĕre, ui, ūtum,* (cum, statuo). To constitute; build, erect; station, place; appoint, arrange, manage.

*Consto, āre, stĭti, stātum,* (cum, sto). To stand together, halt.

*Consuesco, ĕre, ēvi, ētum,* (cum, suesco). To be accustomed.

*Consuetūdo, ĭnis,* f. (cor.suesco). Custom, usage, habit.

*Consul, ŭlis,* m. (consŭlo). Consul, *Roman chief magistrate.*

*Consulāris, e.*     Consular; *subs.* one who has been consul, one of consular rank.

*Consulātus, us,* m. (consul).     Consulship.

*Consŭlo, ĕre, sului, sultum.*     To consult, consider; *with dat.* to consult for one's good.

*Consummo, āre, āvi, ātum.*     To finish, accomplish, complete.

*Consŭmo, ĕre, sumpsi, sumptum,* (cum, sumo).     To consume, wear out, waste, use, employ.

*Contĕgo, ĕre, texi, tectum,* (cum, tego).     To cover.

*Contemno, ĕre, tempsi, temptum,* (cum, temno).     To contemn, despise, disregard.

*Contemptus, us,* m. (contemno).     Contempt, scorn, disregard.

*Contendo, ĕre, tendi, tentum,* (cum, tendo).     To contend, strive, attempt, labor; betake one's self, go.

*Contentio, ōnis,* f. (contendo).     Effort, contest, struggle, exertion.

*Contentus, a, um.*     Content, contented.

*Confĭnens, entis,* (contineo).     Adjoining, continuous; *subs.* f. continent.

*Continentia, ae,* f. (contineo).     Forbearance, self-control.

*Contineo, ĕre, tinui, tentum,* (cum, teneo).     To hold, keep, check.

*Continuo, āre, āvi, ātum,* (continuus).     To connect, unite, continue.

*Contra,* adv., and prep. with acc.     Against, opposite to, contrary to; on the contrary.

*Contra-dico, ĕre, dixi, dictum.*     To contradict, object to.

*Contrăho, ĕre, traxi, tractum,* (cum, traho).     To collect, incur, contract.

*Contrarius, a, um,* (contra).     Contrary to, opposite.

*Contrucĭdo, āre, āvi, ātum,* (cum, trucido).     To slay, kill, mangle.

*Contŭeor, tuēri, tuĭtus sum,* dep. (cum, tueor).     To survey, look upon, behold; consider, ponder.

*Convalesco, ĕre, lui,* (cum, valesco).     To gain strength, recover.

*Conveniens, entis,* (convenio).     Becoming, fit, proper.

*Convenienter, ius, issĭme,* adv. (convenio).     Fitly, suitably, agreeably, consistently.

*Convenio, ĭre, vēni, ventum,* (cum, venio).     To convene, assemble, meet, agree, harmonize, befit.

*Converto, ĕre, verti, versum,* (cum, verto).     To turn, change, alter, convert.

*Convinco, ĕre, vici, victum,* (cum, vinco).     To conquer, convict.

*Convivium, ii,* n.     Feast, banquet.

*Convŏco, āre, āvi, ātum,* (cum, voco).     To assemble, call together.

*Copia, ae,* f.     Abundance, supply, ability, power; *pl.* forces, stores, supplies.

*Coram,* adv., and prep. with abl.     In the presence of, before.

*Corinthus, i,* f.     Corinth, a city of Achaia, (162).

*Corinthius, a, um,* (Corinthus).     Corinthian, subs. *Corinthius, ii,* m. a Corinthian, (45).

*Coriolānus, i,* m.     Coriolanus, a surname given to *Caius Marcius,* derived from *Coriŏli,* the name of a town which he had taken in war, (174).

H

*Coriŏli, ŏrum,* m. pl.  Coriŏii, a town in Latium, (174).

*Cornelia, ae,* f.  Cornelia, the mother of the Gracchi, (131).

*Cornelius, ii,* m.  Cornelius, the name of a distinguished Roman gens, including the *Scipios ;* as, *Publius Cornelius Scipio,* (190, 194).

*Cornelius, a, um.*  Belonging to the Cornelian family, (120).

*Cornu, us,* n.  Horn, wing of an army.

*Corōna, ae,* f.  Garland, crown.

*Corpus, ŏris,* n.  Body, community.

*Corrĭgo, ĕre, rexi, rectum,* (cum, rego).  To reform, correct.

*Corripio, ĕre, ripui, reptum,* (cum, rapio).  To seize, lay hold of.

*Corrumpo, ĕre, rūpi, ruptum,* (cum, rumpo).  To corrupt, bribe, seduce.

*Crassus, i,* m.  Crassus, a Roman name, (93).  *Marcus Licinius Crassus,* a Roman general, (204).

*Creber, bra, brum.*  Frequent, numerous.

*Credo, ĕre, credĭdi, credĭtum.*  To trust, believe.

*Cremĕra, ae,* f.  The Cremera, a river of Etruria, in Italy, (175).

*Creo, āre, āvi, ātum.*  To appoint, elect, make.

*Cresco, ĕre, crēvi, crētum.*  To grow, increase.

*Crimen, ĭnis,* n.  Crime, accusation.

*Crimĭnor, āri, ātus sum,* dep. (crimen).  To accuse.

*Crinis, is,* m.  Hair.

*Critias, ae,* m.  Critias, one of the thirty tyrants at Athens, (228).

*Crixus, i,* m.  Crixus, a leader in the war of the gladiators, (204).

*Crucio, āre, āvi, ātum,* (crux).  To pain, afflict, torture.

*Crudēlis, e.*  Cruel.

*Crudēlĭtas, ātis,* f. (crudēlis).  Cruelty.

*Crudēlĭter, ius, issĭme,* adv. (crudēlis).  Cruelly.

*Cubĭtum, i,* n.  The elbow, a cubit.

*Culpa, ae,* f.  Fault, blame.

*Cultūra, ae,* f. (colo).  Agriculture, cultivation.

*Cultus, us,* m.  Culture, necessaries, as food, clothing, etc.

*Cum,* prep. with abl.  With.

*Cum,* conj. = quum.

*Cumae, ārum,* f.  Cumae, an ancient city and colony in Campania, on the sea-coast, renowned for its Sibyl, (49, 7).

*Cunctatio, ōnis,* f. (cunctor).  Delay.

*Cunctor, āri, ātus sum.*  To delay, hesitate.

*Cunctus, a, um.*  All, all together, entire.

*Cupĭde, ius, issĭme,* adv. (cupĭdus).  Eagerly.

*Cupidĭtas, ātis,* f. (cupĭdus).  Desire, wish.

*Cupĭdus, a, um,* (cupio).  Desirous, having desires, avaricious, covetous, fond of.

*Cupio, ĕre, īvi* or *ii, ītum.*  To desire.

*Cur,* adv.  Why, wherefore.

*Cura, ae,* f.  Care, management, anxiety.

*Cures, ium,* f. pl.  Cures, the ancient capital of the Sabines, (159).

*Curia, ae,* f.  Senate-house ; ward.

*Curiatii, ŏrum,* m. pl.  The Curiatii,

three brothers who were selected from the Alban army to engage in combat with the three Horatii, also brothers, from the Romans, (160). See note on "*Horatiôrum et Curiatiôrum*," (160).

*Curius, ii,* m. Curius, a Roman name, (27).

*Curo, âre, âvi, âtum.* To care for, take care of.

*Curro, êre, cucurri, cursum.* To run.

*Currus, us,* m. (curro). Chariot.

*Cursor, ôris,* m. Cursor, surname of *Lucius Papirius,* dictator in the Samnite war, (178).

*Cursus, us,* m. (curro). Course.

*Custodia, ae,* f. Care, charge of, custody, confinement.

*Custodio, ire, ivi* or *ii, itum,* (custos). To guard, preserve, watch.

*Custos, ôdis,* m. and f. Guard, keeper.

*Cynicus, i,* m. A Cynic philosopher, a Cynic.

*Cynoscephälae, ârum,* f. pl. Cynoscephalae, "Dogs' Heads," two hills in Thessaly, (197).

*Cyprus, i,* f. Cyprus, an island in the Mediterranean sea, near Asia Minor, (27, 11).

*Cyrus, i,* m. The name of two eminent Persian princes; *Cyrus, the Great,* the founder of the Persian empire, (13), and *Cyrus, the son of Darius,* (225).

### D.

*Damnatio, ônis,* f. Condemnation.

*Damno, âre, âvi, âtum,* (damnum). To condemn; *capitis damnâre,* to condemn to death.

*Damnum, i,* n. Loss, damage.

*Darius, ii,* m. Darius, a celebrated king of Persia, (215).

*Datis, is,* m. Datis, one of the generals of Darius, (215).

*De,* prep. with abl. From, of, concerning, on the subject of, over.

*Debeo, êre, ui, itum.* To owe, ought.

*Debeor, êri, debitus sum,* dep. To be due, belong.

*Debilito, âre, âvi, âtum.* To weaken, disable.

*De-cêdo, êre, cessi, cessum.* To depart, withdraw, die.

*Decem,* indecl. Ten.

*Decemplex, icis,* (decem, plico, *to fold*). Tenfold.

*Decem-vir, viri,* m. A decemvir.

*De-cerno, êre, crêvi, crêtum.* To decide; contend, fight; decree, intrust by decree.

*Decet, decuit,* impers. It is seemly, becoming, becomes.

*Decido, êre, cidi, cisum,* (de, caedo). To cut off; decide, determine.

*Decimus, a, um,* (decem). Tenth.

*Decipio, êre, cêpi, ceptum,* (de, capio). To deceive.

*De-clâro, âre, âvi, âtum.* To make clear, manifest; declare, pronounce.

*Decrêtum, i,* n. (decerno). Decree.

*Decus, ôris,* n. Ornament, honor.

*De-dêcus, ôris,* n. Disgrace.

*Dedicatio, ônis,* f. (dedico). Dedication.

*Dedico, âre, âvi, âtum,* (de, dico). To dedicate.

*Deditio, ônis,* f. (dedo). Surrender.

*De-do, êre, didi, ditum.* To surrender; devote one's self to, give one's self up to.

*De-dūco, ěre, duxi, ductum.* To bring down, conduct; remove; lead.

*De-fatigo, āre, āvi, ātum.* To weary, fatigue.

*Defectio, ōnis,* f. (deficio). Failure, eclipse, defection.

*De-fendo, ěre, fendi, fensum.* To defend, ward off.

*De-fěro, ferre, tŭli, lātum.* To offer, exhibit, bestow, present: carry *or* bear away.

*Deficio, ěre, fēci, fectum,* (de, facio). To fail, spend itself; be eclipsed; desert, revolt.

*De-flāgro, āre, āvi, ātum.* To burn, burn down, consume, destroy.

*Deformis, e,* (de, forma). Deformed, ugly.

*De-fungor, gi, functus sum.* To discharge, execute; die.

*De-glŭbo, ěre, —, gluptum.* To flay, to skin.

*Dein* or *deinde,* adv. Then, afterwards.

*Deiotārus, i,* m. Deiotarus, a king of Galatia, (206).

*Dejicio, ěre, jēci, jectum,* (de, jacio) To throw down, overthrow, slay.

*De-lecto, āre, āvi, ātum.* To allure; to delight, please.

*Delectus, a, um,* (deligo). Chosen.

*Deleo, ěre, ēvi, ētum.* To destroy, efface, put an end to.

*De-liběro, āre, āvi, ātum.* To deliberate.

*Deliciae, ārum,* f. pl. Delights, pleasures; delight, darling, beloved.

*Delĭgo, ěre, legi, lectum,* (de, lego). To choose, select; love.

*Delirium, ii,* n. Madness, dotage, instances of it.

*Delos* or *Delus, i,* f. Delos, a small island in the Aegean sea, (27, 10).

*Delphi, ōrum,* m. pl. Delphi, a town of Phocis, celebrated for the temple and oracle of Apollo, (217).

*Demarātus, i,* m. Demaratus, the father of Tarquinius Priscus, (182).

*De-mergo, ěre, mersi, mersum.* To plunge in, bury in, sink.

*De-mitto, ěre, mǐsi, missum.* To let down, drop, send away, send.

*Democrĭtus, i,* m. Democritus, a celebrated Grecian philosopher, (91).

*Demorior, mŏri, mortuus sum,* (de, morior). To die.

*Demosthěnes, is,* m. Demosthenes, the most celebrated of the Grecian orators, (92, 7).

*Demum,* adv. At length, finally.

*Denarius, ii,* m. Denarius, a Roman silver coin, worth about sixteen cents.

*Deni, ae, a.* Ten by ten, ten at a time.

*Denĭque,* adv. Finally.

*Dens, dentis,* m. A tooth.

*De-nūdo, āre, āvi, ātum.* To make naked, strip.

*Denuntiatio, ōnis,* f. (denuntio). Denunciation, warning.

*De-nuntio, āre, āvi, ātum.* To declare, denounce.

*Denuo,* adv. Again, afresh.

*De-pello, ěre, pŭli, pulsum.* To drive away, expel.

*De-pōno, ěre, posui, posĭtum.* To

lay down *or* aside, deposit, depose.

*De-popŭlor, ări, ătus sum.* To pillage, depopulate.

*De-porto, āre, āvi, ātum.* To carry off *or* away.

*Depraedor, āri, ātus sam,* (de, praedor). To ravage, plunder.

*Deprehendo, ĕre, di, sum,* (de, prehendo). To seize, catch, detect, surprise.

*De-pugno, āre, āvi, ātum.* To fight.

*Derelictio, ōnis, f.* (de, relinquo). Neglect, disregard.

*De-scrībo, ĕre, scripsi, scriptum.* To describe; impose; assess; designate; divide.

*Desĕro, ĕre, serui, sertum,* (de, sero). To abandon, desert.

*De-sidĕro, āre, āvi, ātum.* To long for, wish, desire earnestly.

*Desilio, īre, silui, sultum,* (de, salio). To alight, dismount.

*Desīno, ĕre, sivi or sii, situm,* (de, sino). To cease, desist.

*Desipio, ĕre,* (de, sapio). To be void of understanding, be foolish, be delirious.

*De-sisto, ĕre, stĭti, stĭtum.* To desist, leave off.

*Dŭsperatio, ōnis, f.* (despēro). Despair, desperation.

*De-spēro, āre, āvi, ātum.* To despair.

*Despicio, ĕre, spexi, spectum,* (de, specio). To despise, disregard.

*Destĭno, āre, āvi, ātum.* To destine, appoint, design.

*De-sum, esse, fui.* To fail, be wanting.

*De-terreo, ĕre, ui, ĭtum.* To deter.

*Detineo, ĕre, tenui, tentum,* (de, teneo). To detain, hinder.

*Detrăho, ĕre, traxi, tractum,* (de, traho). To draw *or* take away *or* from, detract.

*Detrimentum, i, n.* Loss, damage, detriment, harm.

*Deus, i, m.* God, deity. See 51, 5.

*De-vasto, āre, —, ātum.* To devastate, pillage.

*De-venio, īre, vēni, ventum.* To come down, arrive, reach.

*De-vinco, ĕre, vici, victum.* To conquer.

*Dexter, tra, trum.* Right, on the right hand.

*Dextra, ae, f.* The right hand.

*Di.* See *Dis.*

*Diadēma, ătis, n.* Diadem.

*Diagŏras, ae, m.* Diagoras, a Rhodian athlete, who distinguished himself in the Olympic games, (143).

*Diăna, ae, f.* The goddess Diana, the daughter of Jupiter and Latona, and sister of Apollo, (97).

*Dico, ĕre, dixi, dictum.* To say, call.

*Dictător, ōris, m.* (dico). Dictator, *an officer appointed by the Romans in times of great danger.*

*Dido, us,* or *ōnis, f.* Dido, the foundress of Carthage, daughter of Belus, (44, III.)

*Dies, ēi, m. and f.* Day.

*Diffĭcĭle, ius, līme,* adv. (difficĭlis), With difficulty.

*Diffĭcĭlis, e,* (dis, facĭlis). Difficult. 163, 2.

*Digĭtus, i, m.* Finger.

*Dignĭtas, ātis, f.* (dignus). Dignity, rank, office.

*Dignor, ări, ătus sum,* (dignus). To deem worthy, deign.

*Dignus, a um.* Worthy.

Di-lābor, lăbi, lapsus sum, dep. To fall asunder, go to pieces; flee; scatter, disperse.

\ Dilātio, ōnis, f. Delay, delaying.

; Dilĭgens, entis, (dilĭgo). Fond of, mindful, diligent, observant.

Dilĭgenter, ius, issĭme, adv. (dilĭgens). Carefully, diligently, earnestly.

Diligentia, ae, f. (dilĭgens). Diligence.

Dilĭgo, ĕre, lexi, lectum, (dis, lego). To choose, love.

Dimĭco, āre, āvi, ātum, (dis, di, mico). To encounter, fight.

Di-mitto, ĕre, mīsi, missum. To dismiss, let go.

Diogĕnes, is, m. Diogenes, the noted Cynic philosopher of Greece, (135).

Dion, ōnis, m. Dion, brother-in-law of the tyrant Dionysius of Syracuse, (31).

Dionysius, ii, m. Dionysius, tyrant of Syracuse, (26).

Diripio, ĕre, ripui, reptum, (dis, di, rapio). To lay waste, pillage.

Diruo, ĕre, dirui, dirŭtum, (dis, di, ruo). To destroy, demolish.

Dis, or di, insep. prep. Asunder, not.

Dis-cēdo, ĕre, cessi, cessum. To depart, retire from.

Disceptatio, ōnis, f. Debate, quarrel.

Disciplīna, ae, f. Discipline, instruction.

Discipŭlus, i, m. (disco). A learner, scholar, disciple.

Disco, ĕre, didĭci. To learn.

Discordia, ae, f. Strife, discord.

Discordo, āre, āvi, ātum, (discors, discordant). To differ, be at variance, disagree.

Discrīmen, ĭnis, n. Danger, crisis.

Dis-curro, ĕre, curri, cursum. To run different ways, run about, separate.

Dispergo, ĕre, spersi, spersum, (dis, di, spargo). To scatter, disperse.

Displiceo, ĕre, plicui, plicĭtum, (dis, placeo). To displease.

Dis-pŭto, āre, āvi, ātum. To compute, estimate; examine, investigate, discuss.

Dis-sĕro, ĕre, serŭi, sertum. To examine, argue, discuss.

Dissidium, ii, n. Dissension.

Dis-simĭlis, e. Unlike, dissimilar.

Dissimŭlo, āre, āvi, ātum. To dissemble, conceal, omit.

Dis-sĭpo, āre, āvi, ātum. To dissipate, scatter.

Dis-solvo, ĕre, solvi, solūtum. To destroy, abolish, dissolve.

Dis-tribuo, ĕre, tribui, tribūtum. To distribute.

Districtus, a, um, (distringo). Busy, occupied with.

Distringo, ĕre, strinxi, strictum, (di, stringo). To occupy, engage attention.

Ditio, ōnis, f. Rule, sway.

Diu, diutius, diutissĭme, adv. Long, for a long time.

Diutĭnus, a, um, (diu). Of long duration, lasting.

`Diuturnĭtas, ātis, f. (diuturnus). Long time.

Diversus, a, um. Diverse, unlike, opposite.

Dives, ĭtis. Rich.

Divĭco, ōnis, m. Divico, a distinguished Helvetian general, (85, 5).

Divĭdo, ĕre, divĭsi, divĭsum. To divide, allot.

Divīnus, a, um. Divine.

*Divitiae, ārum, f.* (dives). Riches, wealth.

*Divus, a, um.* Divine; *subs.* god, goddess.

*Do, dăre, dedi, datum.* To give, grant, impute, allow.

*Doceo, ēre, ui, tum.* To teach.

*Doctrīna, ae, f.* Instruction, learning, erudition, doctrine.

*Doctus, a, um,* (doceo). Learned, skilled.

*Documentum, i, n.* Lesson, proof, specimen, mark.

*Dolabella, ae, m.* Dolabella, a Roman name. *Publius Cornelius Dolabella,* son-in-law of Cicero, (122).

*Doleo, ēre, ui, ĭtum.* To grieve.

*Dolor, ōris, m.* (doleo). Pain, grief.

*Dolus, i, m.* Artifice, deceit.

*Domesticus, a, um,* (domus). Domestic, private, personal.

*Domicilium, ii, n.* (domus). Habitation, abode.

*Dominatio, ōnis.* Rule, tyranny.

*Dominātus, us, m.* Rule, sovereignty.

*Domĭnus, i, m.* Master, owner.

*Domo, āre, ui, ĭtum.* To subdue.

*Domus, us* or *i, f.* House, home; *domi,* at home.

*Donec, conj.* Until.

*Dono, āre, āvi, ātum,* (donum). To give, present with.

*Donum, i, n.* (do). Present, gift.

*Dormio, īre, īvi* or *ii, ĭtum.* To sleep, slumber, rest.

*Dos, dotis, f.* Gift, dowry.

*Drusus, i, m.* Drusus, son of the Emperor Tiberius, (146).

*Dubitatio, ōnis, f.* (dubĭto). Doubt, hesitation.

*Dubĭto, āre, āvi, ātum.* To doubt, hesitate.

*Dubius, a, um.* Doubtful; *neut. of ten subs.* doubt.

*Ducenti, ae, a.* Two hundred.

*Duco, ēre, duxi, ductum.* To lead, conduct; *with uxōrem,* to marry.

*Duillius, ii, m.* Duillius, a Roman name. *Caius Duillius,* a Roman commander and consul in the first Punic war, (185).

*Dulcis, e.* Sweet, pleasant, agreeable.

*Dum, conj.* While, until, provided.

*Dum-mŏdo, conj.* So long as, provided that.

*Duo, ae, o.* Two, both. 175.

*Duodĕcim, indec.* (duo, decem). Twelve.

*Duodecĭmus, a, um,* (duodĕcim). Twelfth.

*Duodequadragesĭmus, a, um.* Thirty-eighth.

*Duo-de-viginti, indec.* Eighteen.

*Duplex, ĭcis.* Double.

*Duplĭco, āre, āvi, ātum,* (duplex). To double, increase.

*Duritia, ae, f.* (durus). Hardiness, austerity, rigid temperance, hardship.

*Durus, a, um.* Hard, harsh, rude.

*Dux, ducis, m.* and *f.* (duco). Leader, guide, general.

## E

*E* or *ex, prep. with abl.* From, out of, of.

*Ebriĕtas, ātis, f.* Drunkenness.

*E-disco, ēre, didĭci.* To learn by heart, commit to memory.

*E-do, edĕre, edĭdi, edĭtum.* To set forth, publish; do, perform, make, utter.

E-doceo, ěre, docui, doctum. To teach one thoroughly, inform, instruct.

E-dūco, ěre, duxi, ductum. To lead out or forth.

Effěro, āre, āvi, ātum. To enrage, madden, render unmanageable.

Effěro, ferre, extūli, elātum, (ex, fero). To bring forth, carry forth or out; elate.

Efficio, ěre, fēci, fectum, (ex, facio). To effect, occasion, accomplish, make, render.

Effluo, ěre, fluxi, fluxum, (ex, fluo). To flow out, pass away, disappear.

Effugio, ěre, fūgi, fugĭtum, (ex, fugio). To flee, escape from, escape.

Effundo, ěre, fūdi, fūsum, (ex, fundo). To pour out, pour; indulge in; squander, waste.

Egeo, egěre, egui. To need, to want, require, to be without.

Egeria, ae, f. Egeria, a prophetic nymph from whom Numa professed to receive instructions, (159).

Ego, mei, I. Egŏmet, I myself. 184, 6.

Egredior, egrĕdi, egressus sum, dep. (e, gradior). To go or come out, to go forth, to go, to run away.

Egregie, adv. (egregius). Excellently, remarkably.

Egregius, a, um. Excellent, distinguished.

Ejicio, ěre, ejēci, ejectum, (e, jacio). To throw or drive out, expel; reject.

E-labor, elābi, elapsus sum, dep. To slip away, get off, escape.

E-labōro, āre, āvi, ātum. To labor, exert one's self.

Elegantia, ae, f. Elegance, taste, propriety.

Elementa, ōrum, n. pl. The first principles, rudiments, elements.

Elephantus, i, m. Elephant.

Elĭgo, ěre, elēgi, electum, (e, lego). To choose, elect.

Elŏquens, entis, (elŏquor). Eloquent.

Eloquenter, ius, issĭme, adv. (elŏquens). Eloquently.

Eloquentia, ae, f. Eloquence.

E-lŏquor, lŏqui, locūtus sum, dep. To speak out, utter, declare, tell.

Emax, ācis, (emo). Eager to buy, fond of buying.

E-mergo, ěre, mersi, mersum. To emerge, come to light, rise in importance.

Eminentia, ae, f. Eminence, excellence.

Emineo, ěre, ui. To stand out, be prominent or conspicuous.

E-mitto, ěre, misi, missum. To send forth or away; let go.

Emo, ěre, emi, emptum. To buy, purchase.

Emolumentum, i, n. Effort, exertion; gain, profit, advantage.

Enim, conj. For, indeed.

E-niteo, ěre, nitui. To shine forth; be distinguished.

Ennius, ii, n. Ennius, a celebrated Roman poet, (120).

Eo, adv. Thither; therefore; eo usque, so far, to such an extent.

Eo, īre, īvi or ii, ĭtum. To go; walk, sail, ride, pass. 295.

Eŏdem, adv. (idem). To the same place.

Epaminondas, ae, m. Epaminondas, a celebrated Theban general, (92, 5).

*Ephesius, a, um.* Ephesian, relating to Ephesus, of Ephesus, born at Ephesus, (97).

*Epigramma, ătis,* n. Inscription, epigram. 58, 2.

*Epīrus, i,* f. Epirus, a province in the north of Greece, (180).

*Epistŭla, ae,* f. A letter, epistle.

*Epŭlae, ārum,* f. pl. Food, banquet, feast.

*Epŭlor, āri, ātus sum,* (epŭlae). To feast.

*Eques, ĭtis,* m. (equus). Horseman. *Pl.* cavalry.

*Equester, tris, tre,* (eques). Equestrian.

*Equĭdem,* conj. Indeed, truly, by all means.

*Equitātus, us,* m. Cavalry.

*Equus, i,* m. Horse: *ex equo,* from a horse, on horseback.

*Eretria, ae,* f. Eretria, an important city on the island of Euboea, (16).

*Erga,* prep. with acc. Towards.

*Ergo,* adv. Therefore ; *as subs. abl.* on account of, for, *with gen.*

*Erĭgo, ĕre, erexi, erectum,* (e, rego). To raise up, animate.

*Eripio, ĕre, eripui, ereptum,* (e, rapio). To snatch or take away.

*Error, ōris,* m. Error, deception.

*Erudio, ĭre, ĭvi or ii, ĭtum.* To instruct, refine, discipline.

*Erudītus, a, um,* part. (erudio). Learned, instructed in.

*E-rumpo, ĕre, rūpi, ruptum.* To break forth, rush forth.

*Eruo, ĕre, erui, erūtum,* (e, ruo). To root out, destroy.

*Esca, ae,* f. Food, bait.

*Et,* conj. And; *et—et,* both—and.

*Et-ĕnim,* conj. For, truly, because that, since.

*Etiam.* Also, even.

*Etiam-si.* Even if, although.

*Etiam-tum,* conj. Even then, till then, still.

*Etruria, ae,* f. Etruria, a country of Central Italy ; Tuscany, (190).

*Etruscus, i,* m. An Etruscan, inhabitant of Etruria, (171).

*Et-si.* Even if, although, though.

*Euboea, ae,* f. Euboea, an island in the Aegean sea, (84).    [(144).

*Euripīdes, is,* m. An Athenian poet,

*Euphrātes, is,* m. A river in Asia, (24).

*Eurōpa, ae,* f. The continent of Europe.

*Eurybiădes, is,* m. A king of Sparta, (219).

*E-vādo, ĕre, vāsi, vāsum.* To go out ; to turn out, become; escape ; evade.

*E-venio, ĭre, vēni, ventum.* To come forth, happen ; *evēnit, ut,* it chanced, that.

*E-verto, ĕre, verti, versum.* To pull down, overthrow.

*Evŏco, āre, avi, ātum,* (e, voco). To call forth, summon.

*Evŏlo, āre, avi, ātum,* (e, volo). To fly or flee away, hasten away.

*Ex,* prep. with abl. From. See *e* or *ex.*

*Ex-adversum* or *ex-adversus,* adv., and prep. with acc. Opposite, against.

*Ex-anĭmo, āre, āvi, ātum.* To deprive of life or spirit ; kill.

*Ex-ardesco, ĕre, arsi.* To kindle, be inflamed ; break out, *as war.*

*Ex-cēdo, ĕre, cessi, cessum.* To retire, withdraw.

*Ex-cello, ěre, cellůi, celsum.* To elevate; excel, be eminent.

*Excelsus, a, um,* (excello). Lofty.

*Excidium, ii,* n. Destruction, ruin.

*Excipio, ěre, cěpi, ceptum,* (ex, capio). To take out, except.

*Ex-cǐto, āre, āvi, ātum.* To excite, arouse, awaken, strengthen.

*Exclūdo, ěre, clūsi, clūsum,* (ex, claudo). To exclude, shut out, cut off.

*Ex-cogǐto, āre, āvi, ātum.* To devise, think out.

*Excutio, ěre, cussi, cussum,* (ex, quatio). To shake or throw off.

*Exemplum, i,* n. Example.

*Ex-eo, ǐre, ǐvi or ii, ǐtum.* To go from or forth.

*Exerceo, ěre, cui, cǐtum,* (ex, arceo). To exercise, practise.

*Exercǐtus, us,* m. (exerceo). Army, train.

*Ex-haurio, ǐre, hausi, haustum.* To exhaust, impoverish.

*Ex-horresco, ěre, horrui.* To dread, to tremble at.

*Exǐgo, ěre, ěgi, actum,* (ex, ago). To drive out, expel; finish, end; demand.

*Exiguus, a, um.* Small.

*Eximius, a, um.* Excellent, choice, remarkable.

*Exǐmo, ěre, ěmi, emptum,* (ex, emo). To take away or from; exempt; rescue.

*Existimātio, ōnis,* f. (existǐmo). An opinion, judgment, supposition; reputation.

*Existǐmo, āre, āvi, ātum,* (ex, aestǐmo). To judge, think.

*Exitium, ii,* n. (exeo). End, death, destruction.

*Ex-orior, orǐri, ortus sum,* dep., partly of 3d conj. To arise; be derived from. 288, 2.

*Ex-orno, āre, āvi, ātum.* To adorn, beautify, embellish, furnish, equip.

*Exōsus, a, um.* Hating, hated, odious.

*Expedio, ǐre, ǐvi or ii, ǐtum.* To release, extricate; also to be expedient, or profitable.

*Expeditio, ōnis,* f. (expedio). Expedition.

*Ex-pello, ěre, pǔli, pulsum.* To expel, drive away, banish.

*Ex-pěto, ěre, ǐvi or ii, ǐtum.* To seek, request.

*Ex-pleo, ěre, ěvi, ětum.* To fill make full; fulfil.

*Ex-plico, āre, āvi, ātum.* To unfold; adjust; settle.

*Explorātor, ōris,* m. Explorer, spy.

*Ex-pugno, āre, āvi, ātum.* To take, conquer, storm.

*Ex-scindo, ěre, scǐdi, scissum.* To destroy.

*Ex-sculpo, ěre, sculpsi, sculptum.* To erase.

*Exsecrabǐlis, e.* Detestable.

*Exsequiae, ārum,* f. pl. Funeral.

*Ex-sěquor, sěqui, secūtus sum.* To prosecute, accomplish, finish; perform.

*Exsilium, ii,* n. Banishment, exile.

*Exspectatio, ōnis,* f. (exspecto). Expectation, high hope.

*Ex-specto, āre, āvi, ātum.* To await, expect.

*Ex-stinguo, ěre, stinxi, stinctum.* To extinguish, destroy.

*Ex-struo, ěre, struxi, structum.* To build, construct.

*Exsul, ǔlis,* m. and f. An exile.

*Ex-templo,* adv. Immediately.

*Ex-torqueo, ēre, torsi, tortum.* To extort, obtain by force.

*Ex-trăho, ēre, traxi, tractum.* To extract, draw out, remove ; rescue.

## F

*Fabius, ii,* m. Fabius, the name of a distinguished Roman family. *Quintus Fabius Maxĭmus,* the celebrated Roman general who so successfully weakened Hannibal in the first Punic war, (175).

*Fabricius, ii,* m. Fabricius, a distinguished leader of the Romans in the war against Pyrrhus, (182).

*Fabŭla, ae,* f. Report, narrative, fable, story, drama.

*Facies, ēi,* f. A face, appearance.

*Facĭle, ius, līme,* adv. (facĭlis). Easily.

*Facĭlis, e,* (facio). Easy.

*Facĭnus, ŏris,* n. Deed, act ; wickedness, crime.

*Facio, ēre, feci, factum.* To do, act, make, compose.

*Factio, ōnis,* f. Faction, party.

*Facultas, ātis,* f. Capacity, ability, resource, opportunity ; *plur.* riches, property, resources.

*Fallo, ēre, fefelli, falsum.* To deceive, foil.

*Falsus, a, um.* False, spurious.

*Fama, ae,* f. Fame, report.

*Fames, is,* f. Hunger, famine.

*Familia, ae,* f. Retinue of slaves, a family.

*Familiarĭtas, ātis,* f. Friendship, intimacy.

*Famŭla, ae,* f. Female slave.

*Fannius, ii,* m. Fannius, a Roman name, (48).

*Fanum, i,* n. Temple.

*Fascis, is,* m. A bundle, parcel.

*Fastidio, īre, īvi or ii, ītum.* To loathe, despise, disdain.

*Fatālis, e,* (fatum). Fated, fatal.

*Fatīgo, āre, āvi, ātum.* To oppress, trouble, weary, importune.

*Fatum, i,* n. Fate, destiny, oracle.

*Fauce,* abl. f. ; plur. *fauces, faucium.* Throat, jaws.

*Faustŭlus, i,* m. Faustulus, the shepherd who brought up Romulus and Remus, (153).

*Faveo, ēre, favi, fautum.* To favor.

*Favor, ōris,* m. (faveo). Favor, kindness.

*Felicĭtas, ātis,* f. (felix). Felicity, success.

*Felicĭter, ius, issīme,* adv. (felix). Happily, prosperously.

*Felis, is,* f. Cat.

*Felix, īcis.* Happy.

*Femĭna, ae,* f. Woman, female.

*Femur, ŏris,* n. Thigh.

*Fera, ae,* f. Wild beast.

*Ferax, ăcis.* Fertile, fruitful, productive.

*Fere,* adv. Almost.

*Ferme,* adv. Almost.

*Ferio, īre.* To strike, beat.

*Fero, ferre, tuli, latum.* To bear, endure ; raise ; say, tell ; propose, as law. 292.

*Ferox, ōcis.* Bold, warlike, savage.

*Ferrum, i,* n. Iron, sword.

*Fertīlis, e.* Fertile, rich.

*Ferus, a, um.* Wild, rude, cruel ; *ferus* and *fera* (subs.), wild animal or beast.

*Fessus, a, um.* Wearied, exhausted.

*Festīno, āre, āvi, ātum.* To hasten.

*Festus, a, um.* Festal ; *festum* (subs.), a festival, feast.

*Fidēlis, e,* (fides). Faithful, trusty.

*Fides, ei,* f. Fidelity, allegiance; protection, confidence, assurance; *in fidem,* under protection.

*Fido, ĕre, fisus sum.* To trust, confide.

*Fiducia, ae,* f. Trust, confidence.

*Filia, ae,* f., dat. and abl. pl. *filiābus.* Daughter. 49, 4.

*Filius, ii,* m. Son.

*Fingo, ĕre, finxi, fictum.* To form, feign, represent.

*Finio, īre, īvi, ītum,* (finis). To finish, put an end to.

*Finis, is,* m. and f. Limit, end; *pl.* territory.

*Finitĭmus, a, um.* Neighboring; *subs.* a neighbor.

*Fio, fiĕri, factus sum,* pass. of *facio.* To be made; become, happen. 294.

*Firme,* adv. Firmly, resolutely.

*Firmĭtas, ātis,* f. (firmus). Firmness, strength.

*Firmus, a, um.* Strong, secure, firm.

*Flagitiōsus, a, um.* Infamous, abandoned.

*Flagitium, ii,* n. Disgrace, shame, base deed.

*Flagro, āre, āvi, ātum.* To burn, be carried on with zeal.

*Flaminius, ii,* m. Flaminius, a Roman consul, defeated by Hannibal at the Lake Trasimenus, (190).

*Flamma, ae,* f. Flame.

*Flecto, ĕre, flexi, flexum.* To bend, turn.

*Fletus, us,* m. Weeping, tears.

*Florens, entis,* (floreo). Blooming, youthful, excellent. *Florens aetas,* youth.

*Floresco, ĕre, florui,* (floreo). To bloom, flourish, prosper; excel.

*Flos, ōris,* m. Blossom, flower.

*Flumen, ĭnis,* n. Stream, river.

*Fluvius, ii,* m. River.

*Foederātus, a, um.* Confederate, allied.

*Foedus, ĕris,* n. League, alliance, treaty.

*Fons, ontis,* m. Spring, fountain.

*Forem, es,* etc.=*essem, es,* etc., Might be; *fore=futūrum esse.* See 297, III. 2.

*Formo, āre, āvi, ātum.* To form, fashion, adjust.

*Fors, fortis,* f. Chance; abl. *forte* as adv., by chance, perchance.

*Forsitan,* (fors, sit, an). Perhaps.

*Fortasse.* Perhaps.

*Forte.* See *fors.*

*Fortis, e.* Brave, valiant.

*Fortiter, ius, issĭme,* adv. (fortis). Bravely.

*Fortitūdo, ĭnis,* f. (fortis). Fortitude, bravery.

*Fortūna, ae,* f. Fortune.

*Forum, i,* n. Market-place, forum.

*Fossa, ae,* f. Ditch, trench.

*Frango, ĕre, fregi, fractum.* To break.

*Frater, tris,* m. Brother.

*Fraus, dis,* f. Fraud, deceit.

*Frequenter, ius, issĭme,* adv. Frequently, in great numbers.

*Fretus, a, um.* Trusting, relying upon.

*Fructus, us,* m. Fruit, produce.

*Frugalĭtas, ātis,* f. Frugality, integrity.

*Frumentum, i,* n. Corn, grain.

*Fruor, frui, fruĭtus* and *fructus sum,* dep. To enjoy.

*Frustra,* adv. In vain.

*Fuga, ae,* f. Flight.

*Fugio, ĕre, fugi, fugĭtum.* To fly, flee, avoid, shun.

*Fugo, āre, āvi, ātum.* To rout, put to flight.

*Fulgur, ŭris,* n. Lightning, thunderbolt.

*Fulguratio, ōnis,* f. Lightning.

*Fulmen, ĭnis,* n. Lightning, thunderbolt.

*Fundamentum, i,* n. Foundation.

*Fundĭtus,* adv. Utterly, entirely.

*Fundo, ĕre, fudi, fusum.* To pour out, shed, rout; also to make, cast.

*Funestus, a, um,* (funus). Deadly, destructive; mournful, sad.

*Fungor, fungi, functus sum,* dep. To discharge, perform, pay.

*Furcŭla, ae,* f. Fork. *Furcŭlae Caudīnae;* see *Caudīnus.*

*Furius, ii,* m. Furius, a Roman family name, as *Marcus Furius Camillus;* see Camillus.

*Furor, ōris,* m. Fury, madness.

*Furtum, i,* n. Theft.

*Futūrus, a, um,* part. (sum). Future.

## G.

*Galatia, ae,* f. Galatia, a country of Asia Minor, (206).

*Gallia, ae,* f. The ancient country of Gaul, (209).

*Gallĭcus, a, um,* (Gallia). Gallic.

*Gallīna, ae,* f. Hen.

*Gallus, i,* m. A cock.

*Gallus, i,* m. (Gallia). A Gaul, a native of Gaul, (39, III.).

*Gaudeo, ĕre, gavīsus sum.* To rejoice, take pleasure in. 271, 3.

*Gaudium, ii,* n. Joy, pleasure.

*Gemĭnus, a, um.* Twin, double.

*Gemma, ae,* f. Gem.

*Gener, ĕri,* m. Son-in-law.

*Genero, āre, āvi, ātum,* (genus). To beget, create, produce.

*Genĭtus, a, um,* part. (gigno). Born, produced.

*Gens, gentis,* f. Family, clan, tribe, nation, race. *Ubīnam gentium,* where in the world?

*Genus, ĕris,* n. Race, family, people, kind.

*Germania, ae,* f. Germany, (39, V.).

*Germānus, i,* m. (Germania). A German, (30).

*Gero, ĕre, gessi, gestum.* To bear, wear; carry on, perform; wage, as war.

*Gestio, ĭre, ĭvi or ii, ĭtum.* To desire, long for.

*Gigno, ĕre, genui, genĭtum.* To bring forth, beget, produce.

*Glaciālis, e.* Icy, freezing.

*Gladiātor, ōris,* m. Gladiator, a fighter at the public games.

*Gladiatorius, a, um,* (gladiator). Gladiatorial.

*Gladius, ii,* m. Sword.

*Glisco, ĕre.* To grow, spread; rise.

*Gloria, ae,* f. Glory.

*Glorior, āri, ātus sum,* dep. To boast, exult, glory.

*Gracchus, i,* m. Gracchus, a Roman name. *Sempronius Gracchus,* the Roman general defeated by Hannibal at the Trebia, (190). *Gracchi, ōrum,* m. pl. The Gracchi, members of the Gracchus family, but especially the two brothers, *Tiberius Cornelius Gracchus* and *Caius Cornelius Gracchus,* famous in the political history of Rome, (131).

*Gradus, us,* m. Step, position, stair.

*Graece,* adv. (Graecus). In the Greek language, in Greek.

*Graecia, ae,* f. Greece, (210).

*Graecus* or *Graius, a, um,* (Graecia). Grecian. Subs. *Graecus* or *Graius, i,* m. A Greek, (30, 8).

*Grammatica, ae,* f. Grammar.

*Grammaticus, a, um.* Of or belonging to grammar, grammatical.

*Grandis, e.* Large, great.

*Grando, inis,* f. Hail.

*Gratia, ae,* f. Favor, gratitude; *pl.* thanks; *gratiā,* abl. for the sake of.

*Gratiis* or *gratis,* adv. For nothing, without pay.

*Gratulatio, ōnis,* f. Gratulation, congratulation.

*Gratus, a, um.* Pleasing, acceptable; grateful.

*Gravis, e,* Heavy, severe.

*Gravitas, ātis,* f. (gravis). Weight; dignity, gravity.

*Graviter, ius, issime,* adv. (gravis). Heavily, severely.

*Gravo, āre, āvi, ātum,* (gravis). To burden, load.

*Grus, gruis,* m. and f. Crane.

*Gubernātor, ōris,* m. Pilot, ruler, governor.

*Guberno, āre, āvi, ātum.* To steer, pilot; direct, manage.

*Gylippus, i,* m. Gylippus, a Spartan commander in the Sicilian expedition, (223).

### H.

*Habeo, ēre, ui, itum.* To have; regard; keep. * *Sermōnem habēre,* to hold a conversation.

*Habito, āre, āvi, ātum,* (habeo). To inhabit, live in, dwell in. 332, I. 2.

*Habitus, us,* m. (habeo). Habit, dress, attire.

*Hamilcar, āris,* m. Hamilcar, the father of Hannibal, (186).

*Hamus, i,* m. Fish-hook, hook.

*Hannibal, ālis,* m. Hannibal, the celebrated Carthaginian general in the second Punic war, (189).

*Hanno, ōnis,* m. Hanno, a Carthaginian general in the second Punic war, (195).

*Hasdrubal, ālis,* m. Hasdrubal, son of Hamilcar and brother of Hannibal, (192). Another of the same name was the brother-in-law of Hannibal, and the founder of New Carthage, in Spain.

*Hasta, ae,* f. Spear.

*Hastile, is,* n. Spear.

*Hastilis, e,* (hasta). Belonging to a spear.

*Haud,* adv. Not.

*Haurio, ire, hausi, haustum.* To drink, draw out, exhaust.

*Hector, ōris,* m. Hector, son of Priam and Hecuba, the bravest of the Trojans, (146).

*Hedēra, ae,* f. Ivy.

*Hellespontus, i,* m. Hellespont, the straits of the Dardanelles.

*Helvetii, ōrum,* m. The Helvetians, a people of Gaul, (42).

*Hercūles, is,* m. Hercules, a celebrated Grecian hero, deified after death.

*Heres, ēdis,* m. and f. Heir, heiress.

*Herennius, ii,* m. Herennius, the father of Pontius Thelesinus, who conquered the Romans at the Caudine Forks, (179).

*Herodŏtus, i*, m. Herodotus, a celebrated Grecian historian, (20).

*Heros, õis*, m. Hero.

*Heu !* interj. Oh ! Ah ! Alas !

*Hiberna, õrum*, n. (hibernus). Winter-quarters.

*Hic, haec, hoc.* This, he, she, it.

*Hic*, adv. Here, in this place.

*Hiems, ĕmis*, f. Storm, winter.

*Hiĕro, õnis*, m. Hiero, king of Syracuse at the time of the first Punic war, (185).

*Hierosoly̆ma, ae*, f. or *õrum*, n. pl. Jerusalem, the capital of Judea, (206).

*Hinc*, adv. (hic). Hence, on this account, on this side; *hinc—hinc*, on the one side—on the other side.

*Hippias, ae*, m. Hippias, son of Pisistratus, tyrant of Athens, (97).

*Hispania, ae*, f. Spain, (97).

*Hispānus, a, um.* Spanish ; subs. *Hispānus, i*, m. A Spaniard, (194).

*Historia, ae*, f. History.

*Hodie*, adv. To-day.

*Hoedus, i*, m. A kid, young goat.

*Homĕrus, i*, m. Homer, the celebrated Greek epic poet, (134).

*Homo, ĭnis*, m. and f. Human being, man.

*Honestas, ātis*, f. (honestus). Honor, honesty.

*Honeste, ius, issĭme*, adv. (honestus). Honorably, nobly, honestly.

*Honestus, a, um*, (honor). Full of honor, honorable, creditable, worthy, virtuous.

*Honor* or *honos, õris*, m. Honor, rank, dignity.

*Honorifĭce, centius, centissĭme*, adv. (honorificus). Honorably. 305.

*Honŏro, āre, āvi, ātum*, (honor). To honor, reverence.

*Hora, ae*, f. Hour.

*Horreo, ēre, horrui.* To shudder, shudder at, dread.

*Horatii, õrum*, m pl. See *Curiatii ;* also note on " *Horatiõrum et Curiatiõrum*, (160).

*Horatius, ii*, m. See *Cocles* and *Pulvillus.*

*Hortensius, ii*, m. Hortensius, a Roman name. *Quintus Hortensius Hortālus*, a celebrated orator in the time of Cicero, (84, 91).

*Hortor, āri, ātus sum*, dep. To exhort, incite.

*Hospĭta, ae*, f. Guest.

*Hostia, ae*, f. Victim.

*Hostīlis, e*, (hostis). Hostile.

*Hostilius, ii*, m. Hostilius, a Roman name. *Tullus Hostilius*, the third king of Rome, (160). *Caius Hostilius Mancīnus*, a Roman consul, (201).

*Hostis, is*, m. and f. Enemy.

*Humānus, a, um*, (homo). Human.

*Humĭlis, e.* Humble, small, low.

*Humo, āre, āvi, ātum.* To bury.

*Hypānis, is*, m. Hypanis, a river of Sarmatia, (85).

### I.

*Ibĕrus, i*, m. Iberus, a river of Spain, now the Ebro, (25).

*Ibi*, adv. There, in that place.

*Ico, ĕre, ici, ictum.* To strike; make, ratify.

*Idem, eădem, idem.* The same; sometimes best rendered by also.

*Idoneus, a, um.* Suitable, fit.

*Igĭtur,* conj. Therefore, accordingly.

*Ignāvus, a, um.* Slothful, indolent.

*Ignis, is,* m. Fire.

*Ignŏro, āre, āvi, ātum.* To be ignorant of, not know.

*Ignosco, ĕre, ignōvi, ignōtum.* To excuse, forgive, overlook.

*Ilienses, ium,* m. Inhabitants of Ilium, Trojans, (146).

*Ilium, ii,* n. Ilium, or Troy, sometimes applied to the city, and sometimes to the district, (236).

*Ille, a, ud.* That; he, she, it.

*Illustris, e.* Illustrious, famous.

*Illustro, āre, āvi, ātum,* (illustris). To enlighten, illumine, illustrate, celebrate.

*Illyrĭcus, a, um,* or *Illyrius, a, um.* Illyrian, of or pertaining to Illyria, a country on the northeastern coast of the Adriatic, (245). Subs. *Illyrĭcus* or *Illyrius, i,* m., an Illyrian.

*Imāgo, ĭnis,* f. Image, figure, picture.

*Imbecillus, a, um,* or *imbecillis, e.* Weak, feeble.

*Imbuo, ĕre, imbui, imbūtum.* To imbue, impress.

*Imitātio, ōnis,* f. Imitation.

*Imĭtor, āri, ātus sum,* dep. To imitate, copy, portray, counterfeit.

*Immatūrus, a, um,* (in, matūrus). Young, immature.

*Immĕmor, ŏris,* (in, memor). Unmindful, forgetful.

*Immitto, ĕre, mĭsi, missum,* (in, mit-

to). To send or let in; let go; bring forward.

*Inmortālis, e,* (in, mortālis). Immortal.

*Immortalĭtas, ātis,* f. (immortālis.) Immortality.

*Immunĭtas, ātis,* f. Immunity, exemption.

*Imo* or *immo,* adv. Yes indeed, indeed, by all means.

*Impatiens, entis,* (in, patiens). Impatient.

*Impatienter, ius, issĭme,* adv. (impatiens). Impatiently.

*Impedimentum, i,* n. (impedio). Impediment, obstacle; *pl.* baggage.

*Impedio, īre, ivi* or *ii, ītum.* To impede, embarrass; hinder, prevent.

*Impello, ĕre, pŭli, pulsum,* (in, pello). To impel, induce.

*Impensa, ae,* f. Expense, cost.

*Imperātor, ōris,* m. (impĕro). Commander, emperor.

*Imperītus, a, um,* (in, perītus). Unskilled, ignorant.

*Imperium, ii,* n. (impĕro). Command, power, rule, sway, reign.

*Impĕro, āre, āvi, ātum.* To command, rule, govern.

*Impĕtro, āre, āvi, ātum.* To accomplish, obtain.

*Impĕtus, us,* m. Attack, fury.

*Impiĕtas, ātis,* f. (impius). Want of respect, irreverence, impiety.

*Impius, a, um,* (in, pius). Undutiful, irreverent, impious, abandoned.

*Impōno, ĕre, posui, posĭtum,* (in, pono). To place or put in or to; enjoin; impose.

*Imprŏbo, āre, āvi, ātum,* (in, probo).
To reject.

*Imprudenter, ius, issĭme,* adv. (im-
prūdens, *imprudent*). Imprudently.

*Impūbes, ĕris.* Youthful, young.

*Impugno, āre, āvi, ātum,* (in, pugno).
To assail, attack.

*Impulsus, us,* m. (impello). Instigation.

*In,* prep. with acc. or abl. Into, to,
for, against, *with acc. ;* in, on, *with
abl.*

*Inānis, e.* Empty, void ; vain, foolish, useless.

*Incendium, ii,* n. (incendo). Fire,
conflagration.

*Incendo, ĕre, cendi, censum.* To set
on fire, inflame, excite.

*In-certus, a, um.* Uncertain.

*Incesso, ĕre, cessīvi* or *cessi.* To attack.

*Inchoo, āre, āvi, ātum.* To begin,
commence.

*Incĭdo, ĕre, cĭdi, cāsum,* (in, cado).
To fall into *or* upon, fall in with,
happen.

*Incido, ĕre, cĭdi, cīsum,* (in, caedo).
To cut, destroy.

*Incipio, ĕre, cēpi, ceptum,* (in, capio).
To begin, undertake.

*Incitamentum, i.* n. (incĭto). Incen-
tive, inducement.

*Incitātus, a, um,* (incĭto). Running ;
*equo incĭtāto,* at full speed.

*In-cĭto, āre, āvi, ātum.* To incite,
hasten, spur on ; inspire.

*In-clino, āre, āvi, ātum.* To incline,
bend ; *pass.* to sink, go to ruin.

*Incŏla, ae,* m. and f. (incŏlo). Inhabitant.

*In-cŏlo, ĕre, colui, cultum.* To dwell,
abide in, inhabit.

*In-colūmis, e.* Safe, uninjured.

*In-credibilis, e.* Incredible.

*Incrementum, i,* n. Growth, increase.

*Incursio, ōnis,* f. (incurro). Attack,
inroad.

*Inde,* adv. Thence, from that
place.

*Indecōre,* adv. Disgracefully.

*India, ae,* f. India, an extensive
country of Asia, (242).

*In-dīco, ĕre, dixi, dictum.* To declare, publish, appoint.

*Indigeo, ĕre, indigui.* To need ;
part. *indĭgens,* as *adj.* or *subs.* indigent, an indigent person.

*Indignatio, ōnis,* f. (indignor). Scorn,
indignation.

*Indignor, āri, ātus sum,* (indignus).
To disdain, scorn ; be indignant.

*In-dignus, a, um.* Unworthy, harsh,
indecent.

*In-domitus, a, um.* Unsubdued, invincible.

*In-dubitātus, a, um.* Undoubted, certain.

*Induciae,* or *indutiae, arum,* f. pl.
Truce.

*In-dūco, ĕre, duxi, ductum.* To induce, lead into, overlay, adorn
with, gild.

*Indurātus, a, um,* (indūro). Obdu-
rate, hardened.

*In-dūro, āre, āvi, ātum.* To harden.

*Industria, ae,* f. Industry.

*In-eo, ire, īvi* or *ii, ĭtum.* To enter,
go into ; *gratiam inire,* to obtain
the favor of, conciliate. 295.

*Inermis, e,* (in, arma). Unarmed.

*Infāmis, e.* Infamous, notorious·

*Infans, antis,* adj. Speechless,
dumb ; *subs.* an infant.

*In-fĕliz*, *īcis*. Unhappy, unfortunate.

*Infensus*, *a*, *um*. Exasperated, enraged.

*Inferior*, *ius*. Inferior. 163, 3.

*In-fĕro*, *ferre*, *tŭli*, *illātum*. To carry against, wage against. 292, 2.

*Infesto*, *āre*, *āvi*, *ātum*, (infestus). To infest, trouble.

*Infestus*, *a*, *um*. Infested, troublesome, hostile.

*In-finītus*, *a*, *um*. Great, infinite, boundless, of unlimited power.

*In-flammo*, *āre*, *āvi*, *ātum*. To set on fire, burn, inflame, arouse.

*Informis*, *e*, (in, forma). Shapeless, deformed.

*In-frendo*, *ĕre*, —, *fressum*, *frēsum*. To gnash with the teeth.

*Infringo*, *ĕre*, *frēgi*, *fractum*, (in, frango). To infringe, break.

*Infūla*, *ae*, *f.* Fillet, head-dress, badge of office.

*In-gĕmo*, *ĕre*, *ui.* To groan, lament.

*Ingenium*, *ii*, *n.* Character, genius, intellect, power.

*Ingens*, *entis*. Great, mighty.

*Ingratis* or *ingrātis*, adv. Against one's will.

*In-grātus*, *a*, *um*. Disagreeable, offensive, ungrateful.

*In-gredior*, *grĕdi*, *gressus sum*, dep. (in, gradior). To enter, encounter.

*In-haereo*, *ĕre*, *haesi*, *haesum*. To cleave *or* stick to, to stick fast, adhere.

*In-hio*, *āre*, *āvi*, *ātum*. To gape, stand open; desire, long for.

*Inhumanītas*, *ātis*, *f.* (inhumānus). Barbarity, incivility, inhumanity.

*Inimīcus*, *a*, *um*, (in, amīcus). Hostile; *subs.* an enemy.

*Inīquus*, *a*, *um*, (in, aequus). Unfavorable, unjust.

*Initium*, *ii*, *n.* (ineo). Beginning; *pl.* sacred mysteries.

*Injicio*, *ĕre*, *jēci*, *jectum*, (in, jacio). To throw in; cause; inspire with.

*Injuria*, *ae*, *f.* Injury, wrong.

*Injuste*, *ius*, *issĭme*, adv. (injustus). Unjustly.

*In-justus*, *a*, *um*. Unjust, oppressive, severe.

*In-nŏcens*, *entis*. Innocent.

*In-notesco*, *ĕre*, *notui*. To become known.

*In-noxius*, *a*, *um*. Harmless, innocent.

*In-numerabĭlis*, *e*. Innumerable.

*In-opinātus*, *a*, *um*. Sudden, unexpected.

*Inquam*, defective. To say. See 297, II. 2.

*Insania*, *ae*, *f.* Insanity, folly.

*Inscitia*, *ae*, *f.* Ignorance.

*In-sĕquor*, *sĕqui*, *secūtus sum*. To follow, pursue.

*Insidiae*, *ārum.* *f.* pl. Ambush, treachery, plot.

*Insigne*, *is*, *n.* Mark, sign; *pl.* badges of office, insignia.

*Insignis*, *e*. Distinguished, noted.

*In-simŭlo*, *āre*, *āvi*, *ātum*. To blame, accuse, charge.

*In-sisto*, *ĕre*, *stĭti*, *stĭtum*. To persist; urge; entreat.

*In-sŏlens*, *entis*. Unusual, insolent.

*Insolenter*, *ius*, *issĭme*, adv. (insŏlens). Insolently.

*Inspecto*, *āre*, *āvi*, *ātum*. To look at, to look on.

*Inspicio*, *ĕre*, *spexi*, *spectum*, (in, spe

cio). To consider, inspect, look on.

*Instauro*, *āre*, *āvi*, *ātum*. To renew.

*Instituo*, *ĕre*, *stitui*, *stilūtum*, (in, statuo). To institute, establish.

*Institūtum*, *i*, n. (instituo). Habit, manner, custom, institution.

*In-sto*, *stāre*, *stiti*, *stātum*. To stand in *or* upon a thing, be near to; to urge, insist, beg earnestly.

*Instrumentum*, *i*, n. (instruo). Implements, movables, goods.

*In-struo*, *ĕre*, *struxi*, *structum*. To prepare, build, furnish with, equip.

*Insŭla*, *ae*, f. Island.

*In-sŭper*. Moreover.

*In-tactus*, *a*, *um*. Unharmed.

*Intĕger*, *gra*, *grum*. Whole, entire, unhurt; just, impartial, neutral.

*Integrĭtas*, *ātis*, f. (intĕger). Integrity, probity, honesty.

*Intelligentia*, *ae*, f. (intellĭgo). Intelligence, discernment, understanding.

*Intellĭgo*, *ĕre*, *lexi*, *lectum*. To understand, perceive, know.

*Inter*, prep. with acc. Between, among, in the midst of.

*Intercipio*, *ĕre*, *cēpi*, *ceptum*, (inter, capio). To catch; intercept, take from.

*Interclūdo*, *ĕre*, *clūsi*, *clūsum*, (inter, claudo). To prevent, cut off.

*Inter-dum*, adv. Sometimes.

*Inter-ea*, adv. In the mean time.

*Inter-eo*, *ĭre*, *ĭvi* or *ii*, *ĭtum*. To perish. 295.

*Inter-est*, impers. It concerns, it is important.

*Interfector*, *ōris*, m. (interficio). Murderer.

*Interficio*, *ĕre*, *fĕci*, *fectum*, (inter, facio). To kill, slay.

*Intĕrim*, adv. In the mean time, meanwhile.

*Interĭmo*, *ĕre*, *ĕmi*, *emptum*, (inter, emo). To deprive of, to kill.

*Interior*, *ius*. Interior, inland. 166.

*Interĭtus*, *us*, m. (intereo). Destruction.

*Interjicio*, *ĕre*, *jĕci*, *jectum*, (inter, jacio). To place between; *anno interjecto*, at the expiration of a year.

*Internecio*, *ōnis*, f. Slaughter.

*Inter-nuncius* or *internuntius*, *ii*, m. Messenger.

*Interregnum*, *i*, n. An interreign, interregnum.

*In-territus*, *a*, *um*. Fearless, undismayed.

*Inter-rŏgo*, *āre*, *āvi*, *ātum*. To ask, question.

*Inter-rumpo*, *ĕre*, *rūpi*, *ruptum*. To break down, interrupt.

*Inter-sĕro*, *ĕre*, *serui*, *sertum*. To allege, interpose.

*Inter-sum*, *esse*, *fui*. To be present at, take part in.

*Inter-venio*, *ĭre*, *vēni*, *ventum*. To intervene, occur.

*Intestinus*, *a*, *um*. Intestine, civil.

*Intra*, adv., and prep. with acc. Within.

*Intro*, *āre*, *āvi*, *ātum*. To enter.

*Intro-eo*, *ĭre*, *ĭvi* or *ii*, *ĭtum*. To enter. 295.

*In-tueor*, *tuēri*, *tuĭtus sum*. To look at, observe.

*Intus*, adv. Within.

*In-usitātus*, *a*, *um*. Unusual, extraordinary.

*In-utĭlis*, *e*. Useless.

*In-vādo, ēre, vāsi, vāsum.* To invade, seize.

*In-venio, īre, vēni, ventum.* To find, invent, devise, meet with.

*Inventrix, īcis,* f. (inventor). Inventress.

*In-vīcem,* adv. By turns, one another.

*In-victus, a, um.* Unconquered, invincible.

*In-video, ēre, vīdi, vīsum.* To envy.

*Invidia, ae,* f. Envy, hatred.

*Invīsus, a, um.* Odious, hateful.

*Invīto, āre, avi, ātum.* To invite, allure.

*Invītus, a, um.* Unwilling.

*Ionia, ae,* f. Ionia, a country in the western part of Asia Minor, (224).

*Iōnes, um,* m. pl. The Ionians.

*Iphicrātes, is,* m. Iphicrates, a celebrated Athenian general. He rose from an humble station to the highest offices of state, (49).

*Ipse, a, um.* Self, himself, herself, itself.

*Ira, ae,* f. Anger.

*Irascor, irasci, irātus sum,* dep. To be angry, be in a rage.

*Irātus, a, um,* (irascor). Enraged, angry, angered.

*Irreparabĭlis, e.* Irrecoverable.

*Irrideo, ēre, rīsi, rīsum,* (in, rideo). To ridicule, laugh at, laugh.

*Irrīto, āre, āvi, ātum.* To provoke, irritate, incite.

*Irrumpo, ēre, rūpi, ruptum,* (in, rumpo). To rush into, make an incursion into.

*Is, ea, id.* He, she, it, that, such.

*Isocrātes, is,* m. Isocrates, a famous orator and teacher of rhetoric at Athens, (45).

*Iste, a, ud.* That, such; *sometimes used in contempt.*

*Ister, tri,* m. The river Danube. This name is applied to the lower part of the river, the upper part taking the name Danubius, (215).

*Ita,* adv. Thus, so; to such an extent.

*Italia, ae,* f. Italy, (180).

*Italĭcus* or *Italus, a, um.* Italian; subs. *Italus, i,* m., an Italian, (148).

*Ită-que,* adv. Therefore, and thus, accordingly.

*Iter, itinĕris,* n. Way, march, route, road.

*Itĕrum,* adv. Again, a second time.

## J

*Jaceo, ēre, ui, ītum.* To lie.

*Jacio, ēre, jcci, jactum.* To throw, hurl; *also,* to lay, place, erect.

*Jacŭlum, i,* n. (jacio). Dart, javelin.

*Jam,* adv. Now, already.

*Janicŭlum, i,* n. Janiculum, a hill on the west side of the Tiber, not one of the *seven hills* of Rome, though included within the wall built by Aurelian in the third century, (148).

*Jocus, i,* m., also in the pl. *joca, jocōrum.* Joke, jest. 141.

*Jubeo, ēre, jussi, jussum.* To order, direct.

*Jucundus, a, um.* Pleasing, pleasant, delightful.

*Judaea, ae,* f. Judea, (206).

*Judaeus, a, um.* Jewish; subs. *Judaeus, i,* m., a Jew, (206).

*Judex, ĭcis,* m. and f. (judĭco). Judge, arbiter.

*Judicium, ii,* n. (judex). Judgment, decision, trial.

*Jŭ-dĭco, āre, āvi, ātum.* To judge.

*Jugum, i,* n. Yoke.

*Julius, ii,* m. See *Caesar.*

*Jungo, ĕre, junxi, junctum.* To join, unite; *societātem jungĕre,* to form a partnership.

*Junior, ius,* (juvĕnis). Younger. 168, 3.

*Junius, ii,* m. Junius, a Roman name; as *Caius Junius,* consul and dictator, (20, 7). See *Brutus.*

*Jupĭter, Jovis,* m. Jupiter, king of the gods. 66, 3.

*Juro, āre, āvi, ātum.* To take oath, swear.

*Jus, juris,* n. Right, justice, authority, control; *jure,* with *or* by right, justly, properly.

*Justitia, ae,* f. (justus). Justice.

*Justus, a, um,* (jus). Just.

*Juvenca, ae,* f. Heifer, cow.

*Juvencus, i,* m. A young bullock.

*Juvĕnis, e.* Young; *subs.* a youth. 168, 4.

*Juventus, ūtis,* f. (juvĕnis). Youth; the period of youth.

*Juvo, āre, juvi, jutum.* To help, aid, assist, support.

# L

*L.* An abbreviation of *Lucius.*

*Labiēnus, i,* m. Labienus, a Roman name. *Titus Labiēnus,* the legate of Caesar in Gaul, (56, 14).

*Labor, ōris,* m. Labor, work.

*Labōro, āre, āvi, ātum,* (labor). To labor, strive, take pains; toil; suffer.

*Lac, lactis,* n. Milk.

*Lacedaemon, ŏnis,* f. The city of Lacedaemon *or* Sparta, the capital of Laconia, (94).

*Lacedaemonius, a, um.* Lacedaemonian *or* Spartan; subs. *Lacedaemonius, ii,* m., a Lacedaemonian *or* Spartan, (123).

*Lacesso, ĕre, īvi* or *ii, ītum.* To excite, assail, provoke.

*Laconia* or *Laconĭca, ae,* f. Laconia, a country of the Peloponnesus, (222).

*Laco* or *Lacon, ŏnis,* m. A Laconian.

*Lacrĭma* or *lacrўma, ae,* f. Tear.

*Lacrĭmo* or *lacrўmo, āre, āvi, ātum,* (lacrĭma). To weep, shed tears.

*Lacus, us,* m. Lake. 117.

*Laelius, ii,* m. Laelius, a Roman name. *Caius Laelius,* a celebrated Roman consul and augur, surnamed the Wise. He was the intimate friend of Scipio Africanus the Younger, (65).

*Laetitia, ae,* f. (lactus). Joy, gladness.

*Laetus, a, um.* Glad, joyous, pleased.

*Laevīnus, i,* m. Laevinus, a Roman name. *Publius Valerius Laevīnus,* a Roman consul, (180). *Marcus Valerius Laevīnus,* also a Roman consul and a distinguished commander, (193).

*Laevus, a, um.* Left, on the left hand.

*Lamăchus, i,* m. Lamachus, an Athenian general in the Sicilian expedition, (223).

*Lamia, ae,* m. Lamia, a Roman surname, (71).

*Lanio, āre, āvi, ātum.* To tear in pieces.

*Lassitūdo, ĭnis,* f. Fatigue, weariness.

*Latĕbra, ae,* f.  Retreat, hiding-place, pretence.

*Latīne,* adv. (Latīnus).  In Latin.

*Latīnus, i,* m.  Latinus, an ancient king of the Laurentians in Italy, (149).

*Latium, iĭ,* n.  Latium, a country of *Italy containing Rome, (167).

*Latīnus, a, um,* adj.  Latin; subs. *Latīnus, i,* m., an inhabitant of Latium, a Latin; *pl.* the Latins, (161).

*Latro, ōnis,* m.  Robber.

*Latus, a, um.*  Broad, wide.

*Latus, ĕris,* n.  Side.

*Laudabĭlis, e,* (laudo).  Praiseworthy, laudable.

*Laudo, āre, āvi, ātum,* (laus).  To praise.

*Laurentia, ae,* f.  See *Acca.*

*Laus, laudis,* f.  Praise.

*Lavinia, ae,* f.  Lavinia, daughter of Latinus and wife of Aeneas, (149).

*Lavinium, ii,* n.  Lavinium, a town in Latium, a few miles south of Rome, founded by Aeneas, and named by him after his wife Lavinia, (149).

*Laxo, āre, āvi, ātum.*  To relax, loosen.

*Lectĭto, āre, āvi, ātum,* (lego).  To read often, with eagerness, to read. 332, I. 3.

*Lectus, a, um,* (lego).  Choice, excellent.

*Legatio, ōnis,* f.  Legation, embassy.

*Legātus, i,* m.  Ambassador, lieutenant, messenger.

*Legio, ōnis,* f.  Legion, a body of soldiers.

*Lego, āre, āvi, ātum,* (lex).  To bequeathe as a legacy.

*Lego, ĕre, legi, lectum.*  To choose, elect; read.

*Lentŭlus, i,* m.  Lentulus, a surname of a distinguished Roman family. *Publius Cornelius Lentŭlus,* a conspirator with Catiline, (97, 15).

*Leo, ōnis,* m.  Lion.

*Leonĭdas, ae,* m.  Leonidas, a Spartan king who fell at Thermopylae, (124).

*Lepĭdus, i,* m.  Lepidus, one of the triumvirs with Octaviānus and Antony, (83, 212).

*Lesbos* or *Lesbus, i,* f.  Lesbos, a celebrated island in the Aegean Sea, (49, 12).

*Letālis, e,* (letum).  Deadly, mortal.

*Letum, i,* n.  Death.

*Leuctra, ōrum,* n. pl.  Leuctra, a small town in Boeotia, celebrated for the victory of Epaminondas over the Lacedaemonians, (229).

*Leuctrĭcus, a, um.*  Of or belonging to Leuctra; Leuctrian, (230).

*Levis, e.*  Light, easy.

*Levĭter, ius, issĭme,* adv. (levis).  Lightly, slightly.

*Lex, legis,* f.  Law, condition, terms.

*Liber, bri,* m.  Book.

*Liber, ĕra, ĕrum.*  Free.

*Libĕri, ōrum,* m. pl.  Children.

*Libĕro, āre, āvi, ātum,* (liber).  To liberate, free.

*Libertas, ātis,* f. (liber).  Liberty, freedom.

*Licet,* impers.  It is lawful, is permitted.

*Licet,* conj.  Although, though.

*Licinius, ii,* m.  Licinius, a Roman name.  *Publius Licinius,* a Roman consul and commander in the war with Perseus, (198).  *Marcus Li-*

*cinius Crassus*, proconsul in the war of the gladiators, (204).

*Ligneus, a, um.* Wooden, of wood.

*Ligūres, um*, m. pl. The Ligurians, inhabitants of Liguria in the western part of Italy, (190).

*Lilybaeum, i*, n. Lilybaeum, a promontory on the southwestern coast of Sicily, (188).

*Lis, litis*, f. Strife, quarrel, lawsuit.

*Littĕrae, ārum*, f. pl. Letter, letters; literature. 132.

*Litus, ōris*, n. Shore, sea-shore.

*Locuplēto, āre, āvi, ātum.* To enrich, make rich.

*Locus, i*, m., pl. *loci* or *loca*, n. Place. 141.

*Longe, ius, issĭme*, adv. (longus). Much, greatly, by far.

*Longinquus, a, um.* Remote, distant, long.

*Longitūdo, ĭnis*, f. (longus). Length.

*Longus, a, um.* Long.

*Loquor, loqui, locūtus sum.* To speak, converse.

*Lorīca, ae*, f. Coat-of-mail.

*Lucius, ii*, m. Lucius, a name common among the Romans; as, *Lucius Tarquinius Priscus*, (162).

*Lucretius, ii*, m. Lucretius, a Roman name. *Spurius Lucretius*, the colleague of Publicola in the consulship, (170).

*Lucrum, i*, n. Gain, profit, advantage.

*Lucus, i*, m. Grove.

*Ludus, i*, m. Game, play, sport, school.

*Lugeo, ēre, luxi.* To grieve, mourn, weep for.

*Lumen, ĭnis*, n. A light; the eye.

*Luna, ae*, f. Moon.

*Luo, ĕre, lui, luĭtum* or *lutum.* To pay; expiate, atone for.

*Lupa, ae*, f. A she-wolf.

*Lupus, i*, m. A wolf.

*Lustratio, ōnis*, f. (lustro). Expiatory sacrifice; review attended with sacrifices.

*Lustro, āre, āvi, ātum.* To purify, review.

*Lusus, us*, m. Play, game; jest, sport, fun.

*Lutatius, ii*, m. See *Catŭlus*.

*Lux, lucis*, f. Light, light of day.

*Luxuria, ae*, f. Luxury, excess.

*Lycurgus, i*, m. Lycurgus, the celebrated law-giver of Sparta, (95).

*Lydia, ae*, f. Lydia, a country in Asia Minor, (225).

*Lydus, a, um.* Lydian, pertaining to Lydia; *subs.* a Lydian, (83).

*Lysander, dri*, m. Lysander, a celebrated Spartan general, (225).

## M

*M.* An abbreviation of *Marcus*.

*Macedonia, ae*, f. Macedonia, Macedon, a country north of Thessaly, (193).

*Macĕdo, ōnis*, m. A Macedonian, (230).

*Macedonĭcus, a, um*, adj. Macedonian, (197).

*Magis*, comp. adv. More. See the superlative, *maxĭme*.

*Magister, tri*, m. Master, leader, teacher.

*Magistra, ae*, f. Instructress, teacher.

*Magistrātus, us*, m. Magistracy, magistrate.

*Magnifĭce, centius, centissĭme*, adv. (magnifĭcus). Magnificently, splendidly. 305.

*Magnificenter,* *ius, issĭme,* adv. =
*magnifĭce.*

*Magnificentia, ae,* f. (magnifĭcus).
Magnificence, costliness.

*Magnifĭcus, a, um ;* comp. *magnificentior,* superl. *magnificentissĭmus.*
Splendid ; stately ; high-minded,
magnificent. 164.

*Magnitūdo, ĭnis,* f. (magnus). Greatness, size.

*Magnŏpĕre,* adv. (magnus, opus).
Greatly, earnestly.

*Magnus, a, um ;* comp. *major,* superl. *maxĭmus.* Great, large ;
*in comp. and superl. sometimes*
older, oldest, elder, eldest : *ma-
jŏres,* forefathers, ancestors ; *ma-
jŏres natu,* elders. 165.

*Magus, i,* m. Generally plur. *Magi,
ōrum.* A wise man, *particularly
among the Persians.*

*Majestas, ātis,* f. Majesty, dignity.

*Major.* See *magnus.*

*Male,* comp. *pejus,* superl. *pessĭme,*
adv. (malus). Badly, with ill
success. 305.

*Male-dico, ĕre, dixi, dictum.* To speak
evil of, revile, abuse, rail at.

*Malefĭcus, a, um,* (male, facio.)
Evil-doing, vicious, wicked, hurtful. 164.

*Malo, malle, malui,* irregular. To
prefer. 293.

*Malum, i,* n. Misfortune, evil.

*Malus, a, um ;* comp. *pejor,* superl.
*pessĭmus.* Bad, poor, wicked.
165.

*Mancīnus, i,* m. Mancinus, a Roman consul in the war with the
Numantians, (201).

*Mando, āre, āvi, ātum.* To bid, enjoin, intrust.

*Maneo, ēre, mansi, mansum.* To
remain.

*Manifesto, āre, āvi, ātum.* To show,
manifest.

*Manius, ii,* m. Manius, a Roman
name ; as, *Manius Manlius.*

*Manlius, ii,* m. Manlius, a Roman
name. *Manius Manlius,* a Roman
consul in the third Punic war,
- (199). *Titus Manlius,* a Roman
youth, surnamed *Torquātus* for
his achievements in the Gallic
war, (177).

*Mantinēa, ae,* f. A city of Arcadia,
in the Peloponnesus, (142).

*Manumitto, ĕre, mīsi, missum,* (manus, mitto). To release from one's
power, emancipate, make free.

*Manus, us,* f. Hand ; force.

*Marăthon, ōnis,* m. Marathon, a
town and plain in Attica, celebrated for the victory of Miltiades
over the Persians, (216).

*Marathonius, a, um.* Marathonian ;
of or belonging to Marathon, (97).

*Marcius, ii,* m. Marcius, a Roman
name. See *Ancus, Censorīnus.*

*Marcellus, i,* m. Roman gen'l, (193).

*Marcus, i,* m. Marcus, a Roman
name, (186).

*Mardonius, ii,* m. Mardonius, a Persian general, defeated by Pausanias in the battle of Plataea, (221).

*Mare, is,* n. Sea.

*Marinus, a, um,* (mare). Marine,
of the sea, from or by the sea.

*Marius, ii,* m. Marius, a Roman
name. *Caius Marius,* a distinguished Roman general, the conqueror of Jugurtha, and leader in
the civil war against Sulla. He
was consul seven times, (202).

*Mars, Martis*, m.   Mars, the god of
war ; sometimes put for war itself, (152, 226).

*Massa, ae*, f.   Mass, lump.

*Mater, tris*, f.   Mother.

*Materia, ae*, f., or *materies, ëi*, f.
Material.

*Matricidium, ii*, n.   Matricide.

*Matrimonium, ii*, n.   Marriage.

*Matrōna, ae*, f.   Matron.

*Maxĭme*, adv.   Especially, in the
highest degree.   See *magis*.

*Maxĭmus, a, um ;* superlative of
*magnus*.   Greatest.

*Maximus, i*, m.   Maximus, a Roman
surname ; as, *Quintus Fabius Maxĭmus*, the famous dictator in the
second Punic war, (175).

*Medĭcus, i*, m.   Physician.

*Medius, a, um*.   Middle, midst of,
middle of.   441, 6.

*Medius, ii*, m.   Medius, a Thessalian,
friend of Alexander the Great,
(243).

*Medus, a, um*. Median, Assyrian,(53).

*Mehercŭle*, adv.   By Hercules, truly,
indeed.

*Mel, mellis*, n.   Honey.

*Melior, ius*.   Better.   See *bonus*.

*Membrum, i*, n.   Member, limb.

*Memĭni, isti*, defect.   To remember.
297.

*Memor, ŏris*.   Mindful, endowed
with memory, remembering readily, remembering.

*Memorabĭlis, e*.   Memorable.

*Memoria, ae*, f.   Memory, recollection.

*Memphis, is*, f.   Memphis, a city of
Egypt, (239).

*Menander, dri*, m.   Menander, a
Roman name, (67).

I

*Mendacium, ii*, n.   Untruth, false-
hood, lie.

*Menenius, ii*, m.   See *Agrippa*.

*Mens, mentis*, f.   Mind, reason.

*Mensis, is*, m.   Month.

*Mentio, ōnis*, f.   Mention.

*Mentior, īri, ītus sum*, dep.   To speak
falsely, lie, cheat, deceive.

*Merces, ēdis*, f. (mereo).   Reward,
price, wages.

*Mercor, āri, ātus sum*, dep.   To
trade, buy, purchase.

*Mercurius, ii*, m.   Mercury, the son
of Jupiter and Maia, the god of
eloquence, and the messenger of
the gods, (19).

*Mereo, ēre, ui, ĭtum*.   To deserve,
merit.

*Mereor, ēri, ītus sum*, dep.   To deserve, earn, merit.

*Mergo, ĕre, mersi, mersum*.   To
merge, sink ; destroy.

*Merĭto*, adv. (merĭtum).   With
good reason, with reason, deserv-
edly.

*Merĭtum, i*, n.   Reward, merit.

*Merum, i*, n.   Wine, pure wine.

*Mesopotamia, ae*, f.   Mesopotamia, a
country of Asia, between the Euphrates and Tigris, (24, 10).

*Metallum, i*, n.   Metal, mine.

*Metellus, i*, m.   Metellus, a Roman
name ; as, *Metellus Pius*, (188).

*Metior, īri, mensus sum*, dep.   To
measure, estimate.

*Metius, ii*, m.   See *Suffetius*.

*Meto, ĕre, messui, messum*.   To reap,
mow.

*Metuo, ĕre, ui*.   To fear.

*Metus, us*, m.   Fear, dread.

*Meus, a, um*, voc. sing. masc. *mi*.
My, mine.   185.

*Migro, āre, āvi, ātum.* To migrate, remove.

*Miles, ĭtis,* m. Soldier.

*Militāris, e,* (miles). Military.

*Militia, ae,* f. (miles). Warfare, military service, military affairs.

*Milĭto, āre, āvi, ātum,* (miles). To serve as a soldier, to serve.

*Mille,* subs. and adj. Thousand; *millia,* subs., a thousand, a thousand men.

*Milliarium, ii,* n. Milestone, mile.

*Miltĭādes, is,* m. Miltiades, a celebrated Athenian general, conqueror at Marathon, (39, IV.)

*Minerva, ae,* f. Goddess of wisdom, (22).

*Minĭme,* adv. Least. See *parum.*

*Minĭmus, a, um,* (parvus). Smallest, least.

*Minĭtor, āri, ātus sum,* dep. To threaten, menace.

*Minor, ōris.* See *Armenia.*

*Minor, us,* (parvus). Smaller, less.

*Minuo, ĕre, ui, ūtum.* To lessen, diminish.

*Minus,* adv. Less. See *parum.*

*Mirabĭlis, e,* (miror). Wonderful.

*Mirifĭcus, a, um,* (mirus, facio). Causing wonder, wonderful, marvellous.

*Miror, āri, ātus sum,* dep. To wonder, admire.

*Mirus, a, um.* Wonderful, surprising.

*Miser, ĕra, ĕrum.* Unfortunate, unhappy, worthless, miserable, sad.

*Misereo, ĕre, ui, ĭtum.* To pity; often impersonal; *misĕret me,* I pity.

*Misereor, ĕri, misertus* or *miserĭtus sum,* dep. To pity.

*Miseria, ae,* f. (miser). Misery, affliction.

*Misericordia, ae,* f. Compassion.

*Mithrĭdātes, is,* m. Mithridates, a celebrated king of Pontus, (202).

*Mithrĭdatĭcus, a, um.* Mithridatic; of or belonging to Mithridates, (202).

*Mitis, e.* Mild, gentle, placid.

*Mitto, ĕre, misi, missum.* To send

*Moderāte, ius, issĭme,* adv. (moderātus). With moderation.

*Moderatio, ōnis,* f. Moderation, self-control.

*Moderātus, a, um.* Discreet, moderate.

*Modius* (or *um,* n.), *ii,* m. Measure, *a little more than a peck.*

*Modo,* adv. Now, only, but, provided that; *modo—modo,* sometimes—sometimes.

*Modus, i,* m. Manner, measure, limits.

*Moenia, ium,* n. pl. Walls of a city, city.

*Moles, is,* f. Mole, dam.

*Molestus, a, um.* Unwelcome, irksome, oppressive, troublesome, painful.

*Molitio, ōnis,* f. Undertaking, preparation.

*Mollio, īre, īvi* or *ii, ītum.* To soften.

*Momentum, i,* n. Weight, influence.

*Moneo, ēre, ui, ĭtum.* To advise, warn, admonish.

*Monĭtus, us,* m. (moneo). Advice.

*Mons, montis,* m. Mountain, mount.

*Monstro, āre, āvi, ātum.* To show.

*Mora, ae,* f. Delay.

*Morbus, i,* m. Disease

*Morior, īri* or *i, mortuus sum,* dep. To die. 283.

*Moror, āri, ātus sum,* dep. (mora). To delay, tarry.

*Mors, mortis,* f. Death.

*Morsus, us,* m. Bite.

*Mortālis, e.* Mortal, deadly ; *subs.* mortal, man.

*Mortĭfer, ĕra, ĕrum,* (mors and fero). Deadly, mortal.

*Mos, moris,* m. Custom, manner ; *pl.* character, morals.

*Motus, us,* m. Motion ; commotion, revolt.

*Moveo, ēre, movi, motum.* To move, excite.

*Mox,* adv. Presently, soon.

*Mucius, ii,* m. Mucius, a Roman name. *Mucius Scaevŏla,* a Roman youth who attempted to assassinate Porsena, (172).

*Mucro, ōnis,* m. Point of sword, sword.

*Muliĕbris, e,* (mulier). Belonging to women, womanly, woman's.

*Mulier, ĕris,* f. Woman.

*Multitūdo, ĭnis,* f. (multus). Multitude.

*Mullo, āre, āvi, ātum.* To punish, deprive of by way of punishment ; to fine.

*Multo,* adv. (multus). By far, much.

*Multus, a, um ;* comp. *plus,* n., superl. *plurĭmus.* Much, many. 165.

*Mundus, i,* m. World, universe.

*Munia, ium,* n. pl. Duties, functions of office.

*Munificentia, ae,* f. Munificence, beneficence.

*Munimentum, i,* n. Fortification, defence, covering.

*Munio, īre, īvi* or *ii, ītum.* To fortify, defend.

*Munītio, ōnis,* f. Fortification, rampart.

*Munītus, a, um,* part. (munio). Fortified.

*Munus, ĕris,* n. Reward, present ; service, office.

*Munychia, ae,* f. The Athenian harbor Munychia and the hill which rises above it, (228).

*Murus, i,* m. Wall.

*Mus, muris,* m. Mouse.

*Mutatio, ōnis,* f. (muto). Change.

*Muto, āre, āvi, ātum.* To change, alter.

*Mutuus, a, um.* Mutual.

*Mycăle, es,* f. Mycale, a high promontory or mountain of Ionia, in Asia Minor, (221).

*Myndii, ōrum,* m. pl. Myndians, inhabitants of Myndus, (135).

*Myndus* or *os, i,* f. Myndus, a city of Caria, in Asia Minor, now Mendes, (135).

### N

*Nam,* conj. For.

*Nam-que,* conj. For, but.

*Nanciscor, nancisci, nactus sum,* dep. To obtain, take advantage of.

*Narro, āre, āvi, ātum.* To relate, narrate.

*Nascor, nasci, natus sum,* dep. To be born, be produced, to arise.

*Natālis, e,* (nascor). Of *or* belonging to one's birth, natal; *natālis dies,* birth-day.

*Natio, ōnis,* f. Nation, people.

*Natu,* defective, abl. sing. (nascor). By birth, in age ; *maxĭmus natu,* eldest. 134.

*Natūra, ae,* f. Nature, creation.

*Natus, a, um,* part. (nascor). Born, having been born.

*Naturālis, e,* (natūra). Natural.

*Naufragium. ii,* n. (navis, frango). Shipwreck.

*Nautius. ii,* m. Nautius, a Roman name; as, *Caius Nautius,* the consul, (19, 11).

*Navālis, e,* (navis). Naval.

*Navigatio, ōnis,* f. Navigation, sailing.

*Navīgo, āre, āvi, ātum.* To sail, sail upon, navigate.

*Navis, is,* f. Ship.

*Ne,* adv., and conj. used with imperative and subj. Not, that not, lest; *after verbs of fearing,* that, lest; *nequidem,* or *ne—quidem,* not even.

*Ne,* interrog. particle. 346, II. 1.

*Nec* or *neque,* adv. and conj. Neither, nor; and not, not; *nec—nec, neque—neque,* neither—nor.

*Necessarius, a, um.* Necessary.

*Necesse,* adj. neut. *used chiefly in this form.* Necessary, inevitable.

*Neco, āre, āvi, ātum.* To slay, kill.

*Neglĭgens, entis,* (neglīgo). Negligent, neglectful.

*Neglīgo, ĕre, lexi, lectum.* To neglect, disregard.

*Nego, āre, āvi, ātum.* To deny, refuse.

*Negotium, ii,* n. Business, difficulty; undertaking, work, enterprise.

*Nemo,* (ĭnis, gen. not in good use). No one, nobody.

*Nepos, ōtis,* m. Grandson.

*Neptūnus, i,* m. Neptune, the god of the sea, (155).

*Neque.* See *Nec.*

*Nequeo, īre, īvi,* or *ii, ĭtum,* irreg. like *eo.* To be unable, not to be able. 296.

*Nequidem.* See *Ne.*

*Nequis* or *ne quis, qua, quod,* or *quid.* That no one.

*Nervii, ōrum,* m. Nervians, a people of Belgic Gaul, (28).

*Nescio, īre, īvi* or *ii, ĭtum,* (ne, scio). To be ignorant, not to know.

*Nescius, a, um,* (nescio). Ignorant, unknown.

*Nicias, ae,* m. Nicias, an Athenian statesman and general, (223).

*Nicomēdes, is,* m. Nicomedes, king of Bithynia, (43).

*Niger, gra, grum.* Dark, black, dusky.

*Nigrans, antis.* Black, dusky.

*Nihil,* n. indec. Nothing; *adv.* not, in nothing. 128.

*Nihĭlum, i,* n. Nothing.

*Nilus, i,* m. The river Nile in Egypt, (211).

*Nimis,* adv. Exceedingly, too much.

*Nimius, a, um.* Excessive, too much, too great.

*Nisi,* conj. Unless, if not, except.

*Niteo, nitēre, nitui,* (nix). To shine, glitter, glisten.

*Nitor, niti, nisus* or *nixus sum,* dep. To strive, attempt; to depend *or* rely upon.

*Nix, nivis,* f. Snow.

*Nobĭlis, e.* Noble, famous.

*Nobĭlĭtas, ātis,* f. (nobĭlis). Fame, nobleness; nobility, nobles.

*Nobĭlĭto, āre, āvi, ātum,* (nobilis). To render famous; to ennoble; improve.

*Noceo, ēre, ui, ĭtum.* To hurt, harm, injure.

*Noctu,* abl.  By night.

*Nocturnus, a, um.*  Nocturnal, occurring at night.

*Nolo, nolle, nolui,* irreg.  To be unwilling. 293.

*Nomen, ĭnis,* n.  Name.

*Nomĭno, āre, āvi, ātum,* (nomen). To name, call.

*Non,* adv.  Not; *nonnĭsi,* only.

*Nonagesĭmus, a, um.*  Ninetieth.

*Nonaginta,* indec.  Ninety.

*Non-dum,* adv.  Not yet.

*Nonne,* interrog. particle.  Whether, *expecting answer* yes. 346, II. 1.

*Nonnullus, a, um,* (declined like *nullus*).  Some.

*Nonus, a, um.*  Ninth.

*Nosco, ēre, novi, notum.*  To know, understand, learn.

*Noster, tra, trum.* pron.  Our.

*Notitia, ae,* f. (notus).  Celebrity, note; acquaintance, knowledge.

*Notus, a, um.* part. (nosco).  Known.

*Novem,* indecl.  Nine.

*Noverca, ae,* f.  Step-mother.

*Novo, āre, āvi, ātum,* (novus).  To renew, change; revolutionize.

*Novus, a, um.*  New; *novae res,* revolution.

*Nox, noctis,* f.  Night.

*Nubes, is,* f.  Cloud.

*Nubo, ēre, nupsi, nuptum.*  To veil one's self, to marry, *applied to the bride as she was covered with a veil.*

*Nudus, a, um.*  Naked, uncovered, destitute of.

*Nullus, a, um.*  No one, no. 151.

*Num,* interrog. particle.  Whether,

used both in direct and in indirect questions.  See 346, II. 1.

*Numa, ae,* m.  Numa. *Numa Pompilius,* the second king of Rome, (159).

*Numantia, ae,* f.  Numantia, a city of Spain, (201).

*Numantĭni, ōrum,* m. pl.  Numantians, the inhabitants of Numantia, (201).

*Numen, ĭnis,* n.  A god, deity.

*Numĕro, āre, āvi, ātum,* (numĕrus). To count, reckon, number.

*Numĕrus, i,* m.  Number, quantity.

*Numĭda, ae,* m.  A Numidian, inhabitant of Numidia in Africa, (48).

*Numĭtor, ōris,* m.  Numitor, a king of Alba, grandfather of Romulus and Remus, (154).

*Nummus, i,* m.  Money, a piece of money, a coin.

*Nunc.*  Now.

*Nuncŭpo, āre, āvi, ātum.*  To call, name.

*Nunquam.*  Never.

*Nuntio* (or *cio*), *āre, āvi, ātum,* (nuntius).  To announce, relate.

*Nuntius, ii,* m.  Message, news, messenger.

*Nuptiae, ārum,* f. pl.  Marriage, nuptials.

*Nutrio, īre, īvi* or *ii, ītum.*  To nourish, support.

*Nutrix, īcis,* f.  Nurse.

*Nympha, ae,* f.  Nymph, spouse.

*Nysa, ae,* f.  Nysa, a city in India, (242).

## O.

*O,* interj. O!

*Ob,* prep. with acc. On account of, for.

*Ob-dŭco, ĕre, duxi, ductum.* To draw over, overspread, cover.

*Obedio, ĭre, ĭvi* or *ii, ĭtum.* To obey, serve; be subject to.

*Ob-eo, ĭre, ĭvi* or *ii, ĭtum.* To meet; die. 295.

*Objecto, āre, āvi, ātum,* (objicio). To expose, set forth; endanger. 332, I.

*Objicio, ĕre, jēci, jectum,* (ob, jacio). To expose, offer, present.

*Oblecto, āre, āvi, ātum.* To delight, divert, please.

*Ob-lĭgo, āre, āvi, ātum.* To bind, oblige, put under obligation.

*Oblītus, a, um,* part. (obliviscor). Having forgotten, forgetful.

*Oblivio, ōnis,* f. (obliviscor). Forgetfulness, oblivion.

*Obliviscor, oblivisci, oblītus sum,* dep. To forget.

*Ob-ruo, ĕre, rui, rŭtum.* To destroy, overwhelm.

*Obscūrus, a, um.* Obscure, hidden; mean.

*Obsĕcro, āre, āvi, ātum,* (ob, sacro). To beseech, implore.

*Obses, ĭdis,* m. and f. Hostage.

*Obsideo, ēre, sēdi, sessum,* (ob, sedeo). To besiege, invest.

*Obsidio, ōnis,* f. (obsideo). Siege, blockade.

*Ob-sum, obesse, obfui.* To be hurtful, be injurious, to injure.

*Ob-sto, stāre, stĭti, stătum.* To oppose, prevent.

*Obtemperatio, ōnis,* f. Submission, obedience.

*Ob-tĕro, ĕre, trīvi, trītum.* To crush, wear down.

*Obtineo, ēre, tinui, tentum,* (ob, teneo). To obtain, hold, prevail.

*Obtingo, ĕre, tĭgi, tactum,* (ob, tango). To befall, happen to.

*Ob-trunco, āre, āvi, ātum.* To slaughter.

*Occaeco, āre, āvi, ātum,* (ob, caeco). To darken, obscure, blind, dazzle.

*Occasio, ōnis,* f. Opportunity, occasion.

*Occāsus, us,* m. The setting of the heavenly bodies; setting, evening; the west.

*Oc-cĭdo, ĕre, cĭdi, cāsum,* (ob, cado). To fall down, fall; to set; to perish, die, be ruined.

*Occīdo, ĕre, cīdi, cīsum,* (ob, caedo). To kill, slay.

*Occulte, ius, issĭme,* adv. (occultus). In secret, secretly.

*Occultus, a, um.* Secret, hidden; reserved, dissembling.

*Occŭpo, āre, āvi, ātum.* To occupy, take possession of.

*Occurro, ĕre, curri* (cucurri), *cursum,* (ob, curro). To meet, attack. 273, I. 2.

*Oceănus, i,* m. Ocean.

*Octaviānus, i,* m. (*Caesar*). Octavianus, the first Roman emperor, usually called **Augustus** after his victory at Actium, (213).

*Octāvus, a, um,* (octo). Eighth.

*Octingenti, ae, a.* Eight hundred.

*Octo,* indecl. Eight.

*Octogesĭmus, a, um.* The eightieth.

*Octoginta,* indec. (octo). Eighty.

*Ocŭlus, i,* m. Eye.

*Odi, odisse,* defect. To hate; dislike. 297.

*Odium, ii,* n. Hatred, enmity.

*Oenomaus, i,* m. Oenomaus, a celebrated gladiator, (204).

*Offendo, ĕre, fendi, fensum.* To offend, injure.

*Offensus, a, um,* (offendo). Offended, hostile.

*Offĕro, ferre, oblŭli, oblātum,* (ob, fero). To offer, show; *se offerre,* to present one's self, to offer one's self, *sometimes* as an antagonist, to oppose; expose one's self.

*Officium, ii,* n. Office, duty, kindness, kind office.

*Olim,* adv. Formerly.

*Olympiăcus, Olympĭcus* or *Olympius, a, um.* Olympic, (134).

*Olynthus, i,* f. Olynthus, a city of Thrace.

*Olynthii, ōrum,* m. pl. The Olynthians, (231).

*Omen, ĭnis,* n. Omen, sign.

*Omitto, ĕre, misi, missum,* (ob, mitto). To let go, omit, neglect, disregard.

*Omnis, e.* All, every, whole.

*Oneraria, ae,* f. (onus). Ship of burden.

*Onĕro, āre, āvi, ātum,* (onus). To burden, load, oppress.

*Onustus, a, um,* (onus). Laden, full of.

*Opĕra, ae,* f. Pains, work, labor; care, attention; means.

*Opĭmus, a, um.* Rich, fertile.

*Oportet,* impers. It behooves, one ought. 299.

*Opperior, opperīri, oppertus* or *opperītus sum,* dep. To wait for, await.

*Oppidānus, a, um,* (oppĭdum). Inhabitant of a town, citizen.

*Oppĭdum, i,* n. Town, city.

*Opportunĭtas, ātis,* f. (opportūnus). Opportunity, fitness.

*Opportūnus, a, um.* Suitable, fit.

*Opprĭmo, ĕre, pressi, pressum,* (ob, premo). To put down, defeat, overcome; suppress; oppress.

*Oppugno, āre, āvi, ātum,* (ob, pugno). To attack, storm, take by storm.

*(Ops), opis,* f., nom. sing. not used. Power, resources, wealth, force, aid.

*Optabĭlis, e,* (opto). Wished for, desirable.

*Optĭmus, a, um,* superl. (bonus). Best, most excellent.

*Optio, ōnis,* f. Choice, option.

*Opto, āre, āvi, ātum.* To wish, desire; ask.

*Opŭlens, entis,* or *opulentus, a, um,* adj. Wealthy, rich.

*Opus, ĕris,* n. Work.

*Opus,* nom. and accus. Need, necessary thing, necessary.

*Ora, ae,* f. The shore, coast.

*Oracŭlum, i,* n. Response, oracle.

*Oratio, ōnis,* f. (oro). Oration, speech, language.

*Orātor, ōris,* m. (oro). Orator, messenger.

*Orbis, is,* m. Circle, world; *orbis terrārum,* the world.

*Ordĭno, āre, āvi, ātum,* (ordo). To arrange, establish.

*Ordo, ĭnis,* m. Row, rank, order; bank *as of oars; extra ordĭnem,* out of the common course.

*Orestes, is,* and *ae,* m. Orestes, son

of Agamemnon an l Clytemnestra, (43).

*Oriens, entis,* (orior). Rising; the morning, the east, the countries of the east, the Orient, (213).

*Orīgo, ĭnis,* f. Origin, source.

*Orior, orīri, ortus sum,* dep. To rise, appear, dawn. 288, 2.

*Ornamentum, i,* n. Equipage, ornament, jewel.

*Orno, āre, āvi, ātum.* To adorn, equip.

*Oro, āre, āvi, ātum.* To beg, ask, speak.

*Ortus, us,* m. (orior). A rising; place of rising, the east; birth; beginning.

*Os, ossis,* n. Bone.

*Oscŭlor, āri, ātus sum.* To kiss.

*Ostendo, ĕre, di, sum* or *tum.* To show.

*Ostentum, i,* n. (ostendo). Prodigy.

*Ostia, ae,* f. Ostia, a town at the mouth of the Tiber, (161).

*Ostium, ii,* n. Mouth, door.

*Otium, ii,* n. Leisure, rest, ease, idleness.

*Ovis, is,* f. Sheep.

*Ovum, i,* n. Egg.

## P.

*P.* An abbreviation of *Publius.*

*Paco, āre, āve, ātum* (pax). To subdue.

*Pactum, i,* n. Bargain, contract; *abl. pacto,* way, manner.

*Padus, i,* m. River Po in Italy, (55).

*Paene,* adv. Almost.

*Paenĭtet, ĕre, paenituit,* impers. It causes regret; *paenĭtet me,* it causes me to repent, I repent, am sorry for, regret.

*Palam,* adv. Openly.

*Palatium, ii,* n. Palace.

*Pallium, ii,* n. Cloak, coat, garment.

*Pango, ĕre, pepĭgi, pactum.* To contract, ratify.

*Papirius, ii,* n. See *Cursor.*

*Par, paris,* adj. Equal, a match for, competent for.

*Parātus, a, um,* (paro). Prepared, ready.

*Parco, ĕre, peperci* or *parsi, parsum.* To spare.

*Parens, entis,* m. and f. Parent.

*Parento, āre, āvi, ātum,* (parens). To sacrifice in honor of parents or friends.

*Pareo, ēre, ui, ĭtum.* To obey, be subject to.

*Pario, ĕre, pepĕri, partum.* To bear, bring forth, produce, lay, accomplish, procure.

*Paro, āre, āvi, ātum.* To prepare, equip.

*Pars, partis,* f. Part, portion; party.

*Parsimonia, ae,* f. Frugality, parsimony.

*Partĭceps, partĭcĭpis,* (pars, capio). Sharing, partaking, participant.

*Partim.* Partly, in part; *partim—partim,* some—others, either—or.

*Partior, īri, ītus sum,* dep. To divide, share.

*Parum,* comp. *minus,* superl. *mĭnĭme,* adv. Too little, little, not enough. 305.

*Parvus, a, um,* comp. *minor,* superl. *minĭmus.* Small, little, unimportant.

*Pasco, ĕre, pāvi, pastum.* To feed, graze.

*Pascor, pasci, pastus sum,* dep. To feed, graze, graze upon.

*Passer, ĕris,* m. Sparrow.

*Passus, us,* m. Pace; *mille passus,* a mile.

*Pastor, ōris,* m. (pasco). Shepherd.

*Patefacio, ĕre, fēci, factum,* (pateo, facio). To disclose, lay open, open.

*Pateo, ĕre, ui.* To lie open, be exposed.

*Pater, tris,* m. Father, *sometimes* senator.

*Paternus, a, um,* (pater). Paternal.

*Patior, pati, passus sum,* dep. To permit, keep, endure.

*Patria, ae,* f. Country, native country.

*Patrimonium, ii,* n. Estate, patrimony.

*Patrius, a, um,* (pater). Fatherly.

*Patruus, i,* m. Uncle by the father's side, paternal uncle.

*Pauci, ae, a.* Few.

*Paulātim,* adv. By degrees, gradually.

*Paulus* or *Paullus, i,* m. Paulus, a surname in the Aemilian gens or tribe. *Lucius Aemilius Paulus,* the name of two Roman consuls, one of whom fell in the battle of Cannae, (191); the other conquered Perseus at Pydna, (198).

*Paulo,* adv. (paulus). A little, by a little.

*Paulus, a, um.* Little, small.

*Pauper, ĕris.* Poor, without means; scanty, meagre.

*Pausanias, ae,* m. Pausanias, the leader of the Spartans in the battle of Plataea, (221).

*Pax, pacis,* f. Peace.

*Pectus, ŏris,* n. Breast.

*Pecunia, ae,* f. Money, sum of money.

*Pecus, ŏris,* n. Flock, herd, cattle.

*Pedes, ĭtis,* m. Foot-soldier; *plur.* infantry.

*Pedester, tris, tre.* Pedestrian, on foot, on land; *pedestres copiae,* infantry forces.

*Pellicio, ĕre, lexi, lectum.* To allure, cajole.

*Pellis, is,* f. Skin, hide.

*Pello, ĕre, pepŭli, pulsum.* To drive.

*Pelopĭdas, ae,* m. Pelopidas, a celebrated Theban general, (230).

*Penarius, a, um.* Of *or* for provisions; *cella penaria,* granary.

*Pendeo, ĕre, pependi.* To hang, be suspended.

*Penĕtro, āre, āvi, ātum.* To penetrate.

*Penĭtus,* adv. Inwardly; fully, entirely.

*Per,* prep. with acc. Through, by, during.

*Per-curro, ĕre, percucurri* or *percurri, cursum.* To run through, pass over.

*Percussor, ōris,* m. Assassin, murderer.

*Perdiccas* or *Perdicca, ae,* m. Perdiccas, one of the most distinguished generals of Alexander the Great, (97).

*Perdĭtus, a, um,* (perdo). Lost, abandoned, desperate.

*Per-do, ĕre, dĭdi, dĭtum.* To destroy, waste, lose.

*Per-dūco, ĕre, duxi, ductum.* To conduct, bring to, to extend, build, make.

*Perennis*, *e*, (per, annus). Continual, perpetual.

*Per-eo*, *ire*, *ivi* or *ii*, *itum.* To perish. 295.

*Per-exiguus*, *a*, *um.* Very small, very little.

*Per-fĕro*, *ferre*, *tŭli*, *lātum.* To carry through; bear; suffer.

*Perfidia*, *ae*, f. Perfidy.

*Pergo*, *ĕre*, *rexi*, *rectum*, (per, rego). To go on or to, persevere.

*Pericles*, *is*, m. Pericles, a celebrated Athenian orator and statesman, (222).

*Periculōsus*, *a*, *um*, (pericŭlum). Dangerous.

*Pericŭlum*, *i*, n. Danger, peril.

*Peritus*, *a*, *um.* Skilled in, skilful.

*Per-magnus*, *a*, *um.* Very great.

*Per-mitto*, *ĕre*, *misi*, *missum.* To send; grant, permit; *permittĭtur*, impers., it is permitted.

*Per-multus*, *a*, *um.* Very much, very many.

*Permutatio*, *ōnis*, f. Exchange, barter.

*Per-paucus*, *a*, *um.* Few, very few.

*Per-pĕtro*. *āre*, *āvi*, *ātum.* To finish, achieve.

*Perpetuo*, adv. (perpetuus). Constantly, ever.

*Perpetuus*, *a*, *um.* Perpetual, constant.

*Persa*, *ae*. or *Perses*, *ae*, m. A Persian, (44, II.; 126).

*Per-sĕquor*, *sĕqui*, *secūtus sum*, dep. To follow, pursue, carry on, prosecute.

*Perseus*, *i*, or *Perses*, *ae*, m. Perseus or Perses, the last king of Macedonia, (198).

*Persevĕro*, *āre*, *āvi*, *ātum.* To persevere, persist.

*Persĭcus*, *a*, *um.* Persian, (50, 13).

*Persōna*, *ae*, f. Part, character, person.

*Perspicio*, *ĕre*, *spexi*, *spectum*, (per, specio). To perceive.

*Per-stringo*, *ĕre*, *strinxi*, *strictum.* To graze, wound slightly.

*Per-suadeo*, *ĕre*, *suāsi*, *suāsum.* To persuade.

*Per-terreo*, *ĕre*, *ui*, *itum.* To terrify greatly.

*Pertineo*, *ĕre*, *tinui*, (per, teneo). To pertain to, tend.

*Per-turbo*, *āre*, *āvi*, *ātum.* To disturb, throw into confusion, route, embarrass.

*Per-utĭlis*, *e.* Very useful.

*Per-venio*, *ire*, *vēni*, *ventum.* To reach, come to.

*Perverse*, adv. Perversely, wrongly.

*Pes*, *pĕdis*, m. Foot.

*Peto*, *ĕre*, *ivi* or *ii*, *itum.* To seek, ask; aim at; attack.

*Phaëthon*, *ontis*, m. Phaethon, fabled son of Helios the sun, (71).

*Phalĕrae*, *ārum*, f. pl. Trappings, ornaments for horses.

*Phalērum*, *i*, n. Phalerum, the oldest harbor of Athens; often called *Phalerĭcus portus.*

*Pharnăces*, *is*, m. Pharnaces, son of Mithridates, (205).

*Pharsālus*, *i*, f. Pharsalus, a city in Thessaly, where Pompey was defeated by Caesar, (210). The district was called Pharsalia.

*Philippi*, *ōrum*, m. pl. Philippi, a city in Macedonia, (213).

*Philippus*, *i*, m. Philip, the name of several Macedonian kings, the most celebrated of whom was the father of Alexander the Great, (140, 230).

*Philosophia, ae,* f.  Philosophy.

*Philŏsŏphus, i,* m.  Philosopher.

*Phyle, es,* f.  Phyle, a castle in Attica, (228).

*Picēnum, i,* n.  Picenum, a district in the eastern part of Italy.

*Picēnus, a, um, (Picēnum).*  Of or belonging to Picenum. Picene, (23, 19).

*Piĕtas, ātis,* f.  Dutiful conduct, sense of duty; affection; loyalty; piety.

*Piget, ēre, piguit* or *pigĭtum est,* impers.  It irks, grieves, displeases. 299.

*Pingo, ĕre, pinxi, pictum.*  To paint, depict.

*Piraeus,* or *Piraeeus, i,* m.  The Piraeus, the celebrated port of Athens, (228).

*Pirāta, ae,* m.  Pirate.

*Piscis, is,* m.  A fish.

*Pius, i,* m.  See *Metellus Pius,* (138).

*Placeo, ēre, ui, ĭtum.*  To please, be pleasing to; be determined.

*Placĭdus, a, um,* (placeo).  Quiet, gentle.

*Placo, āre, āvi, ātum.*  To quiet, soothe, calm, appease.

*Plancus, i,* m.  Plancus, a Roman name, (42, 9).

*Plataeae, ārum,* f. pl.  Plataea, a city in Boeotia, (221).

*Plataeenses, ium,* m. pl.  The Plataeans, the inhabitants of Plataea, (216).

*Plato, ōnis,* m.  Plato, one of the most celebrated Grecian philoso-

phers, disciple of Socrates, and instructor of Aristotle, (81).

*Plebs, bis,* f.  Common people, people.

*Plenus, a, um.*  Full, possessed of, rich in.

*Plerumque,* adv. (plerusque).  Commonly, generally, frequently.

*Plerusque, āque, umque.*  Most, many.

*Plurĭmus.*  See *Multus.*

*Plus,* adv.  More.

*Plus, uris,* n. adj.  More, *pl.* many, several.  See *Multus.*

*Pocŭlum, i,* n.  Cup.

*Poēma, ātis,* n.  Poem.

*Poena, ae,* f.  Punishment.

*Poenus, i,* m.  A Carthaginian, (185).

*Poēta, ae,* m.  Poet.

*Polliceor, ēri, ĭtus sum,* dep.  To promise, offer.

*Pollux, ūcis,* m.  Pollux, a celebrated pugilist, brother of *Castor,* (63, 9).  According to some authorities, he was the son of Tyndarus, but according to others, he was the son of Jupiter.  See *Castor.*

*Polycrātes, is,* m.  Polycrates, a celebrated tyrant of Samos, (24, 12).

*Pompa, ae,* f.  Pomp, public procession, procession.

*Pompeius, ii,* m.  Pompey, the name of a Roman gens.  *Cnaeus Pompeius,* a Roman consul and a distinguished commander, defeated by Caesar at Pharsalia, (205).  *Quintus Pompeius,* also consul and commander, defeated in several engagements by the Numantines, (201).

*Pompeianus, a, um,* adj. (Pompeius).

Pompeian, ef *or* belonging to Pompey, (211).

*Pompilius, ii,* m. See *Numa.*

√*Pondus, ĕris,* n. Weight.

*Pono, ĕre, posŭi, posĭtum.* To place, build, pitch.

*Pons, Pontis,* m. Bridge.

*Pontius, ii,* m. Pontius, a Roman name. *Pontius Thelesīnus,* a general of the Samnites, who conquered the Romans at the Caudine Forks, (179).

*Pontus, i,* m. Pontus, a province in Asia Minor, south of the Black Sea, (202).

√*Populatio, ōnis,* f. (popŭlo). Pillaging, booty; people, population.

*Popŭlo, āre, āvi, ātum,* (popŭlus). To depopulate, devastate, pillage; *popŭlor,* dep. = popŭlo.

*Popŭlus, i,* m. People, nation, tribe.

*Porrĭgo, ĕre, rexi, rectum.* To extend, stretch.

*Porsĕna, ae,* m. Porsena, a king of Etruria in Italy, (171).

*Porta, ae,* f. Gate.

*Portendo, ĕre, tendi, tentum.* To portend.

*Portio, ōnis,* f. Portion, share.

*Portus, us,* m. Port, harbor.

*Posco, ĕre, poposci.* To demand, ask.

√*Possessio, ōnis,* f. (possideo). Possession.

*Possideo, ĕre, sēdi, sessum.* To possess.

*Possum, posse, potui,* irreg. To be able. 289.

*Post,* adv., and prep. with acc. Afterwards, after, behind, since.

*Post-ea,* adv. Afterwards.

*Posterĭtas, ātis,* f. (postĕrus). Posterity.

*Postĕrus, a, um;* comp. *posterior,* superl. *postrēmus, postŭmus.* Following, ensuing; *postĕri,* posterity, descendants; *postrēmo, ad postrēmum,* at last. 163, 3.

*Post-fĕro, ferre.* To place after, esteem less; sacrifice.

*Post-pōno, ĕre, posŭi, posĭtum.* To put after, esteem less, postpone; disregard, neglect.

*Post-quam,* or *post quam,* conj. After, after that.

*Postrēmo,* adv. (postrēmus). At last, finally.

*Postrēmus, a, um.* The last; *ad postrēmum,* at last, finally. See *postĕrus.*

*Postridie,* adv. On the following day.

*Postŭlo, āre, āvi, ātum.* To demand.

*Postumius, ii,* m. Postumius, the name of a Roman gens or clan. *Aulus Postumius,* a Roman in whose consulship the first Punic war was brought to a close, (89, 188). *Spurius Postumius,* a Roman consul, defeated by the Samnites at the Caudine Forks, (179).

*Potens, entis,* (possum). Able, powerful.

*Potentĭa, ae,* f. Might, force, power, ability.

√*Potestas, ātis,* f. (potens). Power.

*Potior, potīri, potītus sum,* dep. To obtain, get possession of.

*Potis, e,* comp. *potior,* superl. *potissĭmus.* Able, capable, possible.

*Potius, potissĭme,* adv. (potis); positive not used. Rather than.

*Prae,* prep. with abl. Before, for, on account of, in comparison with.

*Praebeo, ēre, ui, ĭtum.* To show, furnish.

*Prae-cēdo, ēre, cessi, cessum.* To precede, surpass, outstrip.

*Praeceptor, ōris,* m. (praecipio). Preceptor, commander, teacher.

*Praeceptum, i,* n. (praecipio). Maxim, rule, precept.

*Praecipio, ēre, cēpi, ceptum* (prae, capio). To admonish, advise, order.

*Praecipitium, ii,* n. Precipice.

*Praecipĭto, āre, āvi, ātum.* To throw down, precipitate.

*Praecipuus, a, um.* Remarkable, prominent, special.

*Praeclārē, ius, issĭme,* adv. (preclārus). Excellently, nobly.

*Prae-clārus, a, um.* Excellent, noble, distinguished, illustrious.

*Praeclūdo, ēre, clūsi, clūsum,* (prae, claudo). To hinder, preclude, cut off.

*Praeco, ōnis,* m. Herald, crier.

*Praeda, ae,* f. Prey, booty.

*Prae-dīco, ēre, dixi, dictum.* To predict, forewarn.

*Praedictum, i,* n. (praedīco). Prediction, warning.

*Praedĭtus, a, um.* Endued with, possessed of.

*Praedor, āri, ātus sum,* (praeda). To plunder.

*Prae-fāri,* defective. To predict, prophesy; say. 297, II. 3.

*Praefectus, i,* m. Commander, prefect.

*Prae-fĕro, ferre, tŭli, latum.* To prefer, choose; carry *or* bear before.

*Praeficio, ēre, fēci, fectum,* (prae, facio). To place over, put in command.

*Prae-lĕgo, ēre, lēgi, lectum.* To read to another, to read aloud, to lecture.

*Prae-mitto, ēre, mīsi, missum.* To send forward, send in advance.

*Praemium, ii,* n. Reward, premium.

*Praeneste, is,* n. Praeneste, a town in Latium, (182).

*Prae-pōno, ēre, posui, posĭtum.* To place over, intrust with.

*Praesens, entis.* Present; *praesentia, ōrum,* n. pl. present things, the present.

*Praesentia, ae,* f. (praesens). Presence.

*Praeses, ĭdis,* adj. Presiding, ruling, chief; *subs.* head, chief, ruler, governor.

*Praesidium, ii,* n. Guard, garrison.

*Praestabĭlis, e.* Preëminent, distinguished, excellent.

*Praestans, antis,* (praesto). Excellent, eminent.

*Praestantia, ae,* f. Superiority, preeminence.

*Praesto, āre, stĭti, ĭtum,* (prae, sto). To surpass, be superior to; furnish, do, pay, render (as service); evince, show, give.

*Prae-sum, esse, fui.* To preside over, command.

*Prae-tendo, ēre, tendi, tentum.* To pretend, allege.

*Praeter,* prep. with acc. Except, besides.

*Praeter-ea,* adv. Besides, moreover.

*Praeter-eo, ĭre, ĭvi or ii, ĭtum.* To pass by, omit. 295.

*Praeterĭtus, a, um,* (praetereo). Gone by, past; *praeterĭta, ōrum,* n. pl. the past.

*Praeter-vĕhor, vĕhi, vectus sum,* dep.

To be borne over *or* by; to drive *or* sail by; to pass by.

*Praetorius, a, um,* (praetor). Praetorian, belonging to a praetor *or* general; *praetorius,* subs. one who has been praetor.

*Prae-vidĕo, ĕre, vidi, visum.* To foresee.

*Pratum, i,* n. Meadow, pasture.

*Pravus, a, um.* Depraved, bad.

*Preces, um,* f. pl. *dat. acc.* and *abl. sing.* also occur. Prayers, entreaties.

*Precor, āri, ātus sum.* To beseech, pray.

*Premo, ĕre, pressi, pressum.* To press, urge.

*Pretium, ii,* n. Price, worth.

*Pridie,* adv. On the day before.

*Primo, primum,* adv. (primus). At first, first; *quam primum,* as soon as possible.

*Primus, a, um,* superl. (prior). First. 166.

*Princeps, ĭpis,* m. Prince, ruler; chief man.

*Principātus, us,* m. Sovereignty, imperial power.

*Principium, ii,* n. Beginning.

*Prior, us.* Former, previous. 166.

*Priscus, i,* m. Priscus, the surname of *Lucius Tarquinius,* the fifth king of Rome, (162).

*Pristĭnus, a, um.* Ancient, pristine.

*Prius,* adv. Before, first; *priusquam* or *prius quam,* before that, before.

*Privātus, a, um.* Private, personal, *subs.* a private citizen.

*Pro,* prep. with abl. Before, in front of; for, in behalf of, instead of, as; *pro hoste,* as an enemy.

*Probatio, ōnis,* f. Approbation, proof.

*Probātus, a, um,* (probo). Tried, tested, proved, approved.

*Probĭtas, ātis,* f. (probus). Honesty, probity, integrity.

*Probo, āre, āvi, ātum,* (probus). To prove, show; approve.

*Probus, a, um.* Upright, honest.

*Procas, ae,* m. Procas, a Roman name. *Silvius Procas,* a king of Alba, (151).

*Pro-cēdo, ĕre, cessi, cessum.* To step forth, to advance, proceed, come on, succeed.

*Procillus, i,* m. Procillus, a young man sent by Caesar to Ariovistus, (52).

*Pro-clāmo, āre, āvi, ātum.* To cry out, proclaim.

*Pro-consul, ŭlis,* m. Proconsul, one with the authority of consul.

*Procul,* adv. At a distance, far off.

*Pro-cūro, āre, āvi, ātum.* To attend to, have the care of.

*Pro-curro, ĕre, curri* (cucurri), *cursum.* To run forth, project.

*Proditio, ōnis,* f. (prodo). Treachery, treason.

*Prodĭtor, ōris,* m. (prodo). Traitor.

*Pro-do, ĕre, dĭdi, dĭtum.* To disclose, betray.

*Pro-dūco, ĕre, duxi, ductum.* To lead forth, produce.

*Proelium, ii,* n. Battle, conflict.

*Profecto,* adv. Indeed, truly.

*Proficiscor, proficisci, profectus sum.* To depart, set out, go.

*Proflīgo, āre, āvi, ātum,* (pro, fligo). To overthrow, ruin.

*Pro-fundo, ĕre, fūdi, fūsum.* To

pour out, spend; throw away, lavish, dissipate.

*Progredior, grĕdi, gressus sum,* dep. (pro, gradior). To proceed, advance.

*Prohibeo, ēre, ui, ĭtum,* (pro, habeo). To prohibit, prevent.

*Promissus, a, um,* (promitto). Growing long, long.

*Pro-mitto, ēre, misi, missum.* To send forth, promise.

*Promontorium, ii,* n. Promontory.

*Promptus, a, um.* Prompt, ready.

*Pro-nuntio, āre, āvi, ātum.* To publish, proclaim, announce; recite, declaim; act, tell, narrate.

*Propāgo, āre, āvi, ātum.* To propagate; prolong.

*Prope,* adv., and prep. with acc. Near, nearly, near to, close by, near.

*Propĕro, āre, āvi, ātum.* To hasten.

*Propior, ius.* Nearer. See 166.

*Propius,* adv. Nearer.

*Pro-pōno, ēre, posui, posĭtum.* To set forth, state, propose.

*Proprius, a, um.* Peculiar, proper, one's own, characteristic of.

*Propter,* prep. with acc. For, on account of.

*Propter-ea,* adv. Therefore, on that account.

*Pro-pulso, āre, āvi, ātum.* To repel, ward off.

*Prora, ae,* f. Prow, forepart of a ship.

*Prorsus,* adv. Uninterruptedly, straight on, absolutely.

*Pro-rumpo, ēre, rūpi, ruptum.* To rush *or* break forth. *.

*Pro-scribo, ēre, scripsi, scriptum.* To proscribe, outlaw.

*Prosĭlio, īre, ii or ui,* (pro, salio). To leap up, spring forth.

*Prospĕre, ius, rime,* adv. (prospĕrus). Happily, prosperously.

*Prospĕrus, a, um.* Favorable, fortunate, prosperous.

*Prospicĭo, ēre, spexi, spectum,* (pro, specio). To look forward, look, see; look out for, take care of, provide for; discern, descry.

*Prosterno, ēre, strāvi, strātum,* (pro, sterno). To prostrate, overthrow.

*Pro-sum, prodesse, profui.* To profit, avail, be useful.

*Protĭnus,* adv. Directly, immediately after.

*Pro-video, ēre, vīdi, vīsum.* To provide, be on one's guard.

*Provĭdus, a, um,* (provideo). Foreseeing, prudent, cautious, provident.

*Provincia, ae,* f. Province.

*Provocatio, ōnis,* f. (provŏco). Challenge, appeal.

*Provŏco, āre, āvi, ātum.* To challenge, appeal.

*Proxĭmus, a, um.* Nearest, next. 166.

*Prudens, entis.* Prudent, wise, learned, skilled.

*Prudentia, ae,* f. (prudens). Prudence.

*Ptolemaeus, i,* m. Ptolemy, the name of several kings of Egypt, (211).

*Publicŏla, ae,* m. Publicola, the surname of *Valerius,* one of the first consuls at Rome, (169).

*Publicus, a, um.* Public.

*Publius, ii,* m. Publius, a Roman name; as, *Publius Rutilius Rufus,* (139).

*Pudet, ĭre, pŭduit, pudĭtum est,* impers. It shames; *pudet me,* it shames me, I am ashamed.

*Pudor, ōris,* m. Regard, respect, modesty, awe, shame.

*Puella, ae,* f. Girl.

*Puer, ĕri,* m. Boy.

*Puerilis, e,* (puer). Boyish, youthful.

*Pueritia, ae,* f. (puer). Boyhood.

*Pugio, ōnis,* m. Dagger, poniard.

*Pugna, ae,* f. Battle.

*Pugno, āre, āvi, ātum.* To fight.

*Pulcher, chra, chrum.* Beautiful.

*Pulvillus, i,* m. Pulvillus. *Horatius Pulvillus,* a Roman consul in the first year after the banishment of Tarquin, (170).

*Pumilio, ōnis,* m. and f. Dwarf, pigmy.

*Punĭcus, a, um,* (Poeni). Punic, Carthaginian, belonging to Carthage or the Carthaginians. (196).

*Punio, ĭre, ĭvi, ĭtum.* To punish.

*Pupillus, i,* m. Pupil.

*Puppis, is* f. The stern, the hinder part of a ship.

*Pusillus, a, um.* Small, weak; little.

*Puto, āre, āvi, ātum.* To think, imagine, esteem.

*Pydna, ae,* f. Pydna, a town of Macedonia, celebrated for the victory of Paulus over Perseus, (198).

*Pyrenaeus, i,* m. The Pyrenees, a range of mountains between France and Spain, (190).

*Pyrrhus, i,* m. Pyrrhus, a king of Epirus, (183).

*Pythagoras, ae,* m. Pythagoras, a celebrated philosopher of Samos, (94).

*Pythia, ae,* f. Pythia, the priestess of Apollo, at Delphi, (217).

## Q.

Q. or Qu. An abbreviation of *Quintus.*

*Quadragesĭmus, a, um,* (quadraginta). Fortieth.

*Quadraginta,* indecl. Forty.

*Quadrīga, ae,* f. Chariot, four-horse chariot.

*Quadringentesĭmus, a, um,* (quadringenti). The four hundredth.

*Quadringenti, ae, a.* Four hundred.

*Quaero* or *quaeso, ĕre, quaesīvi, quaesītum.* To seek, inquire, ask, implore. *Quaerĭtur,* impers. It is asked, the question is asked.

*Qualis, e.* What, what sort; *talis —qualis,* such—as.

*Quam,* adv. and conj. How; as, than, after: *quam multi,* how many; *with superl.* intensive, *quam maxĭmus,* as great as possible.

*Quam-diu,* adv. How long, as long as.

*Quam-quam,* conj. Although, though.

*Quam-vis.* However, however much, though.

*Quantus, a, um.* How great, how much; *tantus—quantus,* so great as; *quanto,* by how much, as.

*Qua-re.* Wherefore, whereby.

*Quartus, a, um.* Fourth.

*Quasi.* As if.

*Quaterni, ae, a,* distributive. Four by four, four at a time, four each. 174, 2.

*Quatio, ĕre, quassi, quassum.* To shake.

*Quatriduum, i,* n. (quattuor, dies). Space of four days, four days.

*Quattuor,* indecl. Four.

*Quattuordĕcim,* indecl. (quattuor, decem). Fourteen.

*?ue,* appended to another word. And. 587, I. 3.

*Quem-ad-mŏdum,* adv. In what manner, how, as.

*Querĕla, ae,* f. (queror). Complaint.

*Queror, queri, questus sum,* dep. To complain.

*Qui, quae, quod,* rel. and interrog. Who, which, what.

*Quia,* conj. Because.

*Quicunque* (or *cumque*) *quaecunque, quodcunque.* Whoever, whatever.

*Quidam, quaedam, quoddam* or *quiddam.* A certain one, certain.

*Quidem.* Indeed.

*Quies, ĕtis,* f. Rest, quiet.

*Quiesco, ĕre, quiēvi, quiētum,* (quies). To rest, repose, keep quiet.

*Quiētus, a, um,* (quiesco). Quiet, at rest.

*Qui-lĭbet, quaelĭbet, quodlĭbet,* indef. pron. Any one, any.

*Quin.* That not, but that, that.

*Quinctius, ii,* m. Quinctius. *Titus Quinctius,* a Roman general at the time the city was threatened by the Gauls, 321 B. C. (177). *Titus Quinctius Flaminius* gained the victory at Cynoscephalae, (197).

*Quindĕcim,* indecl. Fifteen.

*Quingentesĭmus, a, um,* (quingenti). The five hundreth.

*Quingenti, ae, a.* Five hundred.

*Quinquagesĭmus, a, um,* (quinquaginta). Fiftieth.

*Quinquaginta,* indecl. Fifty.

*Quinque,* indecl. Five.

*Quinquennium, ii,* n. Five years, space of five years.

*Quintus, a, um.* Fifth.

*Quintus, i,* m. Quintus, a common Roman name; as, *Quintus Mucius Scaevŏla,* (172).

*Quippe,* conj. Indeed.

*Quis, quae, quid ?* interrog. pron. Who, which, what ?

*Quis, quae, quid,* indef. pron. Some one, any one. 190, 1.

*Quisnam* or *quinam, quaenam, quodnam* or *quidnam.* Who, which, what.

*Quispiam, quaepiam, quodpiam,* and subs. *quidpiam* or *quippiam,* indef. pron. Any one, any body, any; some one, some thing, some.

*Quis-quam, quaequam, quidquam* or *quicquam.* Any, any one.

*Quis-que, quaeque, quodque* or *quidque.* Every, every one, whoever, whatever; *with superl., intensive, primo quoque tempŏre,* on the very first opportunity.

*Quis-quis, quaequae, quidquid* or *quicquid.* Whoever, whatever.

*Quo.* Where, whither, that, in order that.

*Quo-ad.* Till, until, as long as, as far as.

*Quod,* conj. That, because.

*Quomĭnus,* (quo, minus). That not, from.

*Quomŏdo,* adv. (quo, modo). How, by what means.

*Quondam,* adv. Formerly.

*Quoque.* Also, too.

*Quot,* adj. pl. indec. How many, as many, as; all.

*Quot-annis.* Every year, yearly.

*Quotidie.* Daily, every day.

*Quotus, a, um.* Of what number, how many; what, *often applied to the hour of the day.*

*Quum* or *cum.* When, since; though; *quum—tum,* not only—but also, both—and; *rarely* either —or.

### R.

*Rabies, ēi,* f. Madness, rage.

*Radix, ĭcis,* f. Root, foot, base, *as of a mountain.*

*Ramus, i,* m. Branch.

*Rapīna, ae,* f. Rapine, plunder.

*Rapio, ĕre, rapui, raptum.* To rob, carry off.

*Raptor, ōris,* m. (rapio). Robber, plunderer.

*Raro,* adv. (rarus). Rarely, seldom.

*Rarus, a, um.* Rare, uncommon.

*Ratio, ōnis,* f. A calculating, thinking; reason, understanding; plan, method, kind.

*Ratis, is,* f. Raft.

*Re-bello, āre, āvi, ātum.* To rebel.

*Re-cēdo, ĕre, cessi, cessum.* To withdraw, recede, retire.

*Recens, entis.* Recent, fresh, young, new.

*Recipio, ĕre, cēpi, ceptum,* (re, capio). To receive, recover, resume; *se recipĕre,* to betake one's self, withdraw.

*Recĭto, āre, āvi, ātum,* (re, cito). To repeat, recite.

*Recognosco, ĕre, nōvi, nĭtum,* (re, cognosco). To recognize.

*Recordātio, ōnis,* f. (recordor). Recollection, remembrance.

*Recordor, āri, ātus sum,* dep. To recollect.

*Recte, ius, issĭme,* adv. (rectus). Rightly.

*Rector, ōris,* m. (rego). Director, ruler.

*Rectum, i,* n. (rectus). Right.

*Rectus, a, um,* (rego). Straight, right, correct.

*Recupĕro, āre, āvi, ātum.* To regain.

*Red-do, ĕre, dĭdi, dĭtum.* To restore, return; make; render, repeat, recite, give up, resign; assign.

*Red-eo, īre, ĭvi* or *ii, ĭtum.* To go back, return. 295.

*Redĭgo, ĕre, ēgi, actum,* (red, ago). To force, reduce, compel.

*Redĭmo, ĕre, ēmi, emptum,* (red, emo). To ransom.

*Redĭtus, ūs,* m. (redeo). Return, revenue.

*Re-dūco, ĕre, duxi, ductum.* To lead back, reduce.

*Red-undo, āre, āvi, ātum.* To overflow; to abound.

*Re-fercio, īre, fersi, fertum,* (re, farcio). To fill, stuff, cram.

*Re-fĕro, ferre, tŭli, lātum,* (refero). To bring back, requite, return, render, place among, refer; *refert,* imps. it concerns, matters.

*Refertus, a, um,* part. (refercio). Filled.

*Reficio, ĕre, fēci, fectum,* (re, facio). To repair, restore; recover.

*Refluo, ĕre, fluxi, fluxum,* (re, fluo). To flow back.

*Re-fugio, ĕre, fūgi, fugĭtum.* To retreat.

*Regīna, ae,* f.  Queen.

*Regio, ōnis,* f.  Region, country.

*Regius, a, um,* (rex).  Royal.

*Regno, āre, āvi, ātum,* (regnum).  To reign, rule.

*Regnum, i,* n. (rex).  Kingdom, sovereignty, government.

*Rego, ĕre, rexi, rectum.* To direct, rule, manage.

*Regredior, grĕdi, gressus sum,* dep. (re, gradior).  To return.

*Regŭla, ae,* f. (rego).  Rule, pattern, model.

*Regŭlus, i,* m.  Regulus.  *Marcus Atilius Regŭlus,* a distinguished Roman consul taken prisoner by the Carthaginians in the first Punic war, (186).

*Religio, ōnis,* f.  Religion, obligation.

*Re-linquo, ĕre, lĩqui, lictum.* To leave, desert.

*Reliquiae, ārum,* f. pl.  Remnant, those who escaped.

*Relĭquus, a, um.* The rest, remaining, the other.  *Relĭquum est,* it is left, it remains.

*Re-maneo, ĕre, mansi, mansum.* To remain.

*Remedium, ii,* n.  Remedy.

*Reminiscor, ci,* dep.  To remember.

*Re-mitto, ĕre, mĩsi, missum.* To send back.

*Re-moveo, ĕre, mōvi, mōtum.* To take away, remove.

*Remus, i,* m.  Oar.

*Remus, i,* m.  Remus, the brother of Romulus, (152).

*Renŏvo, āre, āvi, ātum,* (re, novo).  To renew.

*Re-nuntio, āre, āvi, ātum.* To report, announce.

*Repăro, āre, āvi, ātum,* (re, paro).  To renew, repair.

*Re-pello, ĕre, pŭli, pulsum.* To repel, drive back.

*Repente,* adv.  Suddenly.

*Repentīnus, a, um.* Unexpected, sudden.

*Reperio, īre, pĕri, pertum,* (re, pario).  To find.

*Re-pleo, ĕre, ēvi, ētum.* To fill, fill again.

*Re-pōno, ĕre, posui, posĭtum.* To replace, restore, lay up.

*Re-porto, āre, āvi, ātum.* To gain, bear off.

*Reprehendo, ĕre, prehendi, prehensum,* (re, prehendo).  To blame, censure.

*Repudio, āre, āvi, ātum.* To reject, divorce.

*Re-pugno, āre, āvi, ātum.* To resist.

*Re-quīro, ĕre, quisīvi or ii, quisĭtum* (re, quaero).  To seek, demand, require.

*Res, rei,* f.  Thing; affair; state; deed, reality, battle; *res gestae,* exploits ; *res publĭca,* republic.

*Re-scrĭbo, ĕre, scripsi, scriptum.* To write back, reply in writing.

*Resideo, ēre, sēdi,* (re, sedeo).  To sit, remain, sit down.

*Resisto, ĕre, stĭti, stĭtum.* To oppose, resist.

*Respectus, us,* m. (respicio).  Respect, regard.

*Respicio, ĕre, spexi, spectum,* (re, specio).  To look back ; regard, respect.

*Re-spondeo, ĕre, spondi, sponsum.* To reply.

*Responsum, i.* n. (respondeo). Answer, response.

*Res publica, rei publicae,* or *respublica, reipublicae,* f.  Republic. 126.

*Re-spuo, ĕre, spui.* To cast out, eject; reject, refuse, dislike.

*Restituo, ĕre, stitui, stitūtum,* (re, statuo). To restore.

*Re-tardo, āre, āvi, ātum.* To detain, retard, check.

*Retineo, ĕre, tinui, tentum,* (re, teneo). To retain.

*Reus, i,* m. Criminal, defendant.

*Reverentia, ae,* f. Reverence.

*Re-verto, ĕre, verti, versum;* *revertor,* dep. To come back, return.

*Re-vŏco, āre, āvi, ātum.* To recall.

*Rex, regis,* m. King.

*Rhea, ae,* f. Rhea. *Rhea Silvia,* the daughter of Numitor and the mother of Romulus and Remus, (152).

*Rhenus, i,* m. The river Rhine, (208).

*Rhodănus, i,* m. The river Rhone, in Gaul, (208).

*Rhodius, a, um,* (Rhodos, *the island of Rhodes*). Rhodian, of or belonging to Rhodes. *Rhodius, ii,* m. A Rhodian, (143).

*Rideo, ĕre, si, sum.* To laugh, to laugh at.

*Ripa, ae,* f. Bank, *as of a river.*

*Rite,* adv. Rightly, in due form.

*Robur, ŏris,* n. Strength.

*Robustus, a, um,* (robur). Robust, strong.

*Rogatio, ōnis,* f. (rogo). An asking, question; entreaty, request.

*Rogo, āre, āvi, ātum.* To ask, question.

*Roma, ae,* f. Rome, (27).

*Romānus, a, um,* adj. (Roma). Roman; subs. *Romānus, i,* m. a Roman, (26).

*Romŭlus, i,* m. Romulus, the founder of Rome, (154).

*Roscius, ii,* m. Roscius, a Roman name. *Lucius Roscius,* a celebrated tribune of the people and friend of Cicero, (51).

*Rotundus, a, um.* Round, spherical.

*Rufus, i,* m. Rufus, a Roman surname; as, Publius Rutilius Rufus, (139).

*Ruina, ae,* f. Ruin, fall.

*Rullianus, i.* m. Rullianus, a Roman name. *Quintus Fabius Rullianus,* master of the cavalry (*magister equitum*) under the dictator *Papirius Cursor,* (178).

*Rumpo, ĕre, rupi, ruptum.* To break.

*Ruo, ĕre, rui, rultum* or *rutum.* To run, rush forth.

*Rupes, is,* f. Rock, cliff.

*Rursus* (or *um*), adv. Back, again.

*Rus, ruris,* n. Country, *as opposed to city.*

*Rusticus, i,* m. Countryman, farmer, peasant, husbandman.

*Rutilius, ii,* m. Rutilius, a Roman name. *Publius Rutilius Rufus,* a Roman consul, slain in the Social war, (139).

## S.

*S.* An abbreviation for *Sextus, Sp* for *Spurius.*

*Sabini, ōrum,* m. pl. The Sabines, a people of Italy, bordering upon Latium, (157).

*Sacer, sacra, sacrum.* Sacred.

*Sacerdos, ōtis,* m. and f. (sacer). Priest, priestess.

*Sacrificium, ii,* n. Sacrifice.

*Sacro, āre, āvi, ātum,* (sacer). To consecrate.

*Sacrum, i,* n. Sacred rite *or* institution; sacrifice.

*Saepe, ius, issime,* adv. Often.

*Saevio, īre, īvi* or *ii, ītum.* To rage, be cruel.

*Sagacĭtas, ātis,* f. Sagacity, acuteness, shrewdness.

*Sagax, ācis.* Acute, sagacious.

*Sagitta, ae,* f. Arrow.

*Saguntum, i,* n. Saguntum, a town in Spain, on the Mediterranean, (189).

*Saguntini, ōrum,* m. pl. The Saguntines, citizens of Saguntum, (189).

*Salāmis, is* or *īnis,* f. (acc. *Salamī-na*), or *Salamīna, ae,* f. The island of Salamis, off the coast of Attica, (217).

*Salūber, bris, bre,* (salus). Healthful, salubrious.

*Salus, ūtis,* f. Safety; *Salus* personified, the Roman goddess, *Salus,* (20, 7).

*Salutāris, e,* (salus). Healthful, wholesome.

*Salūto, āre, āvi, ātum,* (salus). To salute.

*Salve,* def. verb. Hail. See 297, III. 1.

*Salvus, a, um.* Safe, unhurt.

*Samnītes, ium,* m. pl. The Samnites, the inhabitants of Samnium, in Italy, (178).

*Samus* or *Samos, i,* f. The island Samos, on the coast of Asia Minor.

*Sancte, ius, issime,* (sanctus, *sacred, pure*), adv. Chastely, purely, conscientiously.

*Sanguis, ĭnis,* m. Blood.

*Sannio, ōnis,* m. Sannio, a proper name, (35).

*Sapiens, entis.* Wise; *subs.* a wise man.

*Sapienter, ius, issime,* adv. (sapiens). Wisely.

*Sapientia, ae,* f. (sapiens). Wisdom.

*Sapio, ĕre, īvi* or *ui.* To taste; to have sense, to know, understand, be wise.

*Sardes, ium,* f. Sardis, the ancient capital of Lydia.

*Sardinia, ae,* f. The island of Sardinia, west of Italy, (188).

*Satelles, ĭtis,* m. and f. Lifeguard, attendant.

*Satio, āre, āvi, ātum.* To fill, satisfy, content.

*Satis,* adv., adj., subs. Enough, sufficient, sufficiently; *satis habēre,* to have enough, be content.

*Saturnia, ae,* f. Saturnia, the town and citadel built by Saturn, (148).

*Saturnus, i,* m. Saturn, the most ancient king of Latium, (148).

*Saucius, a, um.* Wounded, injured, hurt, sick, intoxicated.

*Saxum, i,* n. Rock, stone.

*Scaevŏla, ae,* m. See *Mucius,* (172).

*Scelestus, a, um,* (scelus). Wicked, criminal, infamous.

*Scelus, ĕris,* n. Crime, wickedness.

*Scena, ae,* f. Scene, stage.

*Schola, ae,* f. Leisure devoted to learning; a place of learning, a school; a lecture, dissertation.

*Scientia, ae,* f. (scio). Knowledge, science, skill, expertness.

*Scio, scīre, scivi, scitum.* To know, understand, have knowledge.

*Scipio, ŏnis,* m. Scipio, the name of a distinguished Roman family. See *Africānus,* (190).

*Scriba, ae,* m. (scribo). Scribe, clerk.

*Scribo, ĕre, scripsi, scriptum.* To write, prepare.

*Scutum, i,* n. Shield.

*Scythia, ae,* f. · Scythia, an extensive country in the north of Europe and Asia, (215).

*Scythae, ārum,* m. pl. The Scythians, (215).

*Se-cēdo, ĕre, cessi, cessum.* To retire, withdraw.

*Secundum,* adv., and prep. with acc. After, behind, next to ; according to, by the side of, along.

*Secundus, a, um.* Second, favorable, prosperous.

*Sed,* conj. But.

*Sedĕcim,* indec. (sex, decem). Sixteen.

*Sedeo, ĕre, sedi, sessum.* To sit, stay.

*Sedes, is,* f. Seat, abode, residence.

*Seditio, ŏnis,* f. Quarrel, sedition.

*Seditiōsus, a, um,* (seditio). Mutinous, seditious.

*Sedo, āre, avi, ātum.* To allay, quiet.

*Segnis, e.* Slothful, inactive.

*Segnĭter, ius, issĭme,* adv. (segnis). Slothfully.

*Seleucia, ae,* f. Seleucia, a city of Syria on the Orontes, (206).

*Semel,* adv. Once.

*Sementis, is,* f. Seed ; sowing.

*Semianĭmis, e.* Half-alive, half-dead.

*Semper,* adv. Always, ever.

*Sempiternus, a, um,* (semper). Everlasting, imperishable.

*Sempronius, ii,* m. See *Gracchus,* (190).

*Senātor, ōris,* m. (senex). Senator.

*Senātus, us,* m. (senex). Senate.

*Senectus, ūtis,* f. (senex). Old age, age.

*Senesco, ĕre, senui.* To grow old, become aged ; *senescens, entis,* becoming old, aged.

*Senex, senis.* Old, aged. 168, 3.

*Senex, senis,* m. and f. An old man, an aged person.

*Senŏnes, um,* m. pl. The Senones, a powerful people in Gaul, (176).

*Sensim,* adv. (sentio). Sensibly ; slowly, gradually, by degrees.

*Sensus, us,* m. Sensation, sense, perception.

*Sententia, ae,* f. Opinion, sentence, sentiment, maxim, axiom, purpose, decision.

*Sentio, īre, sensi, sensum.* To perceive, feel, experience ; think, judge.

*Sepelio, īre, pelīvi* or *ii, pultum.* To bury.

*Sepio, īre, sepsi, scptum.* To guard, shelter.

*Septem,* indecl. Seven.

*Septĭmus, a, um,* (septem). Seventh.

*Septingentesĭmus, a, um,* (septingenti). The seven hundredth.

*Septingenti, ae, a.* Seven hundred.

*Septuagesĭmus, a, um,* (septuaginta). Seventieth.

*Septuaginta,* indecl. Seventy.

*Sepulcrum, i,* n. (sepelio). Grave, tomb, sepulchre.

*Sepultūra, ae,* f. (sepelio). Burial.

*Sequāni, ōrum,* m. The Sequani, a Gallic people, dwelling · on the river Sequana, (23, 15).

*Sequor, sequi, secūtus sum,* dep. To follow, succeed.

*Sergius, ii,* m. See *Catilīna,* (207).

*Sermo, ōnis,* m. Speech, discourse, conversation.

*Sero, ius, issīme,* adv. (serus). Late, too late.

*Serpo, ĕre, serpsi, serptum.* To spread, extend.

*Serus, a, um.* Late.

*Servilius, ii,* m. Servilius, a Roman name.

*Servio, īre, īvi* or *ii, ītum.* To be a slave, to serve, be subject to.

*Servĭtus, ūtis,* f. (servio). Servitude, slavery.

*Servius, ii,* m. Servius, a Roman name. *Servius Tullius,* the sixth king of Rome, (164).

*Servo, āre, āvi, ātum.* To observe, keep; preserve.

*Servus, i,* m. Slave.

*Seu.* Whether; *seu—seu,* whether —or.

*Sex,* indecl. Six.

*Sexagesīmus, a, um,* (sexaginta). Sixtieth.

*Sexaginta,* indecl. Sixty.

*Sexcentesīmus, a, um,* (sexcenti). Six hundredth.

*Sexcenti, ae, a.* Six hundred.

*Sextus, a, um,* (sex). Sixth.

*Si,* conj. If.

*Sic,* adv. Thus, so.

*Siccus, a, um.* Dry.

*Sicilia, ae,* f. The island of Sicily, (185).

*Sidus, ĕris,* n. A group of stars, a constellation.

*Signifĭco, āre, āvi, ātum,* (signum, facio). To show, indicate, mean, signify.

*Signum, i,* n. Mark, sign, indication, standard.

*Silentium, ii,* n. Silence, stillness, quiet, repose.

*Sileo, ēre, ui.* To be silent, still, quiet; to pass over in silence, not to speak of.

*Silvia, ae,* f. See *Rhea,* (152).

*Silvius, ii,* m. Silvius, the name of several kings of Alba, the first of whom was the son of *Aeneas,* (150, 151).

*Simĭlis, e.* Similar, like. 163, 2.

*Similĭter, ius, līme,* adv. (similis). In like manner, similarly, in a similar way. 305, 2.

*Simonĭdes, is,* m. Simonides, a celebrated lyric poet of Cea, (132).

*Simul,* adv. At the same time.

*Simulātio, ōnis,* f. An assumed appearance, pretence, simulation, deceit, hypocrisy.

*Sin,* conj. But if.

*Sine,* prep. with abl. Without.

*Singulāris, e.* Single, singular, remarkable.

*Singŭlus, a, um.* Single, one by one.

*Sinister, tra, trum.* Left, on the left.

*Sino, ĕre, sivi, situm.* To permit; allow; *situs,* put, placed, situated.

*Sinus, us,* m. Bosom, bay.

*Si-quis* or *siqui, siqua, siquid* or *siquod,* indef. pron. If any, if any one.

*Sitis, is,* f. Thirst, desire.

*Sobrius, a, um.* Sober, temperate, moderate, reasonable.

*Socer, ĕri,* m. Father-in-law.

*Sociālis, e,* (socius). Social, friendly.

*Sociĕtas, ātis,* f. (socius). League, alliance, partnership, society.

*Socius, ii*, m.  Ally, confederate.

*Socrates, is*, m.  Socrates, a celebrated Grecian philosopher, (20, 8).

*Sol, solis*, m.  Sun.

*Solemnis, e.*  Stated, established; religious, solemn.

*Solemniter*, adv. (solemnis).  Solemnly, in due form.

*Soleo, ēre, ĭtus sum.*  To be accustomed, be wont.  271, 3.

*Solĭdus, a, um.*  Solid.

✗ *Solitūdo, ĭnis*, f. (solus).  Solitude.

*Solĭtus, a, um*, (soleo).  Usual.

*Sollertia, ae*, f.  Sagacity, shrewdness.

*Solon, ōnis*, m.  Solon, a celebrated Athenian law-giver and one of the *seven wise men of Greece*, (128).

*Solum*, adv. (solus).  Only, alone.

*Solus, a, um.*  Alone.  151.

*Solūtus, a, um*, (solvo).  Unrestrained, dissolute.

*Solvo, ĕre, solvi, solūtum.*  To loose, unbind; to pay.

*Somnio, āre, āvi, ātum*, (somnium).  To dream.

*Somnium, ii*, n.  Dream.

*Somnus, i*, m.  Sleep.

*Sonĭtus, us*, m. (sono).  Sound, noise.

*Sono, āre, ui, ĭtum.*  To sound, utter, speak, call, express, mean.

*Sonus, i*, m. (sono).  Sound.

*Sophŏcles, is* and *i*, m.  Sophocles, a celebrated Grecian tragic poet, (55).

*Sordĭdus, a, um.*  Sordid, soiled, filthy, base, mean.

*Soror, ōris*, f.  Sister.

*Sors, sortis*, f.  Lot.

*Sparta, ae*, f.  Sparta, the capital of Laconia, in the Peloponnesus; also called Lacedaemon.

*Spartānus, a, um*, adj. (Sparta).  Spartan; subs. *Spartānus, i*, m., a Spartan, (222).

*Spartăcus, i*, m.  Spartacus, a celebrated gladiator who waged war against the Romans, (204).

*Spatium, ii*, n.  Space.

*Species, ēi*, f.  Appearance, guise.

*Spectacŭlum, i*, n. (specto).  Spectacle, show.

*Specto, āre, āvi, ātum.*  To view, witness.  *Spectātus, a, um.*  Tried, proved, illustrious.

*Sperno, ĕre, sprēvi, sprētum.*  To despise, reject, contemn, scorn, spurn.

*Spero, āre, āvi, ātum.*  To expect, hope; flatter one's self.

*Spes, ei*, f.  Hope.

*Spolio, āre, āvi, ātum*, (spolium).  To rob; spoil; despoil.

*Spolium, ii*, n.  Plunder, spoil, booty.

*Spontis*, gen. *sponte*, abl. sing.  Of or for himself, itself, of one's own accord, on one's own account, voluntarily, spontaneously.

*Spurius, ii*, m.  See *Postumius* and *Lucretius.*

*Stabilĭtas, ātis*, f.  Immovability, steadfastness, stability.

*Stadium, ii*, n.  A stade or stadium, a measure equal to 606 English feet; race-course, race-ground.

*Statim*, adv. (sto).  At once, immediately.

*Statio, ōnis*, f. (sto).  Station, post; residence.

*Statua, ae*, f. (statuo).  Statue.

*Statuo, ĕre, ui, ūtum*, (status, *from* sto).  To determine; appoint, place.

*Statūra, ae,* f. (status, *from* sto). Height, size of the body, stature.

*Status, us,* m. (sto). State, condition.

*Stella, ae,* f. Star.

*Sterno, ĕre, stravi, stratum.* To prostrate.

*Sto, stare, steti, statum.* To stand.

*Strages, is,* f. Slaughter, defeat.

*Strangŭlo, āre, āvi, ātum.* To strangle.

*Strenue,* adv. (strenuus). Vigorously, carefully.

*Strenuus, a, um.* Active, valiant.

*Studeo, ēre, ui.* To study, favor, be attached to; to devote one's self to; be zealous.

*Studiōse, ius, issĭme,* adv. (studiōsus). Diligently, earnestly.

*Studiōsus, a, um,* (studium). Eager, desirous, zealous; friendly, studious.

*Studium, ii,* n. Zeal, study, desire, pursuit.

*Stultitia, ae,* f. (stultus). Folly, foolishness, simplicity.

*Stultus, a, um.* Foolish, simple, silly.

*Suadeo, ēre, suasi, suasum.* To advise.

*Sub,* prep. with acc. or abl. Under, at the foot of.

*Sub-dūco, ēre, duxi, ductum.* To take away, withdraw.

*Subĭgo, ĕre, ēgi, actum,* (sub, ago). To subdue, conquer.

*Subĭto,* adv. (subĭtus, *from* subeo). Suddenly, unexpectedly.

*Sublīme,* adv. (sublimĭs). Aloft, loftily, on high.

*Sublīmis, e.* High, on high.

*Sub-mergo, ēre, mersi, mersum.* To dip *or* plunge under; to sink, overwhelm, submerge. *Pass.* To be overwhelmed, to sink.

*Sub-rideo, ēre, rīsi, rīsum.* To smile, laugh.

*Subsidium, ii,* n. The reserve; aid, reinforcement.

*Sub-silio, īre, silui* and *silĭi,* (sub, salio). To leap *or* jump up, leap, jump.

*Sub-sum, esse, fui.* To be at hand *or* near, be under.

*Subter,* prep. with acc. or abl. Below, beneath, under.

*Sub-trăho, ēre, traxi, tractum.* To take away, remove, subtract.

*Sub-venio, īre, vēni, ventum.* To come to; to aid, relieve.

*Sub-verto, ēre, verti, versum.* To overturn, overthrow, destroy, subvert.

*Succēdo, ēre, cessi, cessum,* (sub, cedo). To succeed, come after.

*Successio, ōris,* f. (succēdo). Succession.

*Successor, ōnis,* m. (succēdo). Successor.

*Successus, us,* m. (succēdo). Success.

*Suc-cumbo, ēre, cubui, cubĭtum.* To yield, submit to.

*Suffetius, ii,* m. Suffetius. *Metius Suffetius,* dictator of the Albans. Having been summoned to aid the Romans against the Veientines, he drew off his forces at the very moment of battle, and awaited the issue of the engagement. For this perfidy he was put to death by order of Tullius Hostilius (160).

*Sufficio, ēre, fēci, fectum,* (sub, facio). To substitute; be sufficient, suffice.

J

*Suffundo, ĕre, fŭdi, fusum,* (sub, fundo). To spread over, pour through; suffuse.

*Sui, sibi.* Himself, herself, itself.

*Sulla, ae,* m. Sulla, a distinguished Roman dictator and general, (202).

*Sum, esse, fui.* To be.

*Summa, ae,* f. (summus). Supreme power.

*Summoveo, ĕre, mōvi, mōtum,* (sub, moveo). To remove, displace.

*Summus.* See *Supĕrus.*

*Sumo, ĕre, ·sumpsi, sumptum.* To take, inflict.

*Sumptus, us,* m. (sumo). Expense, cost.

*Super,* prep. with acc. or abl. Over, above, upon; of, concerning, at, at the time of.

*Superbia, ae,* f. (superbus). Pride, haughtiness.

*Superbus, a, um.* Proud.

*Superbus, i,* m. Superbus, the surname of Tarquin, the last king of Rome, (167).

*Supĕro, āre, āvi, ātum,* (supĕrus). To surpass; conquer; pass by, cross.

*Superstitio, ōnis,* f. (supersto). Superstition.

*Super-sum, esse, fui.* To remain, be left, survive.

*Supĕrus, a, um ;* comp. *superior ;* superl. *suprĕmus* or *summus.* High, above; past, former. 163, 3.

*Super-venio, īre, veni, ventum.* To come to, surprise.

*Supplementum, i,* n. Supplies, reinforcement.

*Supplex, ĭcis,* (sub, plico). Humbly

begging, submissive, beseeching, suppliant; *subs.* a suppliant.

*Supplicium, ii,* n. Punishment.

*Supra,* prep. with acc. Above, upon.

*Suprĕmus.* See *Supĕrus.*

*Surripio, ĕre, ripui, reptum,* (sub, rapio). To snatch away; to steal, pilfer, purloin.

*Suscipio, ĕre, cēpi, ceptum,* (sub, capio). To bear, endure; receive; undertake, engage in.

*Suspendo, ĕre, pendi, pensum,* (sub, pendo). To suspend, hang up.

*Suspensus, a, um,* (suspendo). Uncertain, undecided; anxious.

*Suspicio, ōnis,* f. (suspĭcor). Suspicion.

*Suspicio, ĕre, spexi, spectum,* (sub, specio). To suspect.

*Suspĭcor, ari, ātus sum,* (suspicio), dep. To suspect.

*Sustento, āre, āvi, ātum,* (sustineo). To hold up, support, sustain; endure, suffer; delay. 332, I.

*Sustineo, ĕre, tinui, tentum,* (sub, teneo). To sustain, withstand; endure, endure the thought of.

*Suus, a, um.* His, her, its, their; *pl. often,* one's party, friends.

*Syracūsae, ārum,* f. pl. Syracuse, a city in Sicily, (185).

*Syracusāni, ōrum,* m. pl. The Syracusans, the citizens of Syracuse, (223).

T.

*T.* An abbreviation of *Titus.*

*Tabernacŭlum, i,* n. Tent.

*Taceo, ĕre, tacui, tacĭtum.* To be silent, not to speak, to pass over in silence.

*Tacītus, a, um.*  Silent, secret, tacit.

*Tactus, us,* m.  Touch.

*Taedet, ēre, taeduit* or *taesum est,* impers.  It disgusts, wearies.

*Talentum, i,* n.  Talent, sum of money, somewhat more than $1,000.

*Talis, e,* such.

*Tam.*  So; *tam—quam,* so—as.

*Tamen,* conj.  Yet, nevertheless.

*Tametsi,* conj. (tamen, etsi).  Notwithstanding that, although, though.

*Tanăquil, īlis,* f.  Tanaquil, the wife of Tarquinius Priscus, (165).

*Tandem,* adv.  At length.

*Tanquam,* adv.  As, just as.

*Tantum.*  Only.

*Tantus, a, um.*  Such, so great, so much; *tantī esse,* to be worth the while.

*Tarentum, i,* n.  Tarentum, a town of Lower Italy, (184).

*Tarentīni, ōrum,* m. pl.  The Tarentines, the inhabitants of Tarentum, (180).

*Tarpeia, ae,* f.  Tarpeia, a Roman maiden, who betrayed the citadel of Rome to the Sabines, (156).

*Tarpeius, ii,* m.  Tarpeius, one of the seven hills of Rome, also called *Capitolīnus.*  The Capitol was erected upon it.  Afterwards the term *Tarpeius* was applied to the southern summit of the hill, (157).

*Tarquinii, ōrum,* m. pl.  Tarquinii, an ancient town of Etruria, (49, 10).

*Tarquinius, ii,* m.  Tarquin, the name of the fifth king of Rome and of his descendants, as *Tar-*

10

*quinius Superbus,* the last king of Rome; and *Tarquinius Collatīnus,* the colleague of Brutus in the consulship, (169).

*Tectum, i,* n. (tego).  Covering, roof; house, edifice.

*Tego, ĕre, texi, tectum.*  To cover.

*Telum, i,* n.  Weapon.

*Temĕre,* adv.  Rashly.

*Temerĭtas, ātis,* f.  Rashness, indiscretion, temerity.

*Tempestas, ātis,* f. (tempus).  Time; tempest, storm.

*Tempestīve,* adv. (tempestivus, timely).  Seasonably, just at the time, opportunely.

*Templum, i,* n.  Temple.

*Tempus, ŏris,* n.  Time.  *Tempŏra,* times, seasons, events.

*Temulentus, a, um.*  Drunk, intoxicated.

*Teneo, ēre, ui, tentum.*  To hold, keep, occupy; obtain, retain, as in the memory.

*Tento, āre, āvi, ātum,* (tendo).  To try; attack. 332, I.

*Tenus,* prep. with abl.  Up to, as far as.

*Terentius, ii,* m.  See *Varro,* (191).

*Ter-gemĭnus, a, um.*  Threefold; *tergemĭni,* three brothers born at a birth.

*Tergum, i,* n.  Back.

*Termĭno, āre, āvi, ātum,* (termĭnus).  To limit, bound.

*Termĭnus, i,* m.  Limit, boundary; end.

*Terra, ae,* f.  Earth, land, country.

*Terreo, ēre, ui, ĭtum.*  To terrify.

*Terrester, tris, tre,* (terra).  Terrestrial, or land, land (*as adj.*).

*Territorium, ii,* n.  Territory.

*Terror öris*, m. (terreo). Terror, alarm; fear of.

*Tertius, a, um.* Third.

*Testamentum, i*, n. Testament, will.

*Testis, is*, m. and f. Witness.

*Testor, āri, ātus sum*, (testis). To affirm; call to witness.

*Testūdo, ĭnis*, f. Tortoise.

*Thales, is*, m. Thales, a celebrated Grecian philosopher of Miletus, one of the seven wise men, (114).

*Theātrum, i*, n. Theatre.

*Thebae, ārum*, f. pl. Thebes, the capital of Boeotia in Greece, (230).

*Thebānus, a, um*, adj. (Thebae). Theban, (229); subs. *Thebānus, i*, m., a Theban.

*Thelesīnus, i*, m. See *Pontius*, (28, 10).

*Themistōcles, is*, m. Themistocles, a celebrated Athenian commander, (132—134).

*Theocrītus, i*, m. Theocritus, a celebrated Grecian poet, (130).

*Theophrastus, i*, m. Theophrastus, a Grecian philosopher, a disciple of Plato and Aristotle, (129).

*Thermopÿlae, ārum*, f. pl. Thermopylae, the famous defile *or* pass between Locris and Thessaly, where Leonidas fell, (218).

*Thessalia, ae*, f. The country of Thessaly, in Greece, south of Macedonia, (210).

*Thessălus, a, um*, adj. Thessalian; subs. *Thessălus, i*, m., a Thessalian, (243).

*Thessălus, i*, m. Thessalus, a native of Thesprotia, in Epirus, who is said to have formed a settlement in Thessaly, and to have given his name to the country.

*Thorax, ācis*, m. Breastplate, coat-of-mail, corselet.

*Thracia, ae*, f. The country of Thrace, east of Macedonia, (231).

*Thrasybūlus, i*, m. Thrasybulus, an Athenian who liberated the city from the Thirty Tyrants, (136, 228).

*Thucydīdes, is*, m. Thucydides, a celebrated Greek historian, (77).

*Tibĕris, is*, m. The river Tiber, in Italy, (153).

*Tiberius, ii*, m. Tiberius, the second Roman emperor, (145).

*Ticīnus, i*, m. Ticinus, a river in Cisalpine Gaul, famous for the victory of Hannibal over the Romans, (190, 194).

*Tigrānes, is*, m. Tigranes, son-in-law of Mithridates and king of Armenia, (205).

*Timeo, ēre, ui.* To fear.

*Timĭdus, a, um*, (timeo). Cowardly, timid.

*Timoleon, ontis*, m. Timoleon, a Corinthian general, (51).

*Timotheus, ei*, m. Timotheus, an Athenian general, son of Conon, (49, 12).

*Tintinnabŭlum, i*, n. Bell.

*Tiresias, ae*, m. Tiresias, a celebrated blind soothsayer of Thebes, (24, 11).

*Tissaphernes, is*, m. Tissaphernes, a distinguished Persian satrap of Lower Asia, under Darius; afterwards general in the service of Artaxerxes, (225).

*Titus, i*, m. Titus, a Roman emperor, (141). See also *Quinctius*, (177).

*Tollo, ĕre, sustŭli, sublātum.* To

raise, take up, elate; take away; destroy; discard.

*Tondeo, ēre, totondi, tonsum.* To shear, clip, crop; graze, browse; pluck, gather.

*Torquātus, i,* m. Torquatus, surname of *Titus Manlius* and his descendants, (177).

*Torquis, is,* m. and f. Collar, chain for the neck.

*Tot,* indecl. So many.

*Toḧdem,* indecl. Just as many, the same number.

*Totus, a, um.* All, the whole, *sometimes best rendered by adv.* wholly, entirely. 151, 443.

*Tracto, āre, āvi, ātum.* To use, treat, manage.

*Trado, ēre, dĭdi, dĭtum,* (trans, do). To deliver, give, consign to; *also* to relate, say; *tradĭtur* (when impers.), it is said.

*Tradūco, ēre, duxi, ductum,* (trans, duco). To lead across, transport.

*Tragoedia, ae,* f. Tragedy.

*Tragoedus, i,* m. Tragedian.

*Traho, ēre, traxi, tractum.* To draw; protract, delay, detain, derive, influence.

*Trajicio, ēre, jēci, jectum,* (trans, jacio). To throw over; to cross; conduct over, lead over.

*Trano, āre, āvi, ātum,* (trans, no). To swim over.

*Trans,* prep. with acc. Across, beyond.

*Trans-dūco* = tradūco.

*Trans-eo, ïre, ïvi* or *ii, ïtum.* To go over, to cross. 295, 3.

*Trans-fēro, ferre, tūli, lātum.* To transport, transfer, translate.

*Trans-fīgo, ēre, fixi, fixum.* To transfix, to thrust through, to pierce through.

*Transgredior, grēdi, gressus sum,* dep. (trans, gradior). To go *or* pass over.

*Transĭgo, ēre, ēgi, actum,* (trans, ago). To accomplish, finish, pass, spend.

*Transilio, ïre, ïvi, ii* or *ui,* (trans, salio). To leap *or* pass over.

*Transĭtus, ūs,* m. (transeo). Passage.

*Trans-marīnus, a, um.* Transmarine, over the sea.

*Trans-no* = trano.

*Trans-porto, āre, āvi, ātum.* To carry *or* convey from one place to another, carry across, transport.

*Trasimēnus, i,* m. Lake Trasimonus in Etruria, (190).

*Trebia, ae,* f. The river Trebia in Cisalpine Gaul, (190).

*Trecentesĭmus, a, um,* (trecenti). The three hundredth.

*Trecenti, ae, a.* Three hundred.

*Tredĕcim,* indecl. Thirteen.

*Tremo, ēre, tremui.* To shake, quake, tremble, quiver.

*Trepĭdus, a, um.* Alarmed, in terror.

*Tres, tria.* Three.

*Tribūnus, i,* m. Tribune.

*Tribuo, ēre, ui, ūtum.* To bestow, impute, award.

*Tributarius, a, um.* Tributary.

*Tribūtum, i,* n. (tribuo). Tax, tribute.

*Tricesĭmus, a, um.* The thirtieth.

*Triennium, ii,* n. The space of three years, three years.

*Trigemĭnus* = tergemĭnus.

*Trigesĭmus* = tricesĭmus.

*Triginta,* indecl. Thirty.

*Triplex, ĭcis.* Triple, threefold.

*Tripudio, āre, āvi.* To leap, dance.

*Tripus, ŏdis,* m. Tripod.

*Trirēmis, is,* f. (tres, remus). Galley with three banks of oars.

*Trirēmis, e,* adj. Having three banks of oars.

*Tristis, e.* Sad.

*Triumpho, āre, āvi, ātum,* (triumphus). To triumph, have a triumphal procession.

*Triumphus, i,* m. Triumph.

*Troezen, ēnis,* f. (acc. *Troezēna*). Troezen, an ancient city of Argolis, (217).

*Troja, ae,* f. The city of Troy, (33, 6).

*Trojāni, ōrum,* m. pl. (Troja). The Trojans, (149).

*Trojānus, a, um,* (Troja). Trojan, (236).

*Tropaeum, i,* n. Trophy, victory.

*Trucīdo, āre, āvi, ātum,* (trux, caedo). To slay, massacre.

*Trux, trucis.* Fierce, stern.

*Tu, tui.* Thou, you.

*Tuba, ae,* f. Trumpet.

*Tubĭcen, ĭnis,* m. Trumpeter.

*Tueor, ēri, tuĭtus* or *tutus sum,* dep. To look upon; preserve, defend.

*Tullia, ae,* f. Tullia, the daughter of Servius Tullius, and wife of Tarquinius Superbus, (166).

*Tullius, ii,* m. See *Servius,* (164).

*Tullus, i,* m. See *Hostilius,* (160).

*Tum.* Then; *tum—tum,* not only—but also; both—and.

*Tumultuo, āre, āvi, ātum,* (tumultus). To make a noise *or* tumult.

*Tumultus, us,* m. Tumult, sedition.

*Tumŭlus, i,* m. Tomb, grave.

*Tunc,* adv. Then; *tunc tempŏris,* then. 896, 2, 4.

*Tunĭca, ae,* f. Tunic, coat, a garment worn under the toga.

*Turba, ae,* f. Crowd, throng, multitude.

*Turbo, āre, āvi, ātum,* (turba). To disturb, throw into confusion.

*Turgesco, ĕre, turgui.* To swell, to swell with passion.

*Turpĭter, ius, issĭme,* adv. (turpis, base). Basely, disgracefully, in disgrace.

*Turris, is,* f. Tower.

*Tuscŭlum, i,* n. Tusculum, an ancient town in Latium, (172).

*Tutor, ōris,* m. Tutor, guardian.

*Tutus, a, um.* Safe.

*Tuus, a, um,* adj. pron. (tu). Thy, thine, your, yours.

*Tyrannis, ĭdis,* f. (tyrannus). Tyranny.

*Tyrannus, i,* m. Tyrant, monarch

### U

*Uber, ĕris,* n. Udder, dug.

*Ubertas, ātis,* f. Richness, fertility.

*Ubi,* adv. Where, when, *sometimes interrog.*

*Ubii, ōrum,* m. pl. The Ubii, an ancient Germanic people dwelling on the Rhine, (94).

*Ubĭnam,* adv. Where, in what part of?

*Ubīque.* Everywhere.

*Ullus, a, um.* Any, any one. 151.

*Ulterior, us;* superl. *ultĭmus.* Further, more remote; *superl.* last. 166.

*Ultio, ōnis,* f. Revenge.

*Ultra,* adv., and prep. with acc. Beyond, more than.

*Ultro,* adv. Voluntarily, of one's own accord.

*Ulŭlo, āre, āvi, ātum.* To howl, to cry aloud, to shriek.

*Umbra, ae,* f. Shade, shadow.

*Unde,* adv. Whence, *also interrog.* whence?

*Undĕcim,* indecl. Eleven.

*Undequinquaginta,* indecl. Forty-nine.

*Undeviccsĭmus, a, um.* Nineteenth.

*Undīque,* adv. From all quarters or sides.

*Unguentum, i,* n. Ointment, perfume.

*Unguis, is,* m. Nail, claw, talon.

*Ungŭla, ae,* f. Claw, talon, hoof.

*Universus, a, um.* Whole, entire; all together.

*Unquam,* adv. At any time, ever.

*Unus, a, um.* One, alone. 175.

*Unus-quisque, unaquaeque,* etc. (unus, quisque, *both parts declined*). Each, each one.

*Urbs, urbis,* f. City.

*Urgeo, ēre, ursi.* To urge, drive; press upon.

*Usque,* adv. So far as; *usque ad,* even to; *usque eo,* to such an extent.

*Usurpo, āre, āvi, ātum.* To usurp, assume.

*Usus, us,* m. Use, service; experience; need.

*Ut* or *uti,* conj. That, as; *after verbs of fearing,* that not.

*Utcumque* or *utcunque,* adv. However, somewhat.

*Uter, tra, trum,* adj. Which? which of the two? 151.

*Uterque, utrăque, utrumque,* like *uter.* Both, each. 151, 4.

*Utĭlis, e.* Useful.

*Utilĭtas, ātis,* f. (utĭlis). Utility, service, advantage.

*Utor, uti, usus sum.* To use.

*Utrimque* or *utrinque,* adv. On both sides.

*Utrum,* in double questions. Whether.

*Uva, ae,* f. A bunch of grapes, a grape.

*Uxor, ōris,* f. Wife.

## V

*Vaco, āre, āvi, ātum.* To be empty, vacant, to have leisure for; be free from.

*Vacuus, a, um.* Vacant, empty, free from.

*Vadum, i,* n. Ford, shallow water.

*Vagītus, us,* m. Crying.

*Vagor, āri, ātus sum.* To wander about.

*Vagus, a, um.* Wandering, doubtful, uncertain, vague.

*Valeo, ēre, ui, ĭtum.* To have strength, avail, be well.

*Valerius, ii,* m. Valerius, a Roman name. See *Publicŏla, Laevīnus,* (169, 180).

*Valetūdo, ĭnis,* f. (valeo). Habit, state of the body, health, state of health.

*Vanus, a, um.* Empty, vain, false.

*Variĕtas, ātis,* f. (varius). Variety, change.

*Varius, a, um.* Various.

*Varro, ōnis,* m. Varro, a Roman name. *Caius Terentius Varro,* a Roman consul defeated at Cannae, (191).

*Vas, vasis,* n. Vessel, dish, vase.

*Vasto, āre, āvi, ātum,* (vastus). To lay waste, devastate, pillage.

*Vastus, a, um.* Waste, desert, vast.

*Vates, is,* m. and f. Prophet, prophetess.

*Vectigal, ālis,* n. Tax, income, revenue.

*Veho, ĕre, vexi, vectum.* To carry, bear.

*Veientes, um,* or *Veientāni, ōrum,* m. pl. The Veientians, *or* Veientines, the inhabitants of Veii in Etruria, (175).

*Vel,* conj. Or, even; *vel—vel,* either—or.

*Velox, ōcis.* Swift, rapid, fleet.

*Vel-ut,* or *vel-ŭti,* adv. As, like as, as if.

*Venālis, e.* To be sold, for sale, purchasable.

*Vendo, ĕre, dĭdi, dĭtum.* To sell; *sub corōna vendĕre,* to sell as slaves.

*Venēnum, i,* n. Poison.

*Venio, īre, veni, ventum.* To come.

*Venor, āri, ātus sum,* dep. To hunt, chase, pursue.

*Venter, tris,* m. Belly, stomach.

*Ventus, i,* m. Wind.

*Venus, ĕris,* f. Venus, the goddess of love, (28).

*Verbum, i,* n. Word.

*Vereor, ēri, verītus sum,* dep. To fear, to be afraid.

*Verĭtas, ātis,* f. Truth.

*Vero,* adv. and conj. (verus). Truly, indeed; but.

*Verres, is,* m. Verres, a Roman name. *Caius Cornelius Verres* rendered himself notorious by his abuse of power in Sicily, (43).

*Verso, āre, āvi, ātum,* or *versor,* dep. (verto). To turn; busy one's self, be occupied with. 332, I. 2.

*Versus, us,* m. A verse.

*Vertex, ĭcis,* m. (verto). Summit, top.

*Verto, ĕre, verti, versum.* To turn.

*Verum,* conj. But.

*Verus, a, um.* True, real.

*Vescor, vesci.* To enjoy, feed upon, live upon, to eat.

*Vesper, ĕris* or *ĕri,* m. Evening.

*Vespĕra, ae,* f. Evening.

*Vesperasco, ĕre, vesperāvi,* (vesper). To become evening.

*Vesta, ae,* f. Vesta, the goddess of the hearth, to whom a perpetual fire was kept burning, (152).

*Vestālis, e,* adj. (Vesta). Vestal, relating to Vesta, (152).

*Vester, tra, trum.* Your.

*Vestibŭlum, i,* n. Vestibule, entrance.

*Vestio, īre, īvi, ītum,* (vestis). To clothe.

*Vestis, is,* f. Garment.

*Veterānus, a, um,* (vetus). Veteran.

*Veto, āre, ui, ĭtum.* To forbid.

*Veturia, ae,* f. Veturia, the mother of Coriolanus, (174).

*Veturius, ii,* m. Veturius, a Roman name. *Titus Veturius,* a Roman consul defeated by the Samnites at the Caudine Forks, (179).

*Vetus, ĕris.* Old, of long standing, ancient.

*Vetustas, ātis,* f. (vetus). Antiquity, age.

*Vetustus, a, um.* Old, ancient.

*Via, ae,* f. Way.

*Viātor, ōris,* m. Traveller.

*Vicesĭmus, a, um.* Twentieth.

*Vicīnus, a, um.* Neighboring.

*Vicis,* gen. f. Change, reverse, alternation, requital; fate, fortune; in vicem or vicem, in turn, place. 133, 1.

Vicissitūdo, ĭnis, f. (vicis). Change, alternation, vicissitude, succession.

Victor, ōris, m. (vinco). - Conqueror.

Victoria, ae, f. Victory.

Victus, a, um, part. (vinco). Conquered, vanquished.

Vicus, i, m. Village.

Video, ēre, di, sum. To see; pass. videor, etc., to be seen; to seem.

Vigeo, ēre, ui. To flourish, thrive, be in force.

Vigilantia, ae, f. Wakefulness, vigilance.

Viginti, indec. Twenty.

Vilis, e. Low, cheap, base, vile.

Vincio, ĭre, vinxi, vinctum. To bind.

Vinco, ēre, vici, victum. To conquer.

Vincŭlum or vinclum, i, n. Fetter, chain.

Vindex, ĭcis, m. and f. Defender.

Vindĭco, āre, āvi, ātum. To claim; rescue, defend; punish, avenge.

Vinolentus, a, um, (vinum). Full of wine, intoxicated with wine.

Vinum, i, n. Wine.

Vĭŏlo, āre, āvi, ātum. To violate, do violence to; profane, harm.

Vir, viri, m. Man, hero, husband.

Virga, ae, f. Rod, twig.

Virgo, ĭnis, f. Virgin, maiden.

Virgŭla, ae, f. Small rod, rod.

Virtus, ūtis, f. (vir). Manliness, bravery, virtue.

Vis, vis, f.; pl. vires. Power, strength, force; forces; abundance.

Viscus, ĕris, n. Vitals, bowels.

Viso, ēre, si, sum. To view, see, visit.

Vita, ae, f. Life.

Vitis, is, f. Vine.

Vitium, ii, n. Fault, vice, crime.

Vitupĕro, āre, āvi, ātum. To censure, blame, find fault with.

Vivo, ēre, vixi, victum. To live.

Vivus, a, um. Living, alive.

Vocabŭlum, i, n. Designation, name, word.

Voco, āre, āvi, ātum, (vox). To call, name.

Volo, āre, āvi, ātum. To fly.

Volo, velle, volui, irreg. To will, be willing, wish, desire; sibi velle, to mean. 293; 389, 2.

Volsci, ōrum, m. pl. The Volsci or Volscians, a people of Latium, (174).

Volŭcer, cris, cre, (volo). Flying, winged; swift, rapid; subs. a bird.

Volumnia, ae, f. Volumnia, the wife of Coriolanus, (174).

Voluntarius, a, um, (voluntas). Voluntary, willing, spontaneous.

Voluntas, ātis, f. (volo). Wish, inclination, good will.

Voluptas, ātis, f. Pleasure.

Voveo, ēre, vovi, votum. To vow, dedicate, consecrate.

Vox, vocis, f. Voice, word.

Vulgus, i, n. Populace, common people.

Vulnĕro, āre, āvi, ātum, (vulnus). To wound.

Vulnus, ĕris, n. Wound.

Vulpes, is, f. Fox.

Vultus, us, m. Countenance.

## X

*Xanthippus, i,* m.   Xanthippus, a
Spartan commander, who took
Regulus prisoner in the first Punic
war, (186).

*Xerxes, is,* m.   Xerxes, a celebrated
Persian king, (137, 217).

*Xenophon, ontis,* m.   Xenophon, a Greek historian, and the leader of
the Greeks in the famous retreat
of the ten thousand, (142).

## Z

*Zama, ae,* f.   Zama, a town of Numidia, in Africa, famous for the
victory of Scipio over Hannibal,
(196).

THE END

www.ingramcontent.com/pod-product-compliance
Lightning Source LLC
Chambersburg PA
CBHW030119030726
47498CB00007B/2453